LANDSCAPE ARCHITECTURE:
GUIDELINES TO PROFESSIONAL PRACTICE

LANE L. MARSHALL, FASLA

A PUBLICATION OF THE AMERICAN SOCIETY OF LANDSCAPE ARCHITECTS

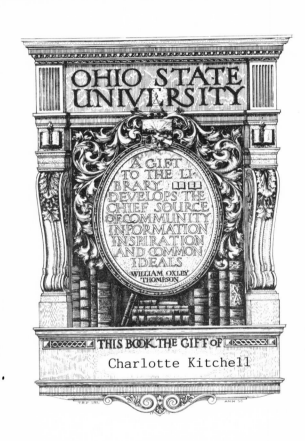

OHIO STATE UNIVERSITY

A GIFT TO THE LIBRARY DEVELOPS THE CHIEF SOURCE OF COMMUNITY INFORMATION INSPIRATION AND COMMON IDEALS

WILLIAM OXLEY THOMPSON

THIS BOOK THE GIFT OF

Charlotte Kitchell

LANDSCAPE ARCHITECTURE:
Guidelines to Professional Practice

Lane L. Marshall, FASLA
Author

James E. Hiss
Illustrator

Cover Design by James E. Hiss
and Stephen Drown

American Society of Landscape Architects
1900 M Street N.W. Suite 320
Washington D.C. 20036
(202) 466-7730

Library of Congress Catalog Card number: 81-69219
ISBN 0-941236-00-5

Project Coordinator: Richard A. Lippman, ASLA Director of Publications
Printed and bound by BookCrafters, Inc., Chelsea, Michigan
Typesetting by Circle Graphics, Washington D.C.

Dedication

This book is dedicated to the present and future students of landscape architecture. Those who have passed this way before you have built a strong and dynamic profession. It's future rests with you. Your skills, your sensitivity, and your energy will be needed in ever increasing measure as the profession continues to mature. In no small way this dedication also goes to the Landscape Architecture Class of 1981 at the Ohio State University.

Lane L. Marshall

The illustrations in this book are dedicated to Mom and Dad, Kathy, Steve, Tom, Mary Jeane, Anne and Laurie with heartfelt thanks and appreciation for your continuous caring and sharing and for showing me the real meaning of "Family."

Jim Hiss

Acknowledgments

A number of very special people deserve an equally special thanks for their role in the preparation of this book. Without their help and encouragement the task would have been overwhelming.

To the reviewers, Jot Carpenter, Debby Weldon, Ed Stone II, Dick Dickinson and Brian Kubota I extend my heartfelt appreciation for your loving attention to the message this book tries to tell. Your long and dedicated hours in reviewing the draft manuscript provided immeasureable help and guidance.

To Larry Walquist I extend a special thanks for allowing me to experiment with the draft manuscript on the students in his professional practice course at Ohio State University. The students were quick to let me know when the material was not making sense. Conversations with these students and with Larry led to a number of clarification rewrites and a correspondingly better product.

I also extend my heartfelt thanks to Jim Hiss, whose creative mind and graphic skills produced the illustrations for the book. Jim's wit and talent brought a renewed vigor to the project's closing hours.

To Bill Swain and Bill Behnke whose friendship and encouragement gave me the stamina and enthusiasm to complete the project. To Bill Swain a special thanks for preparing the foreword to the book.

To my wife, Marian, who read and typed each word and offered wise counsel throughout the book's writing, I extend my loving thanks.

Acknowledgments

Foreword

Any practical response to need presupposes that the need, itself, has been as fully identified as possible, in its time and as far beyond as one can hope to look. Bronowski writes, "And neither need the practical man be unoriginal. If he is to break out of what has been done before, he must bring to his own tools the same sense of pride and discovery which the poet brings to words. Man does not invent by following either use or tradition."

When Frederick Law Olmsted, in 1866, wrote his views on how the ideals of each component of a natural scene could, artfully, be brought together in creation of harmonious compositions, he was, indeed, expressing original thought. His term "landscape architecture," to describe this process, was and is poetic in the highest sense. No other term could be so expressive or concise, considering that no other design profession concerns itself with so wide a range of components. Olmsted, in his life and work nearly always trod a new path, philosophically and practically.

In tracing the growth of the profession of landscape architecture, the author of this book reflects on how its practitioners (and thus the profession) reacted to the times in the years following the founding of the American Society of Landscape Architects in 1899. Ups and downs have been chronicled, the numbers of practitioners doing this and that have been tallied as the years rolled by, but there's a broadening concern that, even in our diversities, the popular "need" which the profession continues to address remains that which was left us by Olmsted. Throughout eight decades the majority of landscape architects seem to have been doing much the same things they've always done, even borrowing some of the earlier forms as we've shaped the natural scene to suit assumed cultural purposes. Consequently, we've attracted new critics because what we do seldom stirs controversy. Without criticism we sometimes tend to be smug about our usefulness to society. Because of our relative obscurity the general public, if they think about it at all, accepts us for what we *say* we are. Of course, that's the crux of the matter. By coasting along, we've fallen into the belief that we're responding to need when, in actuality, we've side-stepped a prime professional responsibility. We haven't taken, often enough, leadership roles in identifying true *need* in given circumstances, "in its time and . . . far beyond." Rather than persist in emulating Olmsted's practice we should be emulating his pioneering spirit.

It seems unlikely that "pioneering," per se, can be taught, but there are ways of stimulating both settled practitioners and newcomers to this profession to consider themselves and their roles as landscape architects in new light. This suggests that we take on the task of the critic, break with tradition which often makes us timid, and examine ourselves and our practices.

This book stretches well beyond tradition and yet it expreses great reverence for the roots of landscape architecture, as rightfully we should, in establishing historical perspective. This book is about professional practice and its purpose is to initiate a process of self-evaluation and consequent self-improvement which will carry landscape architecture into new dimensions. It offers a place to start, in learning to do better what many now do quite well. With mastery comes stability and with stability comes the stimulus and opportunity for innovation.

Had Olmsted been less of a business success, had he and his colleagues of those early days been less willing and able to speak out articulately, the profession would likely not be even as it is today. This reference to "business" is not intended negatively. Rather, it's intended *practically*. It does not imply that the only measure of success is monetary, but it does suggest the obvious: that one must have a measure of financial success to be able to keep going and to improve one's service.

The traditional approaches toward instilling in students and those already at work an understanding of professional practice have fallen somewhat short of the mark. Such educational inadequacy is related less to how the topics usually are covered (contracts, accounting, matters having to do with personnel, office policies, insurance, correspondence, etc.) than it does to the topics which are *not* covered. The teaching of how one should go about providing professional services to real clients has been done, traditionally, on an ad-hoc basis. Those who went through the wars settled for the telling of old soldier's tales to the new recruits. Landscape architects' tales have been, quite probably, as colorful (and nonsubstantive when the chips have been down) as those told by the Dough-boys of WWI and the Yanks of WWII. As a consequence, the greater part of what is learned about the business of providing professional service is learned as it's *done*, by the seat of one's pants.

The need, as met in this book, transcends fundamentals which are the substance of examinations for professional licensure. The need, as perceived by the author (a distinguished practitioner and educator and a tireless advocate of the highest standards for the profession of landscape architecture) is to deal with the basic concept of professionalism, to address those qualities and acquired skills which are essential to successful practice. For the first time in any text written especially for landscape architects, the basic topics of the professionalism are explored. Surely this book will stimulate discussions and seminars on what it means to call oneself a professional among other professionals because, obviously, there's so much more to becoming an effective practitioner, private, public, or in teaching, than can be measured by a registration exam ... which establishes only base-line competencies. Learning all these facets of professionalism takes time, indeed many years. The knowledge and skills needed are those which span and link the arts and sciences.

One can argue that being successful in any professional field requires a large measure of common sense and there's little to be said against that point of view. But, common sense, no matter how developed, is meaningless unless it's exercised in direct application to actual life-situations. While it would be both ambitious and virtually meaningless to undertake the writing of a text which addresses all possible means of applying common sense, it's worth the effort to set forth some precepts in the context of landscape architectural practice. The author identified this need, as well, and a strong thread of practicality and common sense is woven into the fabric of this book.

To the extent that the book contains discussions of contracts and other business-related topics, it might be considered a "how to" book. Yet even in these areas it has a distinctive, non-traditional flavor.

Sharpening candidates (for registration exams) on such matters as contracts, the relationship of construction documents to each other, and the rudiments of record-keeping, preoccupies most teachers. Unfamiliarity with other topics has prevented their being brought up. The third part of this book departs from topical limitations which have made the teaching of professional practice often quite dull and meaningless, both in academic and internship settings. The author speaks from hard-won experience, yet this is not an old soldier's tale because his experience stimulated explorations into "why," into the future rather than the past.

Interpersonal relations, decision-making, the design process, communications, are among the human skills, the practical tools of professionalism which this book carries to the forefront, in answer to the overriding question, "Why?" Intitution, or common sense may have been adequate as the profession emerged and grew, statistically. It's hardly enough, as the profession matures.

William G. Swain, FASLA
Pittsburgh, PA

Foreword notes:

1. J. Bronowski, *Science and Human Values*, N. Y. Harper & Row, Revised edition 1965, Harper Colophon edition 1975

Preface

In 1964 I gave my first lecture on professional practice to landscape architectural students. With only four years of experience behind me, I talked about professional practice as I understood it. I talked about private practice. At that time, private practice and professional practice were thought of as interchangeable terms. This belief received further credence when, in 1972, ASLA published the *Handbook of Landscape Architectural Practice*. While carrying the mantle of Landscape Architectural Practice, the "Handbook" was, in fact, devoted to private practice concerns.

Throughout the past twenty years, however, the profession of landscape architecture was changing, almost daily. At some point during the 1970s the private practice landscape architects became outnumbered by the public and academic practitioners. During this same decade the profession's boundaries were stretched and expanded as practitioners became developers, environmental activists, mortgage bankers, lawyers, industrial consultants, and dozens of other professional types who no longer fit the traditional mold.

In 1978 and 1979 I had the unique opportunity to travel across the length and breadth of this country. On behalf of ASLA, I visited 35 local chapters and 40 landscape architectural degree programs. I talked to thousands of practicing and aspiring landscape architects, and learned first hand about the profession's diversity and the true dimensions of its practice. The unique travel opportunity provided me with a new perspective of the profession. I saw a profession with a special kind of dynamic energy. An energy fueled by diversity and ignited by practitioners who were no longer content to accept narrow professional boundaries or traditional stereotypes.

In 1979 I was asked by ASLA's Board of Trustees to undertake the rewriting of the *Handbook of Landscape Architectural Practice*. Available supplies of the "Handbook" were nearly exhausted and many practitioners felt the material was outdated. I accepted the challenge gladly, but urged from the beginning that the new book should address professional practice in all its diverse forms. No longer, I urged, can a book on professional practice deal solely with private practice concerns.

This book, then, has been designed to capture the full essense of landscape architectural practice. It embraces the professional, human, business and political skills necessary to successfully move us, as individuals, and as a profession into and through the 21st century. It is not a "How To" book. It has no standard forms or sample specifications. It does not explain how to open an office or write a business letter.

The book recognized the profession's special diversity and identifies common threads which continue to bind the profession together. The book suggests that, no matter how one practices, certain skills and knowledge are commonly required. These skills and their application form the backbone of the book. Special attention is given to human and political skills as essential adjuncts to the technical and design skills which are so special to our profession. Attention is also given to the "business" of landscape architecture. No matter how it is practiced, landscape architecture is a professional service business and requires special skills in this area. The business skills, however, are viewed as unique to the professional service enterprise and are presented as common to all landscape architectural practice forms.

This is a hopeful book. It views landscape architecture as a future-oriented profession. It sees great promise for the profession, but urges that new frontiers will only be available to those whose package of professional practice skills are diverse and unbound by traditional stereotype.

Finally, it must be noted that this book was designed as the pivot point for a series of specialized publications on practice specific issues. ASLA's Professional Practice Institute has been charged with the responsibility of developing these publications. They will address practice concerns peculiar to private, public, academic and emerging practice forms. Together with this book, the practice specific publications will provide an in-depth library on the practice of landscape architecture.

Writing this book has been a major and important part of my professional career. Writing it has made me a better practitioner. I can only hope that reading it will encourage all aspiring landscape architects to develop their fullest potential.

Lane L. Marshall, FASLA
June 1, 1981

Contents

PART ONE
A PROFESSIONAL BASE

Chapter One
The Profession Defined

Olmsted coined the term landscape architect while Superintendent of New York City's Central Park in 1858.

The Roots

Frederick Law Olmsted is generally credited as the father of modern landscape architecture. While the historic roots of landscape architecture can be traced back to the Paleolithic period and the first ceremonial and funerary monuments[1], the term landscape architect was, indeed, first coined by Olmsted in 1858.[2]

Olmsted was distressed by the term "landscape gardener," which was in prevalent use when he was appointed superintendent of New York City's Central Park in 1857.[3] The term gardener implied garden, which in turn evoked an image limited in scope to a small and very specific space. Landscape, on the other hand, was a totally comprehensive term that encompassed the garden as well as the mountain and the sky. Olmsted saw his work as an art form not unlike that of architecture. His close friendship and

business association with architect Calvert Vaux, very likely played a significant role in his selection of the term landscape architecture to define his chosen profession. In a letter written in 1866 to the Brooklyn Park Commission Olmsted defined, in eloquent terms, the task of a landscape architect:

A scene in nature is made up of various parts; each part has its individual character and its possible ideal. It is unlikely that accident should bring together the best possible ideals of each separate part, merely by considering them as isolated facts, and it is still more unlikely that accident should group a number of these possible ideals in such a way that not only one or two but that all should be harmoniously related one to the other. It is evident, however, that an attempt to accomplish this artificially is not impossible, and that a proper study of the circumstances relating to the perfect development of each particular detail will at least enable the designer to reckon surely on a certain success of a high character in that detail, and a comprehensive bringing together of the results of his study in regard to the harmonious relations of one, two or more details may enable him to discover the law of harmonious relation between multitudinous details; and if he can discover it, there is nothing to prevent him from putting it into practice. The result would be a work of art, and the combination of the art thus defined, with the art of architecture in the production of landscape compositions, is what we denominate landscape architecture.

Frederick Law Olmsted, 1866[4]

Throughout his life Olmsted saw landscape architecture as a profession dedicated to nature and to humankind. The products of his effort stand today as remarkable evidence of his foresight and talent. Few professions can point with such pride to a modern day founder whose works, plans, and writings speak with such clarity and precision to the needs and aspirations of people, and to the thoughtful and sensitive use of the landscape. Olmsted's life and works bring to landscape architecture a philosophical heritage that is unmatched by any other profession.

The Professions Formal Status

Olmsted's dream of a profession in service to mankind and nature did not take on formal status, however, until 1899 with the founding of the American Society of Landscape Architects. It was several years later, in 1909, when the Society adopted an official definition of the profession.

Landscape Architecture is the art of fitting land for human use and enjoyment.
ASLA Official Minutes 1909-20

Eleven landscape architects founded the American Society of Landscape Architects in 1899 giving formal status to Olmsted's profession.

During this same period the profession began to grow. In 1900, the first program in landscape architectural education was begun at Harvard College. By 1910, the professional society had grown from its 11 original founders to 68 members strong. By 1920, the number had nearly doubled.

The Profession Undergoes Change

Frederick Law Olmsted, Jr. championed the profession during the first quarter of the twentieth century, as his father had done before him. The younger Olmsted promoted the profession in Washington, D.C. and was instrumental in opening up federal employment to landscape architects. In the late 1920s, however, the profession underwent growing pains. While the membership in the professional society grew by 98 per cent during the decade of the twenties, many members withdrew from the society as they entered the burgeoning profession of city planning, largely credited to Olmsted senior's activities in this area. Still others withdrew from the society because its Code of Ethics, adopted in the late 1920s, did not allow them to function as both designers and as contractors. (This Code of Ethics preclusion lasted for more than 50 years and was not officially changed until 1974).

Landscape architects have played an important role in master planning of this nation's national parks.

The second quarter of the twentieth century saw a dramatic increase in the number of landscape architects employed by government agencies. The Great Depression significantly slowed the amount of work available to private practice landscape architects, while at the same time colleges and universities were turning out increasing numbers of graduates. The concept of master planning in the national parks was adopted during this period and prompted wide spread employment of landscape architects in a variety of state and federal projects.

The second world war caused an understandable slow down in the number of new graduates during the 1940's. The professional society grew by only 100 new members during this ten year period. This represented the slowest growth period in the profession's history, but dramatic times lay ahead.

The Growth Years

As the country moved into the second half of the twentieth century, landscape architecture began a period of unprecedented growth. The 1950s produced a 200 percent increase in the membership of the professional society. The G.I. Bill made it possible for war veterans to get federal assistance to attend college, and enrollment in landscape architectural education programs increased sharply in existing programs and many new programs were started. This period produced a new breed of graduate: somewhat older, more mature, highly competitive and always inquisitive; they were to play major roles in the profession's future.

In 1953, California adopted the first registration or licensure law. New York and Connecticut soon followed. By 1960, 5 states had adopted some form of professional licensure for landscape architects.

The unusual growth in numbers of landscape architects during the 1950s was to have an important impact on the profession. By mid-point in the 1960s, the large number of graduates produced in the previous decade was spreading across the country. Not only were they working for the increasing number of private practice firms, but they were being employed by nearly every conceivable form of government agency from local to federal level. Up to this point, the profession was largely confined to the East and

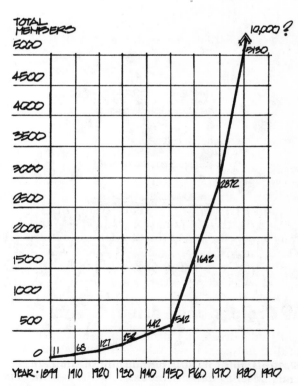

ASLA's membership has grown at a rate which has doubled every decade.

West Coasts, with a few firms located in the major Mid-Western cities. A dramatic geographic spread was taking place during the '60s, however, and by the end of the decade, landscape architects were working in every state and nearly every major city in the country. The profession was "coming of age."

In the 1960s, special attention was drawn to the profession as a result of the nation's increased concern for the environment. More and more young people were being attracted to landscape architecture because of its strong association with the environment, and by 1969 the educational programs were graduating more than 1,000 young professionals a year. The total number of graduates continued to grow and by 1975, the U.S. Department of Labor estimated that more than 20,000 were employed in the country. From a handful of practitioners to 20,000 in just 75 years!

In 1979, the American Society of Landscape Architects celebrated its' 80th birthday during the Society's meeting in New Orleans, Louisiana. More than 1,800 landscape architects from all over the country came together to recognize 80 years of unusual growth. The profession, named by Olmsted in 1858 and formalized in 1899, had grown in unprecedented fashion, and would continue to do so.

ASLA celebrated its 80th birthday during its 1979 Annual Meeting in New Orleans, Louisiana. More than 1800 practicing landscape architects, students and guests attended.

Altering Focus

Throughout its growth period, the profession, in response to external and internal pressures, was frequently compelled to alter its focus. "Public attitudes to ecological matters, social problems, and the changing concept of aesthetics had changed perceptibly during the senior Olmsted's lifetime, and it was a considerably different profession that came into existence after his death (1903). Marked change is apparent in each successive decade of the profession's history. World War I, the 1920, the Depression, World War II, post-war expansion in housing, education, and highways, and a new comprehensive ecological awareness have compelled such changes (in professional focus)."[5]

Despite this changing focus and the ever widening boundaries of the profession, the official definition changed very little during the first half of the twentieth century. In 1950, ASLA's constitution gave this definition:

Landscape Architecture is the art of arranging land and the objects upon it for human use and enjoyment.

ASLA Constitution 1950

During that same time period, the *American College Dictionary* gave this definition:

Landscape Architecture, the art of arranging or modifying the features of a landscape, the streets, buildings, etc. to secure beautiful or advantageous effects.

As the environmental awareness movement of the 1960s opened new opportunities for the profession, suggestions were being made for the redefining of the profession. Dr. Albert Fein, in his *Study of the Profession* released in 1972, recognized the shifts in practice opportunity and recommended the definition be changed as follows:

Landscape Architecture...the art of applying scientific principles to the land—its planning, design, and management—for the Public, Health, and Welfare, with a commitment to the concept of stewardship of the land.

Albert Fein 1972[6]

In 1975, ASLA's Board of Trustees, in response to Fein's recommendation, adopted the following definition:

Landscape Architecture is the art of design, planning, or management of the land, arrangement of natural and manmade elements thereon through application of cultural and scientific knowledge, with concern for resource conservation and stewardship, to the end that the resultant environment serves useful and enjoyable purpose.

ASLA Constitution 1975

As one might expect, the dictionary definition was still lagging far behind. In 1976, Webster's *New Collegiate Dictionary*, No. 8 gave this definition:

landscape architect n.; one whose profession is the arrangement of land for human use and enjoyment involving the placement of structures, vehicular and pedestrian ways, and plantings.

All of this points to the inadequacy of static definitions for a dynamic and expanding profession. Certainly the profession's definition will continue to change. Changing national issues, technological advancement, improved professional credibility, increasing numbers of practitioners, more and better research along with improved methodology, and a host of other factors will insure the continued growth of the profession's dynamic character. To attempt to provide a "definition for all time" would be folly. It is possible, however, to suggest that dedication to nature and mankind are precepts unique to the profession and they will, or should, prevail and direct the profession's growth with equal force during the second eighty years of its history.

Throughout its history, landscape architecture has been viewed as an art or form of artistic expression. Nearly every definition reviewed contains an expressed or implied reference to design, planning, arranging or similar terms which denote specialized artistic and creative skills. Olmsted referred to it as the "law of harmonious relations," which when put into practice, becomes a work of art.

Expanding Horizons

While there has been little change in the artistic perception of the profession over the years, the environmental and social revolution of the 60s and 70s made it clear that the profession included a great deal more than the application of aesthetic principles. Scientific knowledge, the application of new technology and methodology, and the need for collaborative effort have proven to be important aspects of landscape architectural practice. The natural and social sciences have been embraced by the profession as its boundaries expanded to meet and solve new national issues.

Underlying all of this, however, are the two fundamental precepts which have endured throughout the profession's history. The profession's philosophical and practical dedication to the land and to people has set it apart from most other professions and has

been a principal cause of its unique expansion during the twentieth century. These same precepts will continue to provide the profession with a focus that will lead it with clarity of purpose through the twenty-first century as well. No definition need be written to express these special aspects of landscape architecture. As long as they prevail, the profession will continue to expand, for there must never be a lessening of concern for either.

The landscape architect's dedication to the land and to people has withstood the test of time.

Landscape architecture will continue to devote its special skills to the enhancement, preservation, and stewardship of the landscape. Moreover, these skills will be practiced across the widest possible spectrum, from garden to mountain, from a single tree to whole forests, and will focus on the natural systems upon which humankind depends for survival.

Landscape architecture will also continue to devote its special skills to the creation of places which meet and advance the needs of people: places sensitive to the socio-psychological needs, predispositions, and expectations of people. Landscape architects will create spaces which encourage human contact, as well as providing opportunity for privacy. They will create spaces which can be possessed and occupied without emotional or physical stress. Landscape architecture has and will continue to embrace the social and psychological sciences in an effort to make the human habitat enjoyable, safe and productive.

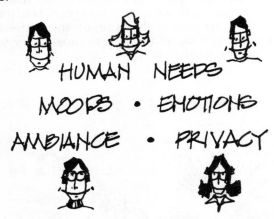

Human needs and expectations are of major concern to the practicing landscape architect.

And so it would seem difficult, if not impossible to provide a precise definition for the profession of landscape architecture. The profession has struggled with this question for years and has survived, and in fact, exhibited dynamic growth without a definition which embraced all of its unique practice forms. While scholars may continue to search for an inclusive definition, landscape architects will continue to expand the profession's boundaries, finding new and dramatic ways to utilize their skills to improve the world in which we live.

Landscape architecture is a profession of unusual diversity, and it is practiced by professionals of equally diverse skills and interests. In order to provide a better understanding of the uniqueness of this profession, Chapter Two will explore the diversity of its practice forms. Just as it is difficult to provide a uniformly applicable definition, so too, is it difficult to understand the profession without a thorough knowledge of its practice diversity.

Chapter One Notes

1. G.A. Jellicoe, *The Landscape of Man, Shaping The Environment, from Prehistoric to the Present Day*, N.Y., N.Y. Viking Press 1975
2. S.B. Sutton, Ed., *Civilizing American Cities*, Cambridge, Mass. The MIT Press, 1979
3. Ibid 2
4. Ibid 2
5. Albert Fein, *A Study of the Profession of Landscape Architecture*, American Society of Landscape Architects, Wash., D.C. LAF, 1972

Chapter Two
Practice Diversity

Landscape architecture is a uniquely diverse profession offering opportunities to specialize or generalize in either the public or private sector.

Introduction

In a traditional sense, landscape architecture has been practiced in three different forms or modes. Olmsted represented one of these modes. He was a private practitioner, and this form of practice has survived since his time. The second practice form was begun in 1900 with the founding of the first educational program in landscape architecture. Academic practice, or teaching, is a time honored form and each year takes on greater importance to the entire profession. The third traditional form is public practice. Public practice roots can be traced, in modern terms, to the mid 1920s, when Frederick Law Olmsted, Jr. successfully encouraged the federal government to hire landscape architects. While it certainly can be argued that other, less traditional forms of landscape architectural practice have been around as long or longer, private, academic and public forms of practice remain best understood by most people. In recent years, however, a fourth area of landscape architecural practice has become recognized.

This fourth area of professional practice is, in fact, not a specific area like the first three, but rather a collection of quite different and unique practice forms which do not fit neatly into the first three molds. This fourth area includes those landscape architects who have combined traditional skills with other specialities and who utilize their talents in vastly different ways. A closeup look at the three traditional practice forms, as well as the fourth area, referred to here as variations and new practice forms, will provide an understanding of the profession's unique diversity.

Private Practice

In the most general of terms, landscape architects in private practice provide professional services and consultation to a client for an openly stated form of compensation or fee. Private practice landscape architects sell only their skills, expertise and time. They do not offer a product or sell material, equipment, or supplies. Nor do they sell installation, maintenance or repair services in connection with their other services. They function in much the same way as a doctor or an attorney. Please keep in mind that these points refer to private practice in a very traditional sense, as defined by early Codes of Ethics. Dozens of variations have appeared in the private practice area over the years and several are discussed later in this book. It is important to point out, however, that a great many landscape architects practice in this traditional mode and that a clear understanding of its form is essential to a proper understanding of all the variations which have evolved from it.

Private practice landscape architects operate in the free enterprise marketplace. As a result, they do not have captive clients and must compete with their collegues for their share of the market. They may be self-employed or work for firms containing other landscape architects. The larger firms may also contain architects, engineers, planners, scientists, economists, and a variety of other specialists depending on the firm's size and area of market emphasis.

The kinds of services offered by private practice firms vary greatly. The size of the firm, geographic location, individual and collective human skills, and the special interests of principal firm members will play a significant role in the services offered. While activities may vary from the design of a small city park to the preparation of a land use plan for an entire region, there is an element of practice common to nearly all of these activities. Almost all private practice activity is project oriented. The services of a private practice landscape architect are normally directed toward finding a solution to a specific problem relating to a particular site. While some private practitioners are called upon to solve conceptual problems which can be generalized to many situations, this is the exception rather than the rule.

Quite frequently, specific solutions to specific projects do have generalizable elements, but more often than not each new project presents a new challenge which requires a new solution. To better understand the services which can be provided by private practice landscape architects, the following outline is provided. The outline demonstrates the variety and comprehensiveness of private practice activity.

Professional Services Outline

I.   **Analysis Services**

    A.   **Client/User Needs**

Determining the needs of clients and the ultimate user is often a complex task.

      1.   Identify and articulate client needs and expectations.
      2.   Identify and articulate user needs and expectations if client is not the eventual user.
      3.   Evaluate and assist in reconciling conflicts between client and user needs.

    B.   **Feasibility Studies**

A large portion of the landscape architect's service effort takes a written form.

      1.   Determine locational and site specific requirements for project site if not yet selected.
      2.   Evaluate site constraints if site is already selected.
      3.   Evaluate economic considerations.
      4.   Determine permitting and approval requirements.
      5.   Evaluate legal considerations.

    C.   **Site Selection and Utilization Analysis**

Analyzing and synthesizing information is an important aspect of landscape architectural practice.

      1.   Survey considered or selected sites to determine:
        a.   Current land use and zoning
        b.   Surrounding land use and character

    c.   Relation to and characteristics of transportation, utilities, community services, recreation, shopping, cultural opportunities and other support concerns

    d.   Natural and environmental characteristics: (soils, topography, drainage, vegetation, etc.)

    e.   Climatological characteristics

    f.   Historical, archaeological, social, and cultural aspects

    g.   Man-made features

    h.   Unusual or unique features

2. Assess relationship to guidelines developed from feasibility and user need studies.

3. Recommended most suitable site.

4. Prepare detailed analysis of project site to clearly identify all problems and opportunities connected with the development of the site.

D.   Preliminary Program

Developing and articulating the design program combines synthesizing and writing skills.

1. Identify functional requirements.

2. Translate site concerns along with client and user needs into design criteria.

3. Identify budgetary and financial requirements.

4. Identify permitting and approvals required.

5. Identify other consultants, along with operational and coordination requirements.

E.   Pre-Testing

1   Pretest design criteria via:

    a.   Citizen survey and Citizen participation programs

    b.   Evaluation of similar or surrogate space

2. Coordinate marketing studies.

Program goals and design criteria should be tested and reviewed by all involved, directly or indirectly with the project.

3. Review program with planning agencies and other permitting groups.

4. Review program with lenders and brokers.

F.   Final Program

The analysis services normally result in the preparation of a final program which gives conclusions, recommendations and outlines the project's design criteria.

1. Define options and identify abilities to meet or exceed program needs.

2. Review with client.

3. Synthesize results of client review and prepare final program in accordance with maximum benefit to client and user.

II.   Design and Planning Services

   A.   Conceptual or Schematic Design

    1.   Site Inventory/Environmental Assessment (see I.C.1).

    2.   Land Use analysis/functional diagram.

    3.   Circulation Analysis (pedestrian and vehicular).

    4.   Special problems assessment.

    5.   Budget analysis.

    6.   Review with client.

Conceptual or schematic design seeks out the most appropriate idealized solution within the practical constraints of the design program.

B. Design Development
1. Preliminary master (site) plan.
2. Design sketches, elevations and special features studies.
3. Budget analysis.
4. Review with client, client's agents and user groups.
5. Final master (site) plan with documentation and back-up material in written form.

The design development drawings expand the level of design detail and provide both 2 and 3 dimensional views of the proposed solution.

III. Review and Approvals

A. Review
1. Assist client with presentations to citizen groups, lending agencies, and approval and permitting agencies.
2. Review with all other consultants and client agents.

B. Approvals
1. Assist client with approval and permitting process and procedures (zoning, environmental impact statements, etc.).
2. Assist client with promotional and marketing activity.

Many aspects of the review and approval process will follow the design development phase and call upon the professional's communication skills.

IV. Contract Drawings and Documents

A. Construction Drawings
1. Staking and layout plans.
2. Grading plans.
3. Planting plans.
4. Irrigation plans.
5. Construction Details.
6. Other drawings peculiar to the project.

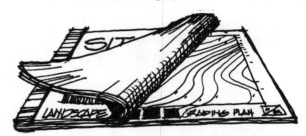

The construction drawings define the physical relationships of design materials; how they look, are joined and fit together and how they relate to each other and to the whole.

B. Construction Documents (see Chapter 13)
1. Bidding Requirement.
2. Contract Documents and General Conditions.

3. Specifications.
4. Materials Summaries.

C. Final Estimates

V. Contract Administration

A. Construction Bidding

Competitive bidding and direct contract negotiation are the two primary ways to select a project contractor.

1. Solicit bids
2. Open and review bids
3. Negotiate contract price when competitive bidding is inappropriate
4. Present recommendations

B. Construction Observation
1. Conduct periodic inspection visits during construction/installation.
2. Prepare observation reports.
3. Advise on change orders.
4. Authorize construction payments.
5. Act as client's agent in all matters pertaining to interpretation of the plans and contract documents.

Observing the project during construction is a most exciting and demanding activity.

VI. Post-Construction Services

A. Post Occupancy Evaluation

B. Maintenance Review and Consulting

VII. Related Services

A. Graphic Design

B. Environmental Assessments and Impact Statements

C. Transportation Planning

D. Recreation Planning

E. Urban and Regional Planning

F. Product Design

G. Expert Witness Testimony

The preceeding list of professional services is comprehensive indeed, but it would be a rare occasion when any private practice firm provided all of the services on a single project. It would also be in error to suggest that the list is complete. As problem solvers, landscape architects are finding more and more ways to utilize their talents on a daily basis, and the list of services is constantly growing. To gain a better understanding of the scope of services offered by private practice firms of varying size and complexity, profiles of three very different firms are given as examples.

Private Firm Profiles

The small private practice office, staffed by less than five landscape architects is the most prevelent office type.

Firm A

Location:	City between 150-200,000 population Southeastern United States
Founded:	1972
No. of Professionals:	2 landscape architects
Other employees:	1 secretary

Both landscape architects are generalists and their practice primarily serves residential, commercial and governmental clients. Their client and project list shows considerable activity in the area of park and playground design for municipalities and county governments. Since the firm was founded, they have averaged 62 clients per year. The firm lists its specialities as follows:

Site Planning
Park and Playground Design
Subdivision Design
Commercial Beautification
Irrigation Design

The medium sized private practice office with 6—15 professionals may have several partners and include other design fields within the organization.

Firm B

Location:	City under 150,000 population Northeastern United States
Founded:	1961
No. of Professionals:	7 landscape architects 1 planner 1 civil engineer
Other Employees:	2 secretaries

This firm is a partnership with three principals and two associates who share in annual distribution of profits. One of the principals is a civil engineer and the other two are landscape architects. While the firm is headquartered in a relatively small community, their market area includes several urban centers, all within daily driving distance. The firm specializes in serving public clients and offers a range of services from comprehensive planning to park design. Their client and project list indicates that since their founding more than 70 percent of their clients have been public agencies.

The firm averages 40 clients per year and their list of specializations includes the following:

Urban and Regional Planning
Park and Recreation Planning and Design
Land Planning and Site Design
Commercial Design

The large private practice offices are often multi-disciplinary in character and may have a large number of principals and associate partners.

Firm C

Location:	City over 1,000,000 population West Coast of United States Branch offices throughout U.S.
Founded:	1951
No. of Professionals:	48 landscape architects 4 architects 8 civil engineers 4 planners 2 social scientists 5 economists 5 ecologists 4 geographers 20 draftspersons 20 administrative persons

Firm C is a multi-disciplinary firm with five senior partners and eight junior partners. The senior partners include three landscape architects, one architect and one engineer. While principally a landscape architectural practice, the firm does promote its architectural and engineering expertise. Primary promotional activities, however, are aimed at the firm's "in-house" multidisciplinary ability to deal with complex projects. The firm's client and project list shows a wide variety of project types in locations around the United States and abroad. Clients include major U.S. and foreign corporations, the National Park Service, many major U.S. cities, and several nationwide development corporations. The firm serves an average of 120 clients each year and lists their service specialties as follows:

Urban and Regional Design
Environmental Planning and Assessment
Resort and Recreation Community Planning
Resource Planning and Management
New Community Planning

These three office profiles provide an overview look at the range of practice activity from very small to very large private firms. Ownership, organization, structure, skill composition, service activity, promotion techniques, and management sophistication varies greatly from one firm to another. In all cases, however, "project" orientation stands out as a common denominator.

The private practice landscape architect is employed by clients who may be private individuals, firms, business, or corporations, or by public agencies from the local to the federal level. They may sell their services to other design firms (primarily architectural), acting as sub-contract consultants. They may provide a very specific area of expertise or they may offer a very wide range of services covering the entire project scope.

Landscape architectural firms sometimes form temporary associations with other design and consulting firms to provide collaborative full service work on a project. This would involve a temporary partnership between two otherwise autonomous firms for a specific project. The division of services and fees is clearly stated in advance, and the association is usually terminated at the completion of the specific project. Some firms have found it convenient, however, to maintain loosely organized but on-going ties with other firms to insure collaborative support when specific projects requiring joint association become available.

The variations on traditional private practice activities are tremendous, and it is difficult to establish a clear cut standard. Limitations on the ways a private practice firm can function are set only by imagination, competence, and professional ethics. All three of these areas will be discussed later in this book, along with some of the practice variations.

Public Practice

Landscape architectural public practice shares many aspects in common with private practice, while being quite different in other aspects.

If one looks closely at the profiles of the public practice agencies and departments which follow, it is possible to find situations which nearly parallel private practice enterprises in scope and nature, while also finding situations which are dramatically different.

To start with the obvious difference, public practitioners work for government or quasi-government employers. They do not compete in the marketplace for "clients," but serve, rather, the stated mission of their agency or department. These mission statements are likely to be highly specific and frequently deal with equally specific areas of practice activity. A city park department, for instance, will be concerned about parks and their use, and will have only limited concern for other areas of landscape architectural practice. Landscape architects in this agency would not be dealing with subdivision design or beautification for a shopping center.

The same circumstances apply to almost every form of public practice. This does not suggest, however, that the services provided by public practice landscape architects are less comprehensive than those offered by their private practice counterparts. The same list of services covered in the private practice section of this book will apply to the services offered by the public practitioner with only minor changes. (see Professional Service Outline)

The mission specific nature of public practice is an obvious difference from private practice, and frequently tends to create specialist practitioners. This is often very appealing to individuals with special interests or an affinity for a certain area of activity. Landscape architects with skills in computer land use modeling and a special affinity for natural resource concerns may well find very meaningful employment in a public agency dealing with large scale land use assessment and visual resource management. Moreover, this same individual may well find a greater number of employment opportunities with government agencies dealing with these issues than with private organizations.

Many private practice landscape architects believe that their public counterparts are largely administrators and managers, and that this fact marks the principal difference between public and private practice. The truth of the matter is that all landscape architects, regardless of practice mode, become administrators and managers as they progress along the path to success. It must be clearly understood that all landscape architects, regardless of practice mode, must develop administrative and managerial skills if they are to advance in their profession.

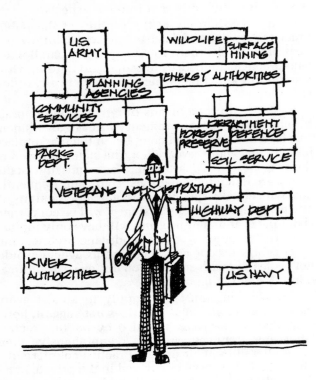

The opportunities for challenging public practice abound. The following list only partially covers the types of agencies and departments of government which employ landscape architects, but does indicate the varied scope of public practice.

City/County Level
City Administration
Parks Departments
Planning Departments
Development Commissions and Authorities
Recreation and other Special Purpose Districts
Engineering and Public Works Departments
Community Service Departments
Redevelopment Agencies
Historic Districts, Agencies and Boards
School Districts
Housing Authorities
Transit Authorities
Regional Level
Port and Airport Authorities
Regional Planning Councils
Water and Flood Management Districts
Forest Preserves

State Level
State Forestry Departments
State Highway Departments (1)
State Departments of Natural Resources (parks, etc.)
State Planning Agencies
State Departments of Conservation
State Departments of General Services
State Agricultural Extension Services
State Universities—Divisions of Plants and Grounds
Multi-State Level
Power and Energy Authorities (TVA)
River Authorities
Multi-State Planning Agencies
Federal Agencies
Department of Defense
    U.S. Navy
    U.S. Air Force
    U.S. Army Corps of Engineers
Department of Housing and Urban Development
Department of the Interior
    Bureau of Land Management
    National Parks Service
    Bureau of Reclamation
    Office of Surface Mining
    Fish and Wildlife Service
Department of Agriculture
    Forest Service
    Soil Conservation Service
Department of Transportation
    Federal Highway Administration
    Federal Aviation Administration
Department of Energy
Veterans Administration
General Services Administration

The list is long, indeed, but can never be complete. Surely some agency, or department, or bureau, or authority, or administration, or board, or whatever has been missed. New government organizations are formed every year and new public practice jobs are created with equal rapidity and will provide ongoing opportunities for landscape architects. The list is also confused by the propensity of agencies at different levels of government to use greatly different names to describe organizations with every similar missions. In other situations, similar names may be used to describe agencies with greatly different missions. The fact remains, however, that opportunities abound in the public practice area for landscape architects.

It is equally important to note that the accomplishments of the public practice area of the profession are significant. The ability to concentrate skills and energies in specific areas of concern has lead to many important state-of-the-art advancements. The pioneering work of the U.S. Forest Service, Bureau of Land Managment and Soil Conservation Service in visual resource assessment and management is an excellent example of this point. State, regional and local public agencies have made equally significant contributions from solar retrofitting of existing park facilities to adoptive re-use of historic areas. This list of unique contributions by the public practice landscape architect grows daily. Public practice is exciting and rewarding work, and represents a significant part of professional landscape architectural practice. The following public practice profiles are given in demonstration of this practice form diversity:

City and county parks departments provide a variety of program development, design and management situations in direct response to local needs and political realities.

A City Parks Department
Location: Southeastern United States
City over 500,000 population

No. of Professionals: 10 landscape architects
2 draftspersons

The department's responsibility includes the ongoing development and improvement of more than 100 existing city parks ranging in size from one-half acre to 400 acres. The city's long range park program calls for the acquisition and development of 200 additional parks during the next 25 years. Park plans are designed by department landscape architects or contracted out to qualified private practice firms depending on project scope and staff work load. All projects are managed by the department staff. Assessment of changing community demographics, cultural patterns, transportation networks, capital improvement budgets and building patterns is an ongoing department task. The assessment data is used to continually modify and update the long range park plans for the community. Staff landscape

architects are responsible for preparation of design and construction documents, field inspection, review and approval of consultant's work product, meetings with community and neighborhood leaders and groups, department and project administration, preparation of budgets and project programming activities.

State park and natural resource agencies find themselves involved in a comprehensive collaborative effort which can directly impact the character of thousands of acres of land.

A State Park and Recreation Department; Development Division
Location: Pacific Coast
No. of Professionals: 31 landscape architects
11 architects
25 engineers
7 delineators
1 estimator
11 technicians
5 secretaries

The Development Division's responsibilities include collaborative effort with a Planning Division, an Acquisition Division, and a Resource Preservation and Interpretation Division in support of a state wide park, recreation, and historic resources program. The Division deals specifically with development of state facilities in support of the overall program. The landscape architectural staff work as members of interdisciplinary teams which include architects and engineers, as well as experts in marine biology, wild life management and plant ecology.

The teams are responsible for the preparation of general plans, construction documents, budgeting, legislation analysis, interagency liaison, coordination of public involvement programs and project administration. Other Division responsibilities frequently include preparation of draft legislation, the preparation of construction development standards, and a variety of special assignments. The Division's landscape architects are given diverse assignments and many hold important administrative positions. Advancement is based not only on technical skill improvement, but also on ability to perform tasks which are designed to develop and improve existing processes and require a high level of interpersonal relationships skills.

Employment with a land resource related Federal Agency can frequently involve direct collaboration with the nation's highest policy makers.

A Federal Government Service Agency Responsible to Cabinet Level Department

Location:	Headquarters: Washington, D.C. Regional Offices: 9 Special Offices: 154
No. of Professionals:	290 landscape architects 20 architects 1200 engineers 492 range conservationists 363 wildlife biologists

313 soil scientists
229 hydrologists
280 computer specialists

This Federal Service Agency employs more landscape architects than any other single organization in the world. With responsibility for the protection and management of more than 187 million acres of federal land, the agency's landscape architects are involved with a wide range of activities including recreation planning, master land use planning, resource assessment and resource management. Staff landscape architects work as members of collaborative teams, which frequently include the full spectrum of professional specialists. The agency is a decentralized federal organization with 9 regional offices and 154 special offices located throughout the country. Most staff landscape architects serve in the 154 special offices, and deal with issues peculiar to their geographical area. Federal lands under the agency's jurisdiction are largely multi-use in nature and are open to private lease concession or permit operation of great diversity. As a result, staff landscape architects are normally called upon to produce land use alternative studies along with impact assessments on visual and recreational values of the land. This agency is also responsible for conducting "state-of-the-art" research in the area of land and resource management.

While many landscape architects are employed in public practice, the actual number changes from year to year. In the mid-1970s, the U.S. Department of Labor estimated that approximately 8,000 were so employed. Probably half of all landscape architects today are practicing in the public sector.

The three profiles also showed the differences in missions and activities which are found between the government levels. The amount of responsibility given to staff landscape architects in public practice is increasing each year, and will continue to do so.

In all three public practice profiles one feature stands out as common to all. Throughout public practice, there is a high level of collaborative design and management effort. While this can obviously be found in the other practice forms as well, it is especially prevalent in public practice. There is ample evidence to suggest, however, that collaborative activity is and will continue to increase in all practice levels as the nature of the profession, and the problems it deals with, increase in complexity.

Public practice is an exciting and demanding practice mode. It is safe to predict that the need for landscape architects in public practice will outstrip the other practice forms in the years ahead. As the demand for public recreation increases and available open space decreases, the need for protecting, managing and enhancing the public domain will continue to grow. It is equally safe to suggest that many innovative and important contributions will continue to be made to the profession by this dedicated group of professionals.

Academic Practice

Academic practice, or professional teaching in landscape architecture, has shown the same dramatic growth in numbers and stature as the other practice forms during the twentieth century. From the first program, with a single teacher in 1900, academic practice grew to nearly 100 programs and 1,000 teachers by the three quarter century mark. As the demand for qualified landscape architects continues into the twenty-first century, so also will the demand for teachers and for qualified educational programs.

Teaching requires a special combination of design, technical and human skills.

Of all the practice forms, academic practice may well be the most demanding as well as the most rewarding. Not only must teachers be highly skilled professional landscape architects, they must also possess the ability to convey their knowledge and experience in an understandable and meaningful way. They must have the skills of two professions;

landscape architecture and teaching.

Moreover, academic practitioners must possess the ability to analyze and evaluate new concepts and issues facing the profession. Traditionally, boundary expanding research and technological advancement has been the province of academic practice. While certainly this responsibility is shared by all practitioners, the academic practitioner's access to research support in the form of quality libraries, computer hardware and software, and a wide variety of special expertise, places a high level of discovery responsibility in their arena. And so a third area of skill and expertise is added to the academic mode: research capability.

A fourth skill is also required. Professional advancement in the academic field is often predicated on the ability to communicate in written form. Many universities and colleges require their faculty to publish state-of-the-art information on a regular basis as a prerequisite for advancement. While the value of this requirement as the principal basis of judging faculty credentials is frequently debated, it has been responsible for a large portion of the current written material available on the state of the profession.

Administrative and managerial skills are also prerequisites in academic practice. Running a landscape architectural program or department with staff members representing a wide variety of skills and interests is not significantly different from running a private or public agency office of equal size. Continuing job advancement requires the acquisition of the same skills in academic practice as the other practice areas. Teaching does, however, have some uniquely different aspects.

The teacher's product is people, tomorrow's landscape architects. While longer to materialize, the rewards for successful academic practice are rich, indeed.

Unlike most other practice forms, where professional satisfaction often comes from built evidence of creativity, the academic practitioner must depend on more long term rewards. Program growth, student success and advancement of the profession within the program's sphere of influence are more standard measures of academic achievement. These returns are slow to emerge and may take entire careers to show their evidence. This does not suggest that the academic practitioner has no short term rewards. Certainly there is great pleasure in watching a young student mature and progress successfully through the curriculum. Life long friendships are made, and the student-teacher relationship is a remarkable and exciting experience.

The profession of landscape architecture depends heavily upon its academic practitioners. While it may seem obvious, the future of the profession will be profoundly affected by the skills of the academic practitioner. Their "product" is people, people who will be tomorrows' landscape architects.

This brief look at the three traditional forms of landscape architectural practice provides an insight to the diversity of the profession. Yet, there is even greater diversity to be explored. A number of variations and totally new practice forms emerged during the late 1960s and the 1970s. The traditional forms, however, do now and will continue to represent the profession's practice mainstream. Each in its own way has a particular form of satisfaction or reward. The private practitioner deals largely with "built" forms upon the landscape. These are tangible objects or improvements which are easily recognized and they can be enjoyed and admired by professional and lay person alike.

The public practitioner tends to work on a broad scale and deals with very natural settings. Admiration is manifested in public recognition that attributes creativity to natural rather than "man-made" actions.

The academic practitioner finds satisfaction in the shaping of people rather than things. Success is measured by the accomplishments and creativity of others: the graduates who have been trained and stimulated by creative teaching.

The increasing number of practice variations and new practice forms indicates, however, that the rewards and satisfactions are not limited to the traditional practice modes.

Variations And New Practice Forms

The landscape architect's special affinity for the land and for people has directed the course of the profession since Olmsted's day. For the most part, and with the benefit of hindsight, the growth of the profession is neither surprising nor unusual. The private, public, and academic forms of practice parallel the course followed by all the design professions, as well as lawyers, doctors and other service professions. With the exception of the dramatically rapid growth of landscape architecture and its special beliefs, its story mirrors most other professions during the twentieth century.

When Larry Halprin addressed the convention of the American Society of Landscape Architects gathered in Atlanta, Georgia in 1978, he expressed the feeling that landscape architecture was more like an ideology than a profession. Halprin suggested that landscape architectures' devotion to the landscape and people's special place in the landscape was a conviction held with a fervor equal to the strongest religious or political beliefs. Taken at its face value, many might believe that this ideological conviction would hold the profession on a rather narrow course. An accounting of the profession's growth and its unique diversity, however, shows that the conviction has had an exactly opposite effect.

This final section of Chapter Two examines, in limited detail, the variations and new practice forms of landscape architecture which have emerged during the twentieth century.

The variations are considerable and new practice forms emerge almost daily. To discuss every variation and new form would be impossible, and would be instantly outdated. What can be accomplished here, however, is an overview designed to demonstrate the expanding variety of professional practice opportunity and provide a basis for understanding future variations.

When one stops for a moment and contemplates the profession and its growth, nearly all the variations and new practice forms appear predictable. Many have emerged as natural reactions to advanced technology and the age of specialization. Others grew from a natural and symbiotic relationship between landscape architecture and the other design professions. Still others developed in response to changing social and cultural patterns and needs. More recently, the profession has become an excellent stepping stone to specialized careers in related fields, especially those with environmental emphasis.

It is often difficult to distinguish new practice forms from new opportunities in an old practice form. The distinction is argumentative, at best, for certainly new opportunity will be met by both new forms as well as restructured existing forms. To save further arguments the term *boundary expansion* might be more appropriately applied to all the variations, new as well as modified existing forms. A number of examples follow:

Specialization

Modern technology has caused, in landscape architecture, as in other design professions, a growing trend toward practice specialization. In some instances this trend has been accomplished by the traditional practice forms. Many government agencies deal with highly specific concerns, and some private practice firms concentrate on specific regional or technological specializations. For the most part, however, specialized practice needs have been met by a variety of new practice forms. A partial list of these new forms would include:

Environmental Specialization:

● *Land Resource Assessment and Management:*
This area involves use of computer modeling and predicting, satellite photography with infrared sensing capabilities, high speed data processing, research methodology testing, and incorporates a wide variety of scientific collaboration. The service effort is frequently regional in scale, but can also be national and international in scope. While services can be provided by private practice firms, it is more common to find consortiums which bring together university research facilities, private foundations, government agencies and private consultants in joint venture efforts. The frequent requirements for sophisticated hardware support facilities and special expertise makes it difficult for any one organization to maintain all under a single entity. The U.S. Forest Service is one of a handful of exceptions to this rule.

Strip and open pit mining reclamation holds great opportunity for landscape architects who have a thorough knowledge of mining operations.

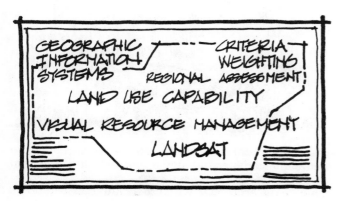

Land resource assessment and management is an environmental specialization pioneered by landscape architects.

● *Mining Reclamation:*
This specialized area was, for many years, the sole province of mining engineers and mining industry trained reclamation experts. In the 1970s, however, a new specialist emerged from the landscape architecture profession. Under the guidance of landscape architects with a thorough knowledge of mining operations, surface mining reclamation began to take on aesthetic and economic values more in keeping with the needs of the industry as well as environmental and political concerns. The term *creative land form modification*, became associated with the reclamation process, and landscape architects were more and more frequently sought out to bring these creative skills to the mining and reclamation team.

While many private practice firms offer these specialized services to both industry and government, the tasks require a complete working knowledge of mining procedures and operations and this is difficult to acquire. As a result, only a few firms have emerged as specialists in this area. These firms have expanded their expertise to include geologists, hydrologists, mining engineers and others associated with special areas of reclamation and associated mining operations.

● *Environmental Impact Assessment:*
Like mining reclamation specialist firms, a new kind of firm has evolved as a result of the Environmental Impact Statement (EIS) activity which became prevalent across the country in the 1970s. Landscape architects pooled their skills with the physical and natural scientists to offer highly specialized services to both business, industry and government. The environmental assessment firms often specialize even further. For example, some firms specialize in problems concerning the routing of power lines while others may deal with marine or coast line projects. Once again their services are normally offered by private practice types of firms. What makes them different from the traditional firms is the unique collection of skills contained within the firms and their specialized markets.

Social and Behavioral Specializations:

● *Design-Behavior Interaction:*

The landscape architect's special affinity for people has lead the profession quite naturally to develop specialists in the area of design-behavior interaction. Specialized firms, university research units, private research institutes, foundations and government agencies are providing in-depth studies which deal with how people use the landscape and how the landscape can be better designed to serve human needs.

This new practice form deals with the linkage between the social and behavioral sciences, and has led to further specializations in the areas of project programming and post occupancy evaluation.

● *Citizen Participation:*

Specialized consultants have emerged from the landscape architectural profession in response to the growing demand for citizen participation at all levels of governmental decision making. Federal law requires citizen participation in the approval process for all federally funded or financially underwritten projects, and state and local governments are following suit. Meaningful citizen participation requires specialized coordination activities as well as an understanding of the impacts and trade-offs of project development. Landscape architects are merging their talents with the skills of social scientists and meeting facilitators to provide these unique new services.

Organizing and facilitating citizen participation in design and land use decision making offers great opportunities to those landscape architects with good organizational and communication skills.

The Entreprenuers

● *General:*

In the early 1920s, a group of landscape architects resigned from the American Society of Landscape Architects when it adopted a Code of Ethics which barred them from growing and selling plant material and/or providing labor for installation or mainte-

nance operations. To do any of these things would have caused them to lose their professional society membership status. For more than 50 years, this group of trained and professionally skilled landscape architects was denied access to the professional society by virtue of its Code of Ethics. In 1974 ASLA revised its Code of Ethics to eliminate the disenfranchisement prohibition. (Before one becomes overly critical of the ASLA it must be pointed out that all of the design professional societies had similar provisions in their Code of Ethics. ASLA was one of the first to eliminate the practice provision in their Code of Ethics). The change in ASLA's Code of Ethics was in direct response to changing times and realization that practice form had little, if anything, to do with professional competence, judgement, or ethical dealings with the general public. The removal of this provision from the Code of Ethics returned a large measure of professional respectibility to a time honored practice form and paved the way for a variety of new practice forms.

● *Design-Build:*

The design-build firms incorporate the features of the conventional design firm and a general contracting firm.

Landscape architects who create and construct their own designs are said to be in a design-build practice form. This simple statement describes an exciting and profitable form of practice. Not only are the traditional "design" skills mandatory, but specialized business skills and capital resources are also necessary ingredients in the design-build process.

While not universally true, most design-build firms do not own or operate nurseries. They are designers and contractors and employ skilled people from both areas. They normally buy nursery stock at wholesale in the same way they buy bricks and lumber, adding a mark-up as they pass these items along to their project clients. They seldom split their activities by acting as designers only or contractors only. Design-build firms suggest that they can offer complete project control from preliminary design to finished product with resulting cost economies, better quality control, and more efficient and timely execution of their work effort. All of these factors result in a better product for their clients. To maintain a high professional standard, design-built firms operate in a highly competent manner and identify for a prospective client exactly how they operate and how their charges are to be determined. Fees are stated in advance and consulting services are closely related to those provided by the traditional private practice firms.

● *Self-Client:*

This somewhat unusual term refers to landscape architects and landscape architectural firms who serve themselves and clients. Unlike the legal adage which suggests that "he who defends himself has a fool for a client", the self-client approach in landscape architecture has been anything but foolish.

Like all professionals, landscape architects occasionally derive an income in excess of expenses. To many, this extra income represents an opportunity to invest in other ventures. Also like others, landscape architects are not immune from investing in areas about which they know little or nothing. Some, however, have taken the view that investment in areas where their special expertise will provide them a competitive edge, makes great sense. By training and experience, landscape architects have a special knowledge of the land, of housing, of growth trends, and other conditions affecting the real estate market and the construction industry. Many of these landscape architects have decided to serve themselves as clients.

The self-client is both a designer and a developer or a contractor or both. Normally a separate company or corporation is formed to buy, develop, improve and sell property. This company hires the landscape architect or landscape architectural firm to provide the same services it would to any other client company. Selecting the best site, determining the most appropriate use, providing design and consulting services, helping to secure financing, zoning and other approvals, overseeing construction, developing promotional tools, and coordinating the overall project are services provided in the same way they would to any other client. The fees for these services, however, are only a fringe benefit to the self-client. The potential profits to be made as a contractor-developer far outweigh the profits to be made by providing professional services. The landscape architect self-clients are doing for themselves what they do for other clients on a regular basis. If they are successful they can make a lot of money for their conventional clients, why not do the same for themselves? As self-clients they are putting their special skills as landscape architects to work for themselves, and enjoy the increased benefits as a result.

● *Industry Related Ownership:*

Industries and other design related professions often find it profitable to own landscape architectural firms which are allowed to operate independently from the parent company. A large architectural-engineering firm, for example, may purchase or develop a landscape architectural firm without absorbing them into the parent organization. The landscape architectural firm is allowed to operate independently, soliciting its own clients, while at the same time servicing the parent company's projects.

A similar situation would be a large development company owning a landscape architectural firm and allowing it to operate at "arms length", while providing specialized services to the owner company. In the same fashion, a landscape architectural firm might purchase or organize support firms which would operate independently while providing direct support to the landscape architectural firm. Such arrangements might include controlling interest in a commercial art firm, marketing firm, engineering firm, construction firm or some other specialized organization purchased to broaden the profit base and provide specialized support services. While these support service and related specialities are more frequently absorbed into the operational framework of the parent company, the "arms length" approach is not at all uncommon. As design professionals become more sophisticated in the business world the benefits of such subsidiary operations become more appealing and frequency of such organizational structures increases.

The Age of Consultants

Landscape architecture, like most technical professions, generates its fair share of highly specialized consultants. From expert witnesses' providing court testimony on land use, zoning or aesthetics, to experts in recreating historic gardens, landscape architects have parlayed their special interest and expertise into a wide variety of profitable consulting ventures.

These expert consultants come from all practice areas and frequently travel widely to offer their special services. A private practice consultant in the South East, for example, is a land use specialist and works closely with a nationally prominent condemnation attorney. The land use consultant provides technical advice on preparation of trial arguments in condemnation lawsuits and testifies as an expert witness during trials. The consultant's relationship with the attorney takes him across the length and breadth of the country.

A midwest academic practitioner provides another example. As a specialist in the behaviorial aspects of park and playground design, the consultant provides expert consultation to private and public park designers over a wide geographic area.

Specialized consulting can be interesting and exciting. The greatest opportunities in this area come to those who have developed, over years of practice activity, specialized and often unique skills, which can be marketed to other firms, public agencies, industry, and the legal profession.

The Stepping Stone

More and more frequently landscape architecture is being viewed as an ideal bridge to related but quite different fields of professional endeavor. This approach has been commonly followed, for some time, by those who wish to become city planners or golf course architects. Both of these professional activities have alternative means of acquiring entry level skills, but landscape architecture is usually seen as one of the more desirable stepping stones.

There are, however, many other, less obvious, professional fields which can be accessed by means of an undergraduate education in landscape architecture. Combining landscape architecture with a masters level degree in business administration can open doors in the fields of mortgage banking, marketing management in land related corporations, and industrial organizations. Similarly, a second degree in public administration or resource planning can provide access to a variety of excellent governmental positions which have a land related mission.

During the 1970s many university law schools began admitting undergraduate landscape architects with appropriate pre-law training. These dual degree holders are practicing specialized law in such areas as zoning, land use and environmental protection.

The variations and new forms of landscape architectural practice are exciting, indeed. Are they really new practice forms or merely expansions of the traditional forms? It doesn't really matter. What is important is the recognition of the profession's unusual ability to expand its boundries. Unique expansion potential sets landscape architecture apart from its sister professions, and marks a vitality that will continue to serve it well for decades to come.

Landscape architectural practice in all of its forms is a part of a larger whole. The profession is not, obviously, practiced in a vacuum, but rather within a larger framework that requires collaboration as well as understanding of the broader industry which the profession serves. The following chapter looks at this broader base as it discusses the profession's role within the industry as a whole.

Chapter Two Notes

1. Jot D. Carpenter, "Study of State Highway Departments", 1978 (unpublished)

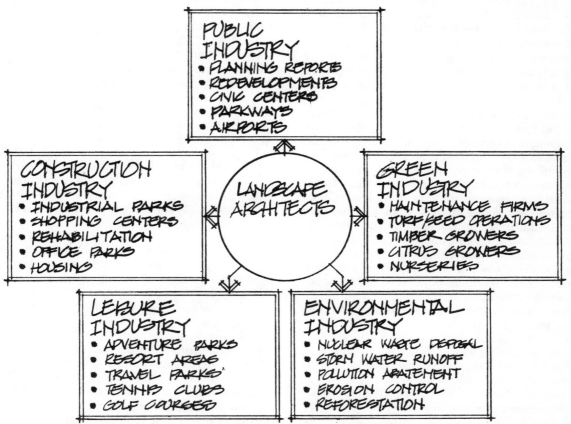

PUBLIC INDUSTRY
• PLANNING REPORTS
• REDEVELOPMENTS
• CIVIC CENTERS
• PARKWAYS
• AIRPORTS

CONSTRUCTION INDUSTRY
• INDUSTRIAL PARKS
• SHOPPING CENTERS
• REHABILITATION
• OFFICE PARKS
• HOUSING

LANDSCAPE ARCHITECTS

GREEN INDUSTRY
• MAINTENANCE FIRMS
• TURF/SEED OPERATIONS
• TIMBER GROWERS
• CITRUS GROWERS
• NURSERIES

LEISURE INDUSTRY
• ADVENTURE PARKS
• RESORT AREAS
• TRAVEL PARKS
• TENNIS CLUBS
• GOLF COURSES

ENVIRONMENTAL INDUSTRY
• NUCLEAR WASTE DISPOSAL
• STORM WATER RUNOFF
• POLLUTION ABATEMENT
• EROSION CONTROL
• REFORESTATION

Landscape architecture serves a diverse and constantly growing list of industries.

Introduction

The basic laws of business economics govern landscape architecture just as they do any other service profession, and with the same compelling force which applies to commerce and industry. Make no mistake about it, landscape architecture, whether publicly, privately or academically practiced, is a business. Landscape architects are hired because they supply a service which directly responds to a real market demand. From the landscape architect who consults on the behavioral relevance of playground design to the large collaborative team providing multi-use planning for a national forest, landscape architects are a part of an economic system, ruled by the laws of supply and demand.

Within this economic framework it is possible to identify certain spheres of influence which have a particular bearing on landscape architectural practice. In general terms these spheres of influence can be classified into five areas: The public service industry, the green industry, the construction industry, the leisure industry and the environmental industry. Not everything landscape architects do fall neatly into three areas, but they certainly represent the major generators of demand for landscape architectural services.

The Public Service Industry

The use of the term industry seems strange in this area when one considers that the major representatives of this activity are government agencies. Most economists, however, will argue that government is an industry. While it may not always compete in the open marketplace for the delivery of services, it is ruled by the same laws of supply and demand. The argument is purely academic. The fact remains that most public services are offered by government or institutional agencies.

The public service industry is a major influence on the practice of landscape architecture. In the broadest sense, the landscape architectural related service industry includes all those programs and activities of government and other institutions, from the local to the federal level, which deal with the land and improvements upon the land as well as a large number of closely related activities. Across the full public spectrum this includes a tremendous amount of activity.

Of all the public service institutions, government and its myriad agencies has the greatest influence on the profession. Even a casual glance at a city's capital improvement budget, for example, provides an accurate summary of the physical impact local government can have on the landscape. Add to this annual figure additional expenditures for bond issues, special assessments, revenue sharing, grants, emergency funding and contingency funding and the impact is enormous. Moreover, government is also in the business of planning, programming, and policy making which can have an even greater impact on the landscape. The "paper" business of government is just as real as the capital improvement business, and has an equal influence on the market for landscape architectural services.

Roads, parkways, utilities, parks, airports, flood control projects, ports, redevelopment projects, civic centers, government buildings, recreation studies, planning reports, zoning activities, beautification projects, and dozens of other activities are carried out by municipalities and counties across the country every year. Add to this similar activities of regional, state, multi-state, and federal agencies and you have identified this country's major industry.

From all of this it is not difficult to understand why so many landscape architects are directly employed by government and its agencies. Estimates during the late 1970s suggested that half of all the landscape architects active in the United States were employed by government agencies. With the demand for public service growing each year, it is reasonable to predict an equal growth of landscape architects employed in this industry.

The public service industry's influence on private practice is equally dramatic. Many private practice firms deal almost exclusively with government clients, and most successful firms strive for a balance between government and private clients. All of this points to the need for a very important skill, one which is seldom taught in the formal education programs: "Political Savvy". While this skill is important to all methods of practice and used throughout the profession's industry base, it is essential to successfully access the public service industry market.

The issue of political skills is addressed in Chapter 16 of this book, but the importance of these skills cannot be stressed often enough. All too frequently other design professionals are being called upon to provide services which could be better performed by landscape architects. This results largely from a lack of political aggressiveness and understanding of the political process. It is fundamental to the long term survival of landscape architecture, that the importance of the role of government as an industry be understood and that landscape architects train themselves to function within this special arena.

The Green Industry

The landscape architect's relationship with the green industry is probably the best understood of all the industry bases. The relationship goes back to the days of Olmsted and beyond. As an economic market for the profession, the green industry is perceived to hold less opportunity than the other areas. It is, nonetheless, a dynamic and important industry and deserves a careful review.

Whatever market potential the green industry may hold for landscape architecture, the ties between the two are compelling and important. The green industry is represented by a variety of sub-industries

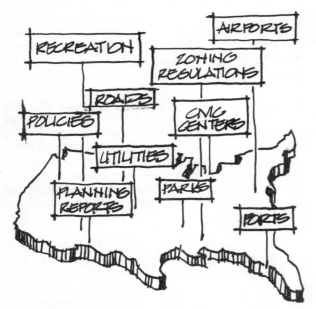

Public service may be the nation's largest industry.

which include retail and wholesale nurseries, turf and seed operations, commercial timber growers, retail and wholesale florists and foilage growers, fruit and citrus growers, landscape contractors, grounds maintenance firms and a host of others. The industry also includes product and grounds equipment manufacturers and suppliers, horticultural chemical and fertilizer manufacturers and suppliers, irrigation manufacturers, suppliers, and installers, and a wide variety of other supporting services.

Landscape architecture will always cherish its traditional ties with the green industry.

The green industry employs the special skills of many scientific professionals including agronomists, arborists, botonists, horticulturalists, foresters, soil scientists, chemists, and many more. Taken in whole, the green industry has gigantic proportions and has played a dramatic role in forces which upgrade the character of the American landscape.

Landscape architects are employed as designers and consultants throughout the green industry. This is most noticeable in the nursery and landscape contracting arms of the industry where landscape architects couple their design skills with marketing and business acumen. Landscape architects are also frequently found as staff counsultants to specialty manufacturers and suppliers to the industry.

The landscape architect's traditional affinity for the land and its resources have always fostered a strong tie between the profession and this active industry. The ties have been ones of mutual understanding and support for common goals and concerns. During the early years of the profession's history the link to the green industry was nearly exclusive and provided the greatest potential source for employment. This link weakened over the years as other industries grew and provided greater service demands. The link continued to weaken during the second half of the twentieth century, and there are today, many landscape architects who have little or no connection with the green industry. Specialists dealing with computer modeling, the behavioral aspects of design, and land use law may have no contact at all.

As long as landscape architects deal with the land, however, the ties between the profession and the green industry will remain strong. The link is formed by a common and prevailing goal to create more handsome and enjoyable landscapes.

The Construction Industry

During the 1950s and 1960s, landscape architecture became inextricably linked with the nation's construction industry. This link finds it roots in the post World War II housing boom and the expansion of suburban America. In the years which followed the second World War, landscape architecture played a major role in the growth of the construction and development industry in America.

The modern day construction industry is multi-faceted and ranges from small building contractors erecting a few single family homes each year to multi-national corporations involved in developing entire communities. The industry divides itself into several categories including, shelter, commercial, industrial, utility, highway, and specialty contractors. Each of these categories is frequently further subdivided by size and geographical location of the construction organization. Some construction industry firms operate in more than one category offering subcontract specialization to a variety of general contractors.

The construction industry is also supported by a tremendous number of manufacturing and supply companies, as well as distributors and manufacturer's agents. The industry is also supported by a large number of service oriented sub-industries which include real estate professionals, marketing and public relations specialists, financial agents, mortgage brokers, investment counselors, and of course, the other design professionals.

During the late 1960s and early 1970s the construction industry saw the land developer emerge as a major industry force. The success of developers like Levitt and Rouse encouraged hundreds of others to move in similar directions. While not always a constructor in the traditional sense, the land developer

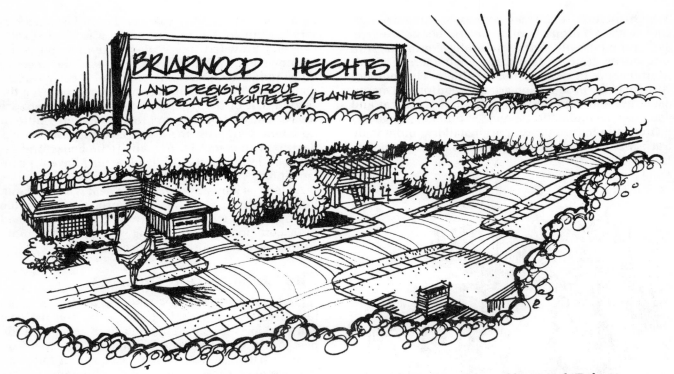

Since the 1950s the landscape architect's link with the construction industry has grown and matured. Today serving this major industry is a primary thrust of many firms.

brought a new level of sophistication to the construction industry. This sophistication included new marketing and sales concepts, new managerial and administration techniques, new and more imaginative ways to finance and underwrite construction costs, and the bringing together, for the first time, of development teams.

Prior to the 1960s, landscape architects were serving the construction industry in highly conventional ways; providing landscape plans for commercial buildings, and housing projects, or office buildings. Most land subdivisions were being designed by engineers. (With a few notable exceptions; Olmsted did his plan for Fairfield outside of Chicago in 1868).

The land developers, however, realized that sound large scale planning required the services of many skilled professional types, including landscape architects. It did not take them long to realize that the landscape architect brought a very special kind of skill to the design team and more often than not the landscape architect was named as team leader. It was during this same period that a number of nationally prominent landscape architects popularized methodological site analysis as an integral step in the land planning process. This systematic approach for determining how the landscape could be most sensi-

tively used also coincided with a growing concern for our nation's natural and ecological heritage. It is not surprising that the landscape architect became so valuable a contributor to the land developer's team. Some landscape architects found that they were so good at this integrated form of practice that they are now leaders of development companies and corporations across the country.

The construction industry represents a major market staple for the private practice landscape architect. Shopping centers, office parks, housing of all sizes, shapes, and forms, industrial parks, golf courses, renewal and rehabilitation projects, and a host of other activities have been an habitual market opportunity for landscape architects. In addition to supplying vast amounts of work to the private practice landscape architect, the construction industry directly employs large numbers of landscape architects. Development companies, real estate companies, turnkey contractors, and many others employ staff landscape architects to guide their daily operations.

It should also be noted that an equally large number of landscape architects are hired by government agencies as an indirect and often direct result of construction industry activities. The myriad of public agencies which have formed as control mechanisms over large scale land development practices find it very helpful to have landscape architects on their staff. While not the largest industry in the world, the construction industry certainly has the largest single impact on the profession of landscape architecture. Perhaps 75% of all landscape architects are directly or indirectly impacted by this constantly fluctuating industry. To survive as a member of, or consultant to, this volatile industry requires a great deal more than basic landscape architectural skills. Business skills, interpersonal relationship skills, the ability to collaborate, compromise, and share rewards are all paramount to success in developing markets in this industry base.

The Leisure Industry

During the second half of the twentieth century the shortened work week and the increasing amount of disposable personal income spawned a major new industry. The leisure industry has shown spectacular growth, and has been led by companies like AMF Alcourt, Holiday Inns and Club Universe. From bowling alleys, to golf courses, to waterslides, the leisure industry is making a mark on the American landscape, and will likely continue to do so.

It may be difficult in the minds of many to separate the leisure industry from the construction industry,

Many landscape architects have turned their special understanding of the land and the game of golf into careers as golf course architects.

From theme parks to waterslides, the leisure industry is making a significant mark on the american landscape.

or for that matter, from the park and recreation arms of the public service industry. Both are certainly involved in this new industry, but what is being suggested here is the emergence of a major new private capital industry that has embraced the American public's leisure time needs in a comprehensive manner never before contemplated by park and recreation directors or the general contractor who builds an occasional theater or skating rink.

The leisure industry is one of the fastest growing market forces in our country, and it offers exciting practice opportunities for landscape architects. Even a partial list of private enterprise activity that meets the leisure time market demand is impressive. The list would include; golf course and tennis club construction, resort operations of all kinds (hotels, motels, travel parks), Theme parks (Disney World, Busch Gardens), Adventure parks (Lion Country Safari, Sea World), and a host of smaller operations from miniature golf courses to skate board ramps. This list can be expanded by a ride along any arterial street in any community in the country. The leisure industry is making a daily mark on the American landscape.

Certainly not all of this activity holds promise for the landscape architect, but much of it does or can. Many landscape architects are also golf course architects, for instance, and their practice is directly affected by the strength of the leisure time industry. Many landscape architects have been reatined to design and plan entire resort facilities including golf courses, ski trails, tennis facilities, and associated activities. Others have been retained to design wave pools, exercise courses, travel trailer parks, and putt-putt golf courses. The National Park Service and the U.S. Forest Service hire a significant number of landscape architects who deal directly with the private leisure industry when looking at mixed use land development or the specific planning of a national recreation area intended for concessionair operation.

There is no reason to doubt the continued growth of the leisure time industry during the twenty-first century. Where the leisure industry utilizes the landscape as either resource or backdrop, the services of the landscape architects will always be in demand.

The Environmental Industry

Serving the environmental industry frequently requires collaboration with a wide variety of other specialists.

The environmental industry is principally a scientific and legal domain. Those who operate within this industry hold advanced degrees in specializa-

tions such as law, marine and micro-biology, hydrology, geology, chemistry, environmental engineering, botany, wildlife management, limnology, ichthyology, meteorology, and a variety of other even more scholarly fields, where Phd's are frequently a prerequisite. In spite of the pedantic sound of this industry there are excellent opportunities for landscape architects to play important roles.

By comparison to most industries, the environmental industry is relatively small. The industry is growing, however, and continued concern for the fragile nature of the environment will insure its continued growth for many years to come.

The environmental industry takes on several forms, but functions in three principal ways: Regulation, Research, and Consultation. The Environmental Protection Agency, Office of Surface Mining, Bureau of Land Management and the Forest Service are the primary government agencies dealing with both protection and with research. State and regional agencies also exist to deal with protection. All of these agencies, however, fall under the public service industry. Their existence, nonetheless, has prompted a sub-industry of semi-public and private organizations whose environmental research and consultation role is of great interest to landscape architects.

A growing number of publically and privately supported foundations and research institutes are exploring ways to assess, manage, and improve environmental conditions throughout the country. Using federal and private research grants these organizations are supplying new knowledge and developing new technology of special value to environmental protection, management and enhancement. In many of these situations research is being conducted by landscape architects as members of research teams, or by special studies involving existing projects, or those under construction. Issues such as storm water run-off, nuclear waste disposal, erosion and sedimentation control, reforestation, and pollution abatement are frequently studied by landscape architects working in concert with specialized research organizations, or with direct grant funds. The landscape architect's special skills as communicator coupled with ability to translate technical matter into lay terms has proven to be very useful to the environmental industry.

The private arm of the environmental industry has shown dramatic growth and frequently interacts with the public service agencies and the research groups. Specialized private practice firms can be found throughout the country, offering the preparation of environmental impact assessments and statements, and consulting to both government and private industry alike.

The environmental industry espouses a set of goals which are uniquely appealing to the profession of landscape architecture. These goals are largely shared in common, providing excellent opportunity for mutual understanding and coordinated effort. As landscape architecture and the environmental sciences move toward century 21, collaboration and intra-professional assimilation will bring about more and more jointly developed answers to the country's environmental concerns. It can be foreseen, as a result, that landscape architecture needs to sharpen its scientific base without losing sight of human needs and expectations.

Some Others

No list is ever complete. Like earlier lists in this book, this outline of five industry categories does not cover all the bases. In closing this chapter, then, a brief review of several additional industry service bases would be appropriate.

Perhaps the most promising of these additional service areas is the burgeoning Alternative Energy Industry. Landscape architects have already played an important role in this area by pioneering site planning techniques which serve energy conservation purposes. Earth sheltered housing, solar access, and passive energy planning are only a few of the alternative energy areas where landscape architects are applying their skills. In the years ahead this industry could become a major market source for landscape architects.

The landscape architect can play a most important role in helping this nation become energy independent.

Surface and Pit Mine Reclamation is another area where landscape architects are making unique contributions to the state of the art. Increased dependence on coal and shale oil for energy will dramatically increase the amount of surface mining across the face of this country. At the same time, growing environmental concerns surrounding mining operations will place the landscape architect in a unique position to serve the mining industry in a highly creative way.

As our nation moves into the 21st century new industries will form and existing industries will restructure to meet the changing demands of the marketplace, as well as changing national interests and goals. Landscape architects will find new and ever expanding areas in which to practice their art. Between the writing and the publication of this book (about 18 monts) new industries have already been formed and others have altered their product or service to be more competitive in the marketplace. To survive in this economic marketplace, the landscape architect must maintain a constant flexibility, always upgrading skill levels and competence, and be ever ready to shift direction to take advantage of new markets. The profession's history has shown a remarkable ability to expand its horizons. To carry this historic trend forward requires only the recognition that market flexibility today is a science. To be prepared to expand the profession's boundaries requires the continued acquisition of skills and competence, and the ability to look ahead and forecast potential new markets.

Collaboration

A look at the Industry/Service Base cannot be complete without a final word concerning the need for professional collaboration. At all levels of practice and within each industry service base, the delivery of services has become highly complex. The amount of information needed to deal with complex design and problem solving issues is usually staggering. Many projects require the skills of several independent professionals, each bringing a special expertise to the effort. It is not uncommon for a complex project to involve as many as a dozen different professional disciplines.

New technology, an ever increasing data base, specialization of services, and increasing project complexity are twentieth century facts of life, and they will continue to dominate professional practice for years to come. The net result, of course, will be the increasing demand for professional cooperation and collaboration.

Landscape architects will, more and more frequently, be asked to coordinate their services with the services of other design professionals, social scientists, environmental scientists, economists, and other consultants with specialized skills. This is not a new idea. In fact, many landscape architects already function in this way. The growing number of multi-disciplinary firms with a variety of specialized expertise is also evidence of response to this trend.

For many professionals, the collaborative trend presents unusual problems. Successful collaboration usually requires a variety of skills not associated with technical competence. These are human skills and deal with interpersonal relations, peer associations, and synergistic activity requiring the ability to compromise and defuse interprofessional misunderstandings. These are issues discussed later in this book in greater detail (see Part III, the Human Skills), but the importance of human and political skills to the collaborative process cannot be overstated.

Successful collaboration often depends on highly refined interpersonal relationship skills. Respecting the skills and contributions of all team members is a must.

An overriding issue with many professionals placed in collaborative situations is who leads the collaborative team. Every team must have a leader, but professional jealousies often confuse real collaborative issues with unnecessary concern over who is to be the prime consultant or team leader.

Logically the team leader should be that professional whose expertise represents the majority concern of the project to be undertaken. Alternatively, the team leader might be that professional with the greatest managerial and leadership skills. Hopefully the prime consultant would fit both of these criteria, for the absence of either will make team collaboration difficult at best.

Frequently landscape architects are reluctant to accept team membership roles which are secondary to other consultants, especially if the project is of a type consistent with their perceived area of expertise. These same firms will often refuse to participate on collaborative teams when they are not chosen as the prime consultant. In many cases their refusal to par-

ticipate leaves a void in the team which is filled by a nonlandscape architect team member. Everyone suffers as a result of this near-sighted concern over who is to be the prime consultant. It occurs among all the design professionals and the damage it causes can be acute.

The age of collaboration is real and its importance will continue to grow. Landscape architects, like all professionals must train themselves to fit collaborative modes with flexibility and a spirit of cooperation aimed at producing the best possible project outcome.

The multi-disciplinary design firm requires almost constant collaboration between its diverse practitioners.

The multi-disciplinary design firm and the larger government agency have become a logical outcome of the need for collaborative effort. Several design disciplines combine together into a single firm with a well defined chain of command. Principals of the firm decide prime professional roles among the expertise within the firm and eliminate the multi-headed appearance of collaborative joint ventures or professional associations which are frequently necessary when several firms join forces to bring the full spectrum of expertise together to solve a complex problem. The multi-disciplinary firm will normally include the skills of architecture, engineering and landscape architecture. Additionally they may include environmentalists, economists, planners, geographers, and others, depending on their area of practice and marketing approach.

PART TWO
PROFESSIONAL SKILLS

ART
PROFESSION
CRAFT
BUSINESS

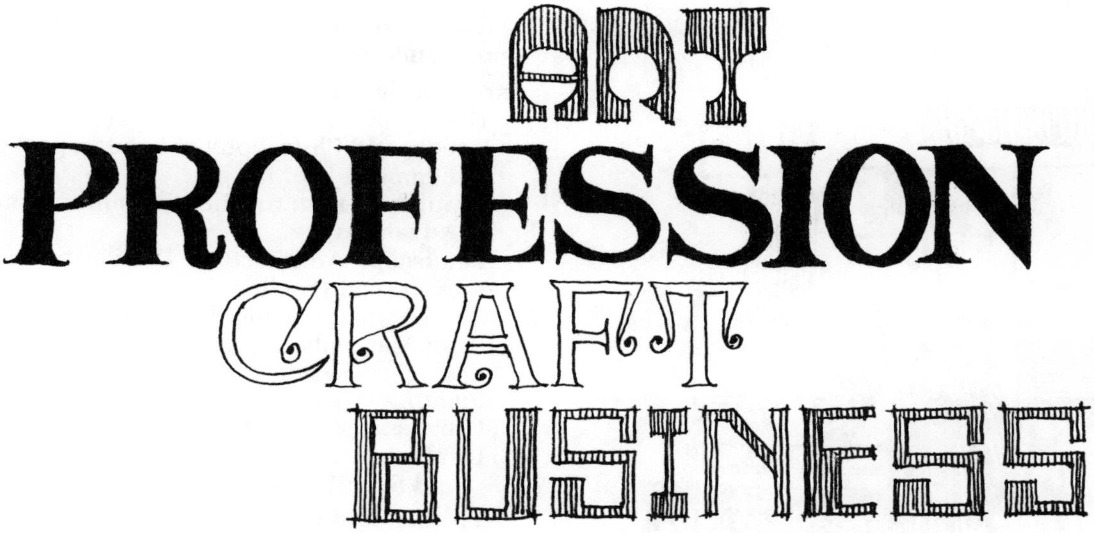

Introduction

The vast majority of practicing landscape architects achieved their career positions through a combination of formal education and practice experience. While a few approached the profession by way of "on the job" training and experience their numbers are small and the ever-increasing demand for greater technical and theoretical skills throughout the profession will reduce the viability of this approach in the years to come. For this reason, Chapter Four will look at formal education as the most frequently accepted method for acquiring the basic skills needed to access the profession. Chapter Four will look at both undergraduate and graduate level education. It will also look briefly at the philosophical process and the accrediting of formal education programs in landscape architecture. Above all, Chapter Four will attempt to articulate the formal educational experience, and its relevance to landscape architectural practice.

Undergraduate Education

"Design being partly a profession, partly a craft, partly an art and partly a business, is searching—consciously or unconsciously—for identity that can sustain and dignify it. It is struggling not only to make good objects, when it can, and to make a living, which it must, but also to make a place for itself in the human community."

Sydney Harris, from "The
Consumer Viewpoint" address,
IDSA Meeting, Kentucky, 1977[1]

The Harris remarks provide an interesting framework for a look at education in the design professions. A profession, a craft, an art, and a business; terms which certainly describe landscape architecture in its broadest sense. For the most part it is the development of basic skills and theory in these areas that formal education should be expected to direct its emphasis. This is not intended to denegrate the unique total experience of undergraduate education. Neither does it preclude the need to learn a host of other skills uniquely common to successful landscape architectural practice. The statement merely suggests that an undergraduate curriculum in landscape architecture must, of necessity, include certain essential skill training within very specific time constraints, while at the same time foster and stimulate an intellectual awareness of the profession's ongoing search for identity and a place for itself in the human community. This is an enormous task, which is being met with an unprecedented high level of success.

Most landscape architects enter the profession by way of formal education, usually an undergraduate degree.

No matter how one chooses to practice, certain basic skills present themselves as common denominators. Studies in these basic skill areas are often referred to as core curriculum courses, and are normally common to all undergraduate programs. The Uniform National Examination used to evaluate minimum professional competency by most states requiring licensure, tests skills in these core areas. Historically, then, undergraduate programs have the responsibility to provide aspiring landscape architects with these basic skills. The undergraduate programs, of course, do a great deal more, but an examination of this fundamental responsibility provides an excellent look at the formal education process.

Base Skills: The Uniform National Examination divides base skills into four testing areas:[2]

1. History
2. Professional Practice
3. Design Theory
   —Conceptual Design
   —Planting Design
   —Master Planning
4. Design Implementation
   —Grading
   —Staking and Layout
   —Details and Specification

To provide skill training in these four general areas most undergraduate programs provide course instruction in the following subject areas:

History of Landscape Architecture
Theory and Philosophy of Landscape Architecture
Fundamentals of Design
Graphic Communication (Beginning and
   Advanced)
Landscape Architectural Design
Professional Practice
Site Engineering and Surveying
Plant Materials
Ecological Systems
Planting Design
Urban and Regional Analysis
Landscape Architectural Construction Drawings
   and Specifications

This list is supplemented by required and elective studies selected by the student, usually from areas of special interest or related subject matter. Studies are further supplemented by field trips, visiting professional critics, intern programs, travel programs, special seminars and public service activities. For more detailed curriculum information, please see the "Landscape Architectural Curriculum Content and Depth Chart" included in the Appendix.

Once again this subject list must be considered incomplete, but most programs in landscape architecture will follow it rather closely, allowing for variations of regional interest, faculty specialization and institutional resources. Variations may also be found between programs of four year and five year duration. The latter programs frequently provide more formalized intern or "on-the-job" training opportunities, travel options, and will allow for greater latitude in the selection and comprehensive use of electives.

All undergraduate programs attempt to teach basic skills in practice world situations. Visiting instructors will often take a design studio course through the redesign of a project already constructed, providing interesting comparisons between student solutions and the constructed project. Public service projects are often undertaken which include the design and construction of community playgrounds and other recreation or beautification activities and allow students to "see" a project from start to finish.

Helping to build a class-room designed project provides a hands-on experience to the student.

Nearly all undergraduate curricula place their emphasis on basic skill development coupled with mind-broadening electives. These programs are concerned with preparing students to function in the practice world in the most competitive manner. The undergraduate programs want their students to be able to pass the Uniform National Examination, and to find the best available jobs. Moreover, they want their graduates to be competent and successful practitioners, and future contributors to the profession's growth.

The profession's educators recognize, however, that undergraduate education is only the beginning of a long educational continuum. Base skill competence does little more than provide entry into the profession, it does not make a proficient landscape architect. The profession's rapid growth and exceptional diversity requires a great deal more than formally taught skills, as the new graduate soon finds out.

Most new graduates soon recognize that they know little or often nothing about some very fundamental skills required for their advancement in the pro-

fession. Most know nothing about business or financial management, very little about interpersonal relationship skills, very little about government systems or political acumen, very little about computers or other micro-processor systems which are becoming more prevalent throughout the profession, even less about the scientific fields with which landscape architecture interacts on an almost daily basis, and less yet about the often frightening scope of the profession they have just entered.

The new graduates' learning experience has just begun, and several roads to professional proficiency are available. A choice between these alternative roads to proficiency must soon be made. A period of apprenticeship and a comprehensive program of continuing education will provide the best opportunity to acquire those skills which could not be taught in the undergraduate education program. (Chapter Five will look at this subject in more detail.) Many students, however, will decide to take an extra step in the formal education process before entering the practice world. For many, graduate education provides a period for specialized training that will greatly enhance their entry level skills and prepare them for the unique boundary expansion areas of the profession. Graduate level programs offer special opportunities for many people and a look at these opportunities is most appropriate.

Graduate Education

A Master's degree in landscape architecture is considered the profession's terminal or final degree. While a few Phd. programs do exist, the MLA meets educational criteria for the profession's top degree. This fact is of special importance to those who wish to pursue academic careers where a terminal degree is a job prerequisite.

The Master's degree is also a prerequisite in a number of other employment areas in addition to teaching. Many specialized government agencies and almost all government planning agencies require an MLA or equivalent degree. Moreover, the Master's degree is more and more frequently seen by all employers as a sign of personal maturity and advanced skill that can provide new dimensions to their current staff, and they have begun to seek out the MLA graduate with increasing regularity.

To the undergraduate landscape architect, a Master's degree represents an advanced or second professional degree, which provdes an opportunity to specialize or sharpen base skills along with the maturing process. Most graduate programs in landscape architecture, however, have experienced a growing trend of enrollment by non-design undergraduate students. Students with undergraduate degrees in business administration, sociology, forestry, the sciences, and many other areas are looking to landscape architecture as a first professional degree through the graduate level programs.

Graduate landscape architecture students come from a wide variety of undergraduate backgrounds adding diversity and a collaborative viewpoint to the programs.

Students may seek out a graduate program because of its specialization, such as land resource management, design-behavior interaction, arid landscapes and so forth, or they may just wish to expand upon their undergraduate landscape architectural degree. Whatever their motivation, if they come from a non-design background, they need exposure to basic skill courses in order to acquire the professional base skills common to the profession. Most Master's programs will require non-design background students to spend an extra year in the program to learn these base skills. Experience has shown that higher levels of maturity and motivation will allow these students to learn in a year many of the technical skills acquired in two or three years by undergraduate students. The remaining core skills are acquired during practice experience and the apprentiseship period.

It is also interesting to note the increasing number of women in the graduate programs and the increasing number of graduate students who have returned to school several years after receiving their undergraduate degrees. (It should be pointed out that these same increases are also noted at the undergraduate level.)

Graduate education across the country shares a number of special responsibilities to the profession.

Much of the profession's boundary expansion has the potential to generate from the graduate programs. Research and practice specialization training should be considered important roles at the graduate level. Unique regional concerns are also more logically dealt with at the graduate level. To teach and discover have long been the credo of formal education. To these credos must be added the term lead. To teach, discover, and lead; three most important roles for formal education. Of these three roles, discovery and leadership must be primary concerns of the graduate programs.

Meaningful research is essential to the profession of landscape architecture, and the profession must look to the graduate programs to initiate research and to promulgate its findings. Beyond this, the academic graduate school community has the obligation to champion their discoveries, and provide the profession with graduates who possess the abilities to take this information into the world of professional practice and put it to practical use.

For many, graduate education offers special advantages. It should quickly be pointed out, however, that the Master's degree in landscape architecture is not the only option for those who wish to expand their skills, nurture their maturing process or acquire specialized knowledge. Many undergraduate landscape architects are finding Master's education in business administration, planning, sociology, political science, environmental science, engineering, architecture, journalism, and a host of other fields representing first professional degree skills are excellent career adjuncts and provide unique theoretical and skill combinations offering outstanding long range opportunities. Many undergraduate landscape architects have even chosen to pursue law degrees bringing their special understanding of and affinity for the land into law practices and Federal agencies who find the combination of exceptional usefulness.

Going forward to graduate school will increase in popularity with both student and employer as the profession continues to expand and increase its utilization of human knowledge. As a career strategy, graduate education may hold special appeal to those landscape architect undergraduates whose love for the profession is not equally matched by design and graphic skills. The profession needs problem solvers across a broad spectrum, and the days of the generalist are slowly diminishing. This inexorable fact allows for whole new set of career opportunities, and the graduate programs may well become the life blood of the profession's future.

With the number of undergraduate and graduate programs in landscape architecture continuing to increase it is essential that a system be maintained to insure the highest possible level of academic quality,

Some undergraduate landscape architects have chosen to pursue law degrees.

... or business administration and financial oriented graduate degrees.

and to further insure that these educational programs keep pace with the needs of the profession as a whole. The American Society of Landscape Architects, through its accrediting procedures, has assumed this responsibility. A review of the accrediting process follows:

Accreditation

In 1958 the National Commission on Accrediting formally approved the American Society of Landscape Architects as the official body for accrediting schools of landscape architecture. ASLA had been performing this task unofficially since the late 1930s. In those early years schools were accredited rather than programs, a cumbersome distinction which caused great confusion in later years. Under this earlier system schools which offered two landscape architectural programs (undergraduate and graduate), by meeting accreditation standards for one of their programs garnered the accreditation mantel for both. Because the standards were different for the two kinds of programs, it was possible through the "school" accreditation approach to provide the seal of approval to a program that did not in fact meet the standards applicable to that particular kind of program or degree.

In the late 1960s the U.S. Department of Health, Education and Welfare (HEW) took on the task of monitoring and controlling the official accreditation bodies. At the same time the National Commission on Accrediting's responsibilities were assumed by the Council on Post Secondary Accreditation (COPA). During this period the accreditation ground rules changed. HEW's endorsement of ASLA as landscape architecture's accrediting body was limited to first professional degree programs. It did not include the right to accredit advanced professional degree programs until such time as special standards could be prepared and approved by HEW. ASLA interpreted this to mean, and appropriately so, that schools were no longer to be accredited. Only those first professional degree programs within schools could be accredited. Where more than one program existed within a school, the school itself was given the option to decide which of the programs was the first professional degree program. As one might expect, the undergraduate program was usually selected.

This procedure, in effect, disenfranchised eligible graduate programs that existed within schools whose undergraduate programs were declared as the first degree program. With the increasing number of graduate programs, this problem intensified and was further aggravated by state registration laws and many state and federal job offerings which required a degree from an accredited program in landscape architecture. With the increasing number of non-landscape architecture undergraduate students enrolled in graduate programs, the problem soon became acute.

In 1979 ASLA, with HEW's blessing, revised its accreditation procedures to allow more than one program at a school to be accredited, if both programs could qualify as a first professional degree program. This policy change recognized that many graduate programs were first professional degree programs because of the large number of non-landscape architecture students enrolled in them. If these programs were providing the non-landscape architecture undergraduate students with base skill training equivalent to the undergraduate program accreditation standards, then they could seek accreditation. This decision by ASLA's Council on Education was a major change in the accreditation process. In the years ahead ASLA's Council On Education will undertake development of standards for accreditation of advanced degree graduate programs (Those programs which accept only undergraduate landscape architecture students).

ASLA's Council on Education has the overall responsibility for setting policy for the accreditation process. The Landscape Architecture Accreditation Board, a sub-group of the Council on Education, along with ASLA's Director of Education and Research, carry the principal load of coordinating the accreditation process itself.

Standards for excellence in landscape architectural education have evolved since the informal accreditation process was begun in the 1930s and they have been continuously updated and improved. Today each program must demonstrate acceptable levels of excellence in the following areas: curriculum content, faculty experience and performance (to include an appropriate ratio of faculty members to students), facilities and organization, and student and alumni performance. The standards for judging excellence are demanding and comprehensive, but they do allow latitude for program variations designed to meet regional concerns and special interest orientation. The Department of Education (formerly HEW) and COPA maintain a constant watch on ASLA's accreditation procedures to insure adherence to due process and the consistent application of the standards.

The overriding purpose of program accreditation is to insure an academic standard which will produce properly educated and technically skilled landscape architectural practitioners. Curriculum standards are keyed to the subject matter tested in the Uniform National Examination, as well as to encourage the incorporation of mind broadening and related subject matter. Faculty and facility criteria are consistent with the standards which prevail throughout the academic world, but also include requisites specific to the nature of landscape architecture.

The accreditation process has served the profession well. The quality of program content, faculty, facilities, and of greatest importance, graduates is exceptional. This statement, furthermore, can be made for all accredited programs across the country. The number of both undergraduate and graduate programs will continue to grow in direct response to the needs of the profession. The accreditation process will likewise continue to provide the assurance that each new program provides and maintains a standard of excellence consistent with the increasing demands for excellence in the practice of the profession.

Formal education provides the aspiring landscape architect with two essential sets of tools. The first set includes those basic technical and theoritical skills needed to enter the profession. The second set includes those skills which allow the educational process to continue in the years ahead. It is this second set of tools which may well prove to be the most essential. Chapter Five looks at this continuum of education, and explores a strategic approach to the accumulation of knowledge and experience required to practice the profession with competency and proficiency.

Chapter Four Notes

1. Louis R. Fishman; *Profile of the Design Professions*, Background Report prepared for Architecture, Planning and Design Program, National Endowment for the Arts, 1978.

With formal education behind the learning process is just beginning.

Introduction

The educational continuum contains five phases beginning with college preparation and continuing through proficiency maintenance and the expansion of professional horizons. Each phase is distinct. They are frequently separated by a specific bench mark or goal accomplishment, but often, especially in the latter phases, they are less easily separated.

The concept of an educational continuum strongly suggests that professional competence in landscape architecture, like all professions, requires an ongoing program of knowledge acquisition, skill sharpening and goal evaluation. More importantly, the concept suggests that this ongoing process must be comprehensive, well coordinated and steadfastly followed. No professional can maintain a level of competence

consistent with the demands of a growing profession without such a program.

Studies have suggested that one fifth of a technical professional's time needs to be spent in the educational continuum just to maintain a constant level of competence; just to keep pace. This time would be equally divided between learning newly developed technology and recovering unused and consequently lost knowledge.[1]

The chart on the following page provides a graphic view of the educational continuum for landscape architects. The formal education phase has already been discussed in detail in Chapter Four. It is appropriate here, then, to look at those phases which follow formal education.

THE CONTINUUM OF LANDSCAPE ARCHITECTURAL EDUCATION

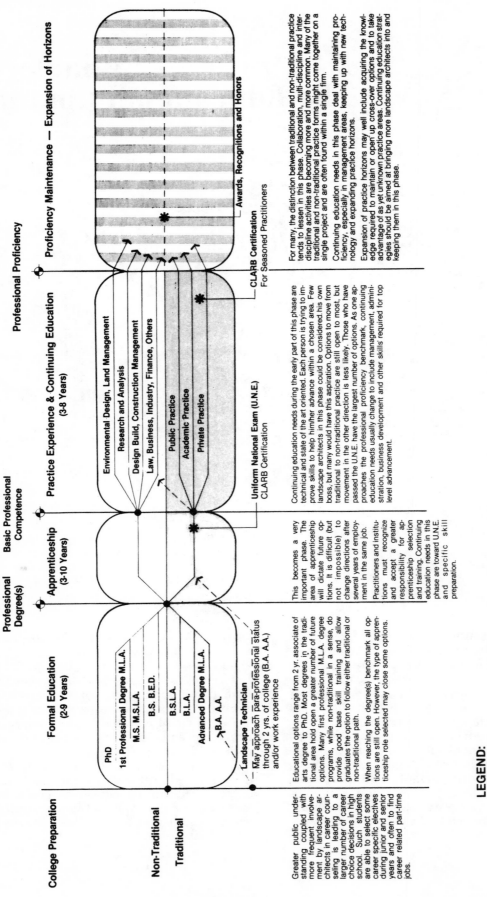

Reprinted from *Landscape Architecture* magazine, November, 1978.

Apprenticeship

Webster's *New Collegiate Dictionary No. 8* defines an apprentice as "one who is learning by practical experience, under skilled workers, a trade, art, or calling". This definition of apprenticeship gives concern to many because it suggests an approach to the acquiring of skills in the absence of formal education. The issue is further confused by the frequent use of the term intern. In the medical profession internship is a formal and required period of practical experience which immediately follows formal education.

The teaching profession also uses the term intern to describe a formal and required period of on-the-job practical experience within the formal educational period. Some programs in landscape architecture have less formalized but similar intern programs within their curriculum.

On the surface both terms seem inadequate to describe that period which follows the formal educational period in landscape architecture. Of the two, however, apprenticeship is suggested as the more appropriate. To avoid further confusion a new definition is recommended for apprenticeship in landscape architecture:

> *Apprenticeship:* A period immediately following formal education devoted to acquiring, through practical experience, basic professional skill competency, under the guidance of skilled practitioners.

Apprenticeship as redefined suggests that formal education must be coupled with a period of on-the-job training in order to produce a professional landscape architect with basic professional competence. The concept is predicated on the fact that certain required skills can only be learned under practical on-the-job conditions. It is difficult and often impossible to accurately simulate in the class room or design studio many practice world conditions which form a significant part of a practicing professionals daily work process. The interaction between client and professional is difficult to simulate in the class room. The interaction between project budget and design, and design and project implementation are nearly impossible to simulate. These and many other critical skills must be mastered before a person is truly competent as a professional. Teaching these skills is the goal of the apprenticeship period.

The teachers during this period are the professionally competent practicing landscape architects, and responsibility to their students (their entry level employees) is no less important than that of their counterparts in the formal education programs.

The apprenticeship period may well be the most important period in the educational continuum. It is during this period that a landscape architect's future may well be determined. If the training during this period is inadequate professional proficiency may never be reached. It is also possible for the training during this period to be so highly specific that future employment options become limited only to those represented by that area of training. This same problem may limit development of those skills required to pass the Uniform National Examination.

A great deal can be learned while serving with the skilled practitioner.

The apprenticeship period is fraught with troubles and concerns for the new landscape architect, but for most it is a period of excitement and mounting professional enthusiasm. It is during this period when self confidence replaces self doubt and when a sense of accomplishment replaces the frustration of hypothetical classroom problem solving. (A nearly universal phenomenon).

The length of the apprenticeship period will vary. It will depend on individual motivation, commitment of the professional teachers, and the area of practice represented by the "first job". For most, the period is 2 to 3 years long, but there are exceptions on both sides of this norm. The goal is basic professional competency and it can be measured in several ways.

Passing the Uniform National Examination is one measure of basic professional competence, and certainly represents a legitimate goal for entry level professionals. An equally important measurement is job advancement. In the same way teachers evaluate their students, employers provide grades in the form of salary increases, increased responsibility, and ad-

The apprenticeship period is a difficult and often confusing time, but it can be a most significant learning experience.

vancement within the organization's hierarchy. The bench mark between apprenticeship and the next continuum phase is not always well defined and may happen quite gradually.

Important career decisions are normally made during the closing portions of the apprenticeship period. Decisions to change practice form, to go back to school, to strike out on one's own, and many others will present themselves during this period. These are difficult decisions, confounded by job longevity and loyalty to current employer, ever growing financial obligations, social and community bonds, and dozens of other real and imagined issues. It is at this point, however, when most landscape architects commit themselves to a long term career choice, either consciously or subconsciously.

The apprenticeship period, then, is a time to sharpen known skills and acquire the new skills to practice the profession with competency. Critical to the success of this period is the role played by the employer/teacher. Some employers expect a recent graduate to step in and be fully productive from the first day on the job. To insure an immediate return on salary investment, these new employees are frequently ''pigeon holed'' and left to do highly repetitive work in areas where their skills are most obvious. For example, a recent graduate with good graphic skills might be put to work doing all of an organization's graphic work and given little chance to see the other aspects of practice. This could pose a real threat to that new employee's apprenticeship period. Both employee and employer should insist on an entry level professional's exposure to all aspects of the organization's activity.

The continuum of education is an individual responsibility, but it can only function in an atmosphere sympathetic to the continuum concept. Employers must reward and encourage employees who take positive steps to advance their skills and acquire new knowledge. At no point is this more important than during the apprenticeship period.

Both employer and employee should insist that the apprenticeship period offer a well rounded exposure to the profession.

Practice Experience and Continuing Education

Following the apprenticeship period comes a period of new skill acquisition and the fine tuning of old skills. While this sounds much the same as apprenticeship, the level of intensity is vastly different. The more frequently skills are used, the more they become habitual and accomplished, freeing time for the learning of new skills, and sharpening recently learned skills.

During this same period, however, there is often a propensity to gravitate toward the work activity which represents those most accomplished skills, with a corresponding avoidance of work which may require the acquisition of new skills. For many, this very natural tendency leads to specialization, for others it may well lead to stagnation. Freed-up time can, and should be, used wisely and comprehensively. Specialization has many merits, but no form of prac-

tice can tolerate avoidance of new skill and knowledge acquisition.

In the early stages of the practice experience and continuing education phase of the continuum, job advancement provides the primary motivation to new skill and knowledge acquisition. Technical and state-of-the-art information is widely sought after by most during this phase as a means of insuring forward movement within a practice organization. During the middle period of this continuum phase, continuing education needs turn to the acquisition of administrative, managerial and business development skills. As job advancement becomes more competitive, managerial and leadership ability plays a significant, if not primary role in all practice activity.

Even the specialist needs to keep pace with the entire profession.

The educational continuum becomes more and more a matter of individual motivation during this continuum phase. While many employers encourage continuing education, their organizational policies seldom insist that staff people follow a comprehensive continuing education program. Job advancement, however, normally rewards those whose skills have advanced to meet new job challenges and expanding competency requirements. Throughout this period professional proficiency is the sought after goal. When contrasted with competency, professional proficiency suggests that skills and abilities are standard setters in the profession.

Measurement of professional proficiency may come in any of several ways. Awards and recognitions for accomplished work and competitions, premier job promotions, special honors, financial security, and other benchmarks may be used by individuals and their peers to judge professional proficiency. Maintaining this proficiency and expanding professional horizons becomes the next and final continuum phase.

Proficiency Maintenance and Expansion of Horizons

The term final continuum phase is used here with great reluctance. The term suggests the end of the line, when in fact, this final phase is, for many, the most exciting of all.

Maintaining proficiency in professional practice becomes increasingly difficult as the years go by. When a professional has reached the top there appears no place left to go. It becomes easy to say, "I've made it, now its time to relax and enjoy the benefits." Most of those benefits have been hard earned and the urge to sit back and enjoy them is certainly human and understandable. It is rare, however, to find a landscape architect prepared to rest on hard earned laurels. Most continue their quest for knowledge and strive to maintain a pace consistent with that of the profession.

Enjoy yourself, yes, but maintain your proficiency.

A head count at any professional seminar or other educational session will reveal participants of all ages and levels of practice success. Wise landscape architects have learned that without proficiency maintenance the profession will soon pass them by.

This final continuum phase contains another element of some excitement to many. Expanding professional horizons, exploring new fields of practice, looking at old methods in new light, the ability to experiment with one's special skills, all become possible to those landscape architects who have maintained their proficiency. If professional proficiency was accompanied with any degree of financial success the ability to extend one's self and take on new challenges is open in a way never before possible in the earlier continuum phases. Much of the profession's boundary expansion has been accomplished by professionals who extended themselves during this horizon expansion phase of their careers.

It is during this continuum phase that the truly accomplished professional acquires the most exciting reward (and useful tool) attainable—CLOUT! The accomplished professional can assemble budgets and modulate policy and coordinate programs and influence people, and, with these clout tools, have a dramatic impact on the profession's image and horizon expansion. The profession's unique leadership role in the area of visual resource assessment and management results from the actions of a handful of "senior" landscape architects who leveraged their clout and severed traditional boundary inhibitions.

Landscape architecture is a profession dependent on the recognition and pursuit of an educational continuum. The pace of our daily lives is fast and often frantic but this pace is laborious when compared to the growing expansion of landscape architecture. New knowledge and technology is matched by new physical and social concerns which can easily outpace our ability to comprehend or function without a comprehensive program of continuing education.

Chapter Five Notes

1. J.K. Wolfe; "Keeping Up to Date in Career Training in the USA", *Electronics and Power*, August, 1965

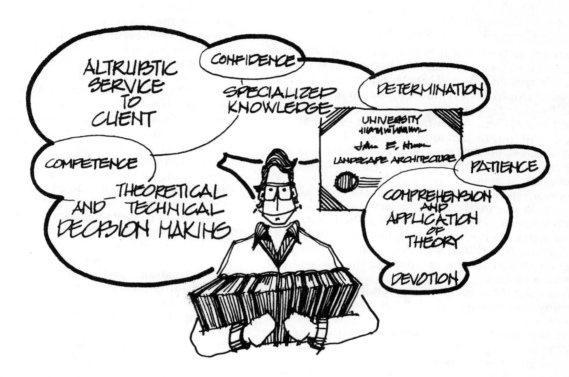

The characteristics of a professional.

Introduction

This chapter is concerned with the concept of professionalism. It begins by defining a profession, discusses professional responsibilities, looks at public images, and concludes with accepted means of professional licensure. The overall intent of this chapter, however, is to identify the comprehensiveness of professionalism and to relate its special meaning to landscape architecture.

For many years landscape architects struggled under the weight of confused public images about what they did for a living. Many believed this to be a curse unique to landscape architecture, one deeply enmeshed in perceived historical garden-oriented roots. The years have proven this viewpoint inaccurate and certainly not unique to landscape architecture. An historical glance backward, for instance, shows that public image problems have been faced by architecture, engineering and even medicine. In fact, nearly every profession has faced image prob-

lems not so very different from those faced by landscape architecture.

There can be no question that landscape architecture is a profession and its increasing contributions to society strengthens the public's view in this regard almost daily. This emerging high regard for the profession of landscape architecture has not been accomplished by massive public relations campaigns or even a major stroke of good luck. The public's view of the profession has changed gradually but continuously as a result of the profession's actions, completed works and involvement in the concerns of humankind.

To insure the continued growth of the profession's stature, it is imperative that all landscape architects understand the meaning of the term professionalism and that they practice according to reasonable and responsible guidelines.

A Profession Defined

The search for a definition of profession begins, as all searches must, with *Webster's New Collegiate Dictionary, No. 8.*

Pro·fes·sion, n.
"a calling requiring specialized knowledge and often long and intensive academic preparation."

So far, so good. Most would agree that landscape architecture meets Webster's criteria: "...specialized knowledge and long and intensive academic preparation." It would be easy, indeed, to stop the search for a definition right here. For, so far, everyone is in complete agreement. But, nothing is ever that easy. First of all, public perceptions of what is and what is not a profession vary greatly. Even Webster goes on to suggest that a profession may be "...vocation, employment or even a calling". These terms are often more closely equated with trades and certainly contribute to the public's misunderstanding of what a profession is. *The British Oxford Dictionary* adds even more confusion by defining a profession as a "...vocation, calling, esp. one that involves some branch of learning or science, as the learned professions (divinity, law, medicine)". To make matters worse, the Oxford Dictionary concludes by suggesting the alternative of "...a carpenter by profession".

Within the Oxford Dictionary definition lies the root of the real problem. In the minds of many people only clerics, lawyers and doctors are "professionals". All others, from architect to carpenter, engineer to welder, landscape architect to gardener, are merely craftspeople, at best skilled trades. They may all claim they are professionals, but they are hardly learned.

The ministry, law, and medicine—the traditional "learned" professions.

When one considers the historic evolution of occupations to professions, it is not difficult to understand the current dilemma. As early as 1711 divinity, law and physics were recognized as professions.[1] All other means of earning a living were occupations or trades. Medicine was to eventually evolve from the practice of physics, but only after more than 100 years of gradual development. Architecture and engineering did not receive formalized recognition until the middle of the 19th century. It is interesting to note that the Royal Institute of Architects and two principal engineering societies were formed several decades before the Medical Act of 1858 which legally defined the practice of medicine.[2]

With the exception, then, of divinity and law, the transition from craft or trade to profession has happened within a relatively short historic period. It is not surprising that many people are confused and find it difficult to recognize even the most highly specialized callings as professions. There is, however, a kind of common perceptional link between divinity, law and medicine which provides the key to end the confusion. Each of the "learned professions" is perceived to serve mankind's well being in a very direct way. Moreover, this service to mankind's well being is usually provided in time of critical need. The cleric soothing a deeply troubled conscience, the doctor treating a serious illness, and the lawyer defending an unjustly accused citizen are highly publicized examples. This perception quite naturally forms the basic public criteria for judging what is and what is not a profession. In this regard, while the design professions are usually credited with direct service to mankind's creature comforts, they are seldom seen as responsible for the salvation of either mind or body.

During the early part of the twentieth century there was a gradual increase in popular or friendly attitudes toward professionals in general. More and more frequently professionals were seen as people who provided a variety of altruistic services to mankind. Morris L. Cogan put it this way:

"A profession is a vocation whose practice is founded upon an understanding of the theoretical structure of some department of learning or science, and upon the abilities accompanying such understanding. This understanding and these abilities are applied to the vital and practical affairs of man. The practices of the profession are modified by knowledge of a generalized nature and by the accumulated wisdom and experience of mankind, which serve to correct the errors of specialism. The profession, serving the vital needs of man, considers its first ethetical imperative to be altruistic service to the client."[3]

The common perceptional link between the "learned" professions is their service to the most basic of human needs.

Cogan's definition suggests a number of essential criteria for a profession and its practitioners.
1. Specialized knowledge
2. An understanding of theory and the ability to apply this theory to practice situations.
3. The ability to temper theoretical and technical decision making with wisdom and an understanding of human frailities, and to overcome the myopia of specialization.
4. The imperative of altruistic service to client.

Within this definition are two extremely important concepts; altruistic service and service to the vital affairs of mankind. It is within the framework of these concepts that landscape architecture has emerged as a true profession. Certainly the practice of landscape architecture meets Gogan's criteria, but it is the profession's unique devotion to the land and mankind that sets it apart, and gives it a modern day conformance with a centuries old definition.

Theodore Caplow provides us with additional insight to the quest for an understanding of the term profession. Caplow suggests five steps which form a logical progression from a trade or craft to profession.[4] These five steps are listed here along with a brief historical assessment specific to the profession of landscape architecture.

Step 1: Establishment of a Professional Association:
The basic purpose of establishing a professional association in Caplow's chronology is to define membership criteria for those who will be allowed to associate themselves with the profession, "to keep out the unqualified". The American Society of Landscape Architects was founded in 1899, and while membership criteria has changed over the years, the attempt to maintain a high level of membership standards has always been evident.

The professional association established in 1899

Step 2: Undergo a Name Change:
In the case of landscape architecture this was a first step and came when Frederick Law Olmsted coined the name landscape architect to replace landscape gardner. The fundamental purpose of this step is consistent with Caplow's belief that a name change reduced identification with the previous occupational or trade status associated with the former name and created a title which could be monopolized.

FREDERICK LAW OLMSTED

Olmsted coined the profession's name in 1858.

Step 3: Adopt a Code of Ethics:

This step is designed to identify a social welfare rationale and provide further criteria for professional conduct. The earliest codes of ethics established real limitations on internal competition and were often arbitrary about methods in which a profession could be practiced. In the early 1970s, however, the U.S. Federal courts found many aspects of professional codes of ethics to be in restraint of trade and thereby in violation of constitutional guarantees. Most professional societies have modified their codes in subsequent years to reflect concerns for quality of practice rather than form of practice. ASLA was among this group and its code is given later in this chapter. The purpose of step 3, however, was very much like steps 1 and 2, to establish the profession as different and requiring a special attention to social welfare.

Step 4: Licensure:

This step is normally achieved through prolonged political agitation to gain public support for legislated control of minimum professional competency. Results are frequently gained in stages beginning with control of examination of those who can use the professional title (title laws) and ending with control over actual performance of professional activities (practice laws). Most professions have chosen a legislative path leading to state registration or licensure laws. Some professions, like accounting and real estate appraising, have chosen to accomplish this control through internal processes such as certification and master's credentials earned by examination.

Licensure examination measures minimal professional competency.

Step 5: Development and Accreditation of Training Facilities:

Steps 4 and 5 may be undertaken simultaneously, according to Caplow, but both are equally important. In the case of landscape architecture, the development of educational programs preceeded licensure, and accreditation of these programs occured simultaneously. Step 5 does suggest, however, that the chronology of professional development includes the setting and control of standards for the training of those who are to enter the profession.

1900
LANDSCAPE ARCHITECTURE at HARVARD UNIVERSITY

If one considers Caplow's steps in the evolution of a profession as only loosely linked by chronological order, it is possible to trace landscape architecture's history as consistent with this prescribed course. It is more than evident that landscape architecture is a profession, by any of the criteria mentioned. It is difficult, nonetheless, to shake the question of confused public image, which raises its head time and time again. Is landscape architecture really perceived as a profession? This is an important issue and deserves to be looked at more closely.

Public Image

No matter how well landscape architecture measures up from an intellectual point of view, its public image must be considered as a more important barometer of the role it is to play in the years ahead. Regrettably, landscape architects, along with most professionals, are suffering a credibility problem in the minds of the nation's general public. Even the once revered physician is now viewed more often with suspicion than with awe.

Wrong doing by any professional brings all other professionals under critical scrutiny and frequently cause a loss of esteem to an entire profession. The age of consumerism has further placed the professional in a suspicious light. Professionals speak in a technical and specialized language—a jargon that is all too often designed to exclude the lay person and impress professional peers. An air of professional superiority coupled with an intellectual countenance often "worn on the sleeve" has given the professions a nonconsumer orientation which is very visible in the public mind.

Attorneys who falsify escrow accounts, engineers and architects involved with "kickbacks" from contractors, or who sell their "seals" to endorse work they had nothing to do with, and a host of other media dramatized un-professional activity has created a general decline in the image the public has of the professions. All of this has lead to an unusual

rash of highly publicized liability and malpractice suits which further damages the reputation of all professionals.

Many landscape architects fear the public image problem goes deeper yet, as it relates to their own profession. The preceived "garden" image of the profession's early roots seems to haunt some landscape architects who cry for massive public relations campaigns which, they are convinced, will cause a dramatic change in the public's view of the profession overnight. While public relations campaigns may well produce meaningful results, the public's image is more likely to be changed by deeds and actions which can be personally experienced rather than by words and pictures.

Landscape architects, through their works, have the power to enhance the daily lives of many people.

Landscape architecture is a small profession when measured by numbers against the other professions. On the surface this may seem to greatly incumber image making by example. When seen in proper perspective, however, landscape architecture is a major profession in terms of the number of people affected by its examples and actions. A popular public park, for instance, may well attract hundreds of thousands of visitors each year. The visitor use and enjoyment of this park will have a far greater impact on public image than would a bridge of equally competent design traversed by an equal number of people. This assumes, of course, that those who use the park know it was designed by a landscape architect.

Few people are impressed by the attractiveness or ambiance of a well designed bridge.

Of paramount importance here is the realization that the average individual rarely seeks out the design professional in the same way they seek out a doctor or a lawyer. Landscape architects are not perceived to be contributors to health and happiness in the way doctors and lawyers are. This places an unusual incumbency on the landscape architect's adoption of practice and conduct codes which advance the critical and vital needs of mankind as mainstays of the profession's ethic. Special attention must be placed by each individual professional on sense of duty, maintenance and continued advancement of knowledge and skills, service to the vital and practical needs of mankind, the highest regard and adherence to ethical standards, and a deep and abiding sense of civic responsibility.

When these fundamental precepts are followed, public image improves automatically. All of these precepts are of basic importance, but the final one, civic responsibility, carries special meaning to the advancement of the public's image of landscape architecture. Civic responsibility which manifests itself in unselfish contribution to community needs, holds the greatest potential for improving the public's image, understanding and empathy for the profession.

Selling one's self comes before selling one's profession.

Take, for example, the young landscape architect who opened a private practice office during the early 1960s. There were no other landscape architects in the community, and selling the profession was a difficult and arduous task. This young landscape architect soon realized that selling himself had to come first before he could sell landscape architecture. He quickly became active in the affairs of the community, serving as a volunteer in areas of pressing community need. In most cases these areas had little to do with landscape architecture but his reputation as a "professional" grew with each passing day. His mannerisms, deportment, problem solving ability, and sincere concern for the well being of the community were perceived by community leaders as highly professional and were quickly transferred to the perception of his special knowledge and training. His success as a landscape architect followed swiftly, and today most people in that community hold landscape architecture in the highest regard. This true account has been repeated time and time again across this nation. Individuals showing concern and taking part in the life of their community have the power to move landscape architecture forward in a way no public relations campaign could ever do. And it is largely by this simple but dramatically effective technique that landscape architecture will continue to grow in stature and prestige.

Duties and Responsibilities

When considering the issues of the duties and responsibilities of a professional, morality, integrity, decency and honesty will not be raised. They are, after all, issues common to all of mankind and hold the same importance to landscape architecture as they do to any form of human contact. Suffice it to say, that without these values a professional will surely fail and by so doing will bring hardship to all.

The landscape architect does, however, subscribe to a credo of special responsibilities to mankind as a whole and to the client and user in specific. In general terms, the landscape architect is committed to the protection, preservation, and enhancement of the earth's natural resources, and of equal importance to the enhancement of mankind's physical and social well being. Within this laudable but mostly general framework, landscape architects are committed to a set of specific responsibilities to their clients, agencies, organizations, and above all to those who will be directly affected by their professional endeavors.

Both the general and the more specific responsibilities have been clearly articulated in the American Society of Landscape Architect's *Code of Ethics and Guidelines for Professional Conduct*: both were approved in their most recent form in 1980 and are reproduced here in their entirety.

ASLA Code of Professional Conduct

At their mid-year meeting in Kansas City, in May of 1980, the ASLA Board of Trustees reviewed and adopted a final proposed draft of a new *Code of Ethics and Guidelines for Professional Conduct for the Society*. The following is the approved wording for the new ethics and conduct codes.

Preamble

This code expresses in general terms the level of professional conduct expected of Fellows, Members and Associates of the Society.

Such a code is no guarantee of moral actions on the part of the members but depends upon the integrity of each individual member to conduct himself or herself in a responsible and straightforward manner both in dealings with clients and other professionals.

A profession should be more than a group of individuals offering a service to the public. It should be an entity with a bond between members based on mutual respect and a dedication to improving the quality of life for all persons.

Code

I. The landscape architect shall exert every effort toward the preservation and protection of our natural resources and toward understanding the interaction of the economic and social systems with these resources.

II. The landscape architect has a social and environmental responsibility to reconcile the public's needs and the natural environment with minimal disruption to the natural system.

III. The landscape architect shall further the welfare and advancement of the profession by constantly striving to provide the highest level of professional services, avoiding even the appearance of improper professional conduct.

IV. The landscape architect shall serve the client or employer with integrity, understanding, knowledge and creative ability and shall respond morally to social, political, economic and technological influences.

V. The landscape architect shall encourage educational research and the development and dissemination of useful technical information relating to planning, design and construction of the physical environment.

Guidelines for Professional Conduct

1. A landscape architect shall make full disclosure to the client or employer any financial interest which even remotely bears upon the services or project.

2. A landscape architect shall truthfully and clearly inform the client or employer of his/her qualifications and capabilities to perform services.

3. A landscape architect shall not make exaggerated, misleading, deceptive or false statements or claims to the public about his/her professional qualifications, experience or performance.

4. A landscape architect shall not give, lend or promise anything of value to any public official in order to influence or attempt to influence the official's judgment or actions in the letting of contracts.

5. A landscape architect shall be free of any constraint from his fellow landscape architects if he wishes to participate in a price or competitive bidding selection when such method is selected by a client, but the landscape architect is encouraged to advocate to the client the public benefit to be derived from selection processes that establish as their primary consideration in the selection of landscape architects the ability and competence of the landscape architect to provide the required services.

6. A landscape architect shall recognize the contribution of others engaged in the planning, design and construction of the physical environment and shall not knowingly make false statements about their professional work nor maliciously injure or attempt to injure the prospects, practice or employment position of those so engaged.

Professional Relations

The age of collaboration was discussed in Chapter Two. Collaboration of any nature carries with it certain responsibilities of an extra professional nature. Principal among these responsibilities is the recognition of the skills and special abilities of collaborators. There is no room for professional jealousies in effective collaboration and team effort. The most common cause of difficulty in professional collaboration is ignorance or misunderstanding of the role that each professional is to play in the joint effort. This problem can be compounded by language (jargon) barriers, technological differences, and disparity in application of practice methodology.

Difficulties may also result from jealousies between professionals or narrowmindedness about the relative importance of collaborative professional roles. While misunderstandings can be easily addressed through effective communication, jealousy and narrowmindedness are insidious and more difficult to deal with. These characteristics obviously have no place in professional collaboration, and professionals who are haunted by them are usually avoided by collaborative teams.

It would be rare, indeed, for a landscape architect, in any form of practice, to follow a career without, at some time, working with another design professional. As equal collaborators, sub-contractors, or consultants on specific types of projects the need for professional respect and responsive relationships is inherent to the nature of design practice. Efforts to strengthen common bonds between collaborative professions is an ongoing and important effort being conducted on many fronts.

At the national level the American Society of Landscape Architects is an active member of the Interprofessional Council on Environmental Design (ICED). This council is composed of the presidents and executive directors from the professional societies of architecture, engineering, landscape architecture and planning. They meet throughout the year to consider issues common to the design professions. Many states have formed state ICED groups which consider state or regional issues. Similar groups have been formed in the larger cities across the country.

This same level of professional interaction is now being extended to include many of the environmental and social science organizations in an attempt to stimulate better channels of communication and to broaden the level of interaction at every conceivable opportunity.

Landscape architecture as a profession does not exist or function in a vacuum. Its future lies in creating a stronger collaborative position among all those professions which espouse mutually compatible goals.

Licensure and the Profession

Theodore Caplow's fourth step in the growth of a profession is establishing official support for the maintenance of the profession. As we have already seen, landscape architecture followed this historic pattern.

For many, professional licensure provides a means of maintaining a competitive position with other already licensed design professionals, namely the architects and engineers. While the legal roots of licensure lie in the public health, safety and welfare laws, efforts to obtain state licensure are often criticized as being exclusionary and self-serving. Existing laws are also coming under similar attack by state legislatures charged with streamlining and reducing state regulatory control powers. These issues are complex and frustrating and accordingly deserve special attention, for licensure is currently an important institution within the profession of landscape architecture.

A Brief History: Licensure or state control of professional activity is not a new concept. It began in the United States in 1772 when Virginia passed the first comprehensive medical practice act. By the end of that century 13 of the 16 existing states had similar medical practice laws and a nearly equal number had statutes controlling the practice of lawyers.[5]

Between 1800 and 1850 however, nearly all of these regulatory laws were repealed. The unprecedented growth of the nation during this period was epitomized by a free market—free enterprise mentality which saw regulations of any kind as un-American and certainly an unnecessary stumbling block to the nation's growth.

It should also be pointed out that during this same period, no professional associations existed to provide political agitation for licensure activity. By the mid-point in the nineteenth century, however, a number of professional associations had been formed and the move for licensure on an organized basis appeared. The following chart demonstrates the effectiveness of this effort:[6]

There is an obvious and strong correlation between professional society formation and the adoption of state licensure. The state of California was the first state to require licensure of landscape architects in 1954. By the early 1960s four more states had joined California.[7] By 1973, 27 states had passed similar licensure laws, and by 1980 the number had increased to 38.

During the 1970s, however, many states enacted "sunset" laws designed to review and eliminate un-necessary existing state regulatory agencies. In two states, Colorado and Oregon, the legislatures voted to eliminate landscape architectural licensure statutes. While several states successfully defended their licensure laws during "sunset" review, and a few new laws have been passed, the future of licensure has been clouded and placed in some jeopardy.

The licensure issue is further confused by the lack of uniformity between the existing laws. No two laws are truly alike. The greatest difference lies in the distinction between a *Title* law and a *Practice* law. Title laws govern the use of the term *landscape architect* and limits its use to those who meet certain criteria. A Practice law limits the performance of activities generally thought of as landscape architectural in nature to those people who meet the licensure criteria.

The licensure criteria are usually the same for both types of laws and include a landscape architectural degree, some practical experience, and the successful passage of a minimum competency examination. The exact specifics of the criteria will differ from state to state.

As each new law was passed, a "grace period", usually six months in duration immediately following adoption, allowed those who already made their living as defined in the law, to register without taking the examination. This provision, referred to as the "grandfather clause" allowed many, who otherwise would be unable to meet the licensure criteria, to register under the law. At the close of the grace period, however, all subsequent registrants were required

Organization	Number of States with Licensure	Year Professional Organization Formed	Years During Which 80% of States Adopted Licensure
American Society of Landscape Architects	38 (1980)	1899	1954–
American Medical Association	50	1847	1871–1915
American Pharmaceutical Association	50	1852	1871–1910
American Institute of Architects	50	1857	1897–1939
American Dental Association	50	1859	1881–1930
National Society of Professional Engineers	50	1934	1921–1950

to meet the full provisions of the law.

In spite of the differences, idiosyncrasies and confusion associated with licensure, it does have a justifiable rationale.

The Rationale

Every state is empowered with the right and duty to protect the public health, safety, and welfare of its citizens. Professional licensure falls under this mandate. The issue being, of course, the 50 states' responsibility to protect their citizens "against the consequences of ignorance, incompetency, and incapacity, as well as deception and fraud."[8] By granting licensure to those practitioners who could meet the criteria, the state could ensure the health, safety and welfare of its citizens. The profession of landscape architecture has found it frequently difficult to convince state legislatures of the applicability of this rationale to the services performed by its practitioners. State legislatures could easily imagine how an incompetently designed building or bridge would jeopardize the health, safety and welfare of the public, but their perceptions of landscape architectural products and services conjured altogether different images.

Those states which adopted landscape architectural licensure laws and similarly those who survived the "sunset" review, have been those states where the profession has been the most active, eloquent, and politically astute.

There is no question in the minds of practicing landscape architects that the profession does have potentially great impact on the public's health, safety and welfare. Articulating these beliefs in the face of opposition from other professional and occupational interest groups, as well as politicians who are under constant pressure to reduce rather than enlarge government regulation, is proving to be more and more difficult. In states where the profession itself is strong, licensure has been successfully defended on the basis of its public health, safety and welfare rationale.

Current and Future Directions

The American Society of Landscape Architects (along with the vast majority of individual landscape architects) is committed to the cause of licensure. State chapters of ASLA have and will continue to mount concerted efforts to gain and to maintain licensure laws. The cause is just and should be defended, but in the end it may prove futile. The energy and costs necessary to mount a licensure drive or to defend a "sunset" review are staggering. The Florida Chapter of ASLA, for instance, reported that their successful effort to defend the existing law during "sunset" review in 1979 cost over $40,000.00 in expenses and included more than 5,000 volunteer hours. If a minimum figure of $25.00 per hour were attached to the volunteer time, the total cost to the landscape architects in Florida would reach $200,000.00.

The nature of the legislative system places the burden of proof concerning licensure on the professionals who seek it. Not only are the costs of this approach staggering, the perceptions of both legislator and lay public become confused and prejudiced by the self-serving appearance of the process.

There is a growing feeling that the costs and energy requirements in the licensure process are much too high. Moreover, many landscape architects feel that the current state laws (with a few exceptions) are much too weak and ineffectual as a result of political compromise. These landscape architects believe a national certification program, similar to that conducted by the American Association of Accountants holds a better future for the profession.

Certification could require even tighter criteria than current licensure laws but would be voluntary in nature. The public, apprised that certified landscape architects meet acceptable standards of competence, could choose between a certified or noncertified professional as their personal requirements dictated.

Whatever the future may hold, the fact remains that a majority of the 50 states currently require licensure of landscape architects by examination. About equally split between title laws and practice laws, these existing laws are real and directly affect the entry of landscape architectural graduates into practice where they exist.

In 1961 the Council of Landscape Architectural Registration Boards (CLARB) was formed to help coordinate the enactment of uniform laws and to equalize and improve the standards for licensure examination. The Uniform National Examination (UNE) used by nearly all the states requiring licensure is prepared each year under CLARB's direction. CLARB also provides assistance to those states seeking licensure as well as those states defending existing laws under "sunset" review. While initially sponsored by the American Society of Landscape Architects, CLARB is now a totally autonomous group composed of representatives from each state licensure board.

ASLA publishes a current list of states requiring registration each year in its *Members Handbook*. UNE Review Manuals are also available from the Environmental Design Press in Reston, Virginia.

Professionalism is a difficult term to define. It can mean many things to many people. But to landscape architects it means a commitment to nature and to people. It means conducting the practice of a truly unique profession with grace and with dignity and with an energy that is contagious.

Chapter Six Notes

1. A.M. Carr-Sanders, "The Professions", *Untangling the Web of Professional Liability*, The Design Professionals Insurance Co. San Francisco, CA 1976

2. IBID 1

3. H.A. Wagner, "Principles of Professional Conduct in Engineering", *The Annals of the American Academy of Political and Social Sciences, 197.* January 1955

4. Theodore Caplow, *Harvard Educational Review*, Winter 1955

5. Dr. Sam Miller, *Professional Licensure of Landscape Architects. An Assessment of Public Needs and Private Responsibilities*, ASLA, 1978, Wash., D.C.

6. IBID 5

7. Reimann-Bueckner-Crandell Partnership, *Candidate Review Manual* Uniform National Examination in Landscape Architecture, Environmental Design Press, 1978

8. IBID 7

PART THREE
THE HUMAN SKILLS

Chapter Seven
Interpersonal Relations

Leadership is an "art" that requires many skills with interpersonal skills at the top of the list.

Introduction

The design professions, like all forms of enterprise, require knowledge, skill and technical expertise which are peculiar or unique to these forms of endeavor. While these specialized "tools of the trade" may be similar in closely related fields, they are usually special enough to give identity and distinguishing character to the majority of different modes of professional endeavor.

Landscape architecture fits this generalization well. Its uniqueness is clearly established by its land, nature, and people ethic, and equally well by the specialized knowledge and technical skill used in its practice. Despite its clearly different character, however, success in the practice of landscape architecture is dependent on mastering a wide variety of skills and expertise common to all other business endeavors. Because these skills are not unique to landscape architecture they are often overlooked in professional degree curriculums and left to chance

acquisition during the years following school. The development of human, business, and political skills are far too important, however, to be left to chance.

Expertise in the human, business, and political skills is as fundamental to successful practice as are the specialized design and technical skills of landscape architecture. The best designer or graphics person may achieve only average success in practice without these "other" skills, while the average designer who possesses strong human, business, and political skills may easily become a very successful practitioner.

The importance of these "other" skills cannot be stressed strongly enough, and much of the remainder of this book will be devoted to a detailed look at their applicability to the practice of landscape architecture. This detailed examination begins with the human or interpersonal skills necessary to successful practice.

The successful practitioner wears many hats.

The School—Work Dichotomy

Understanding the fundamental differences between the school world setting and the work world setting is important to the discussion which follows in this chapter. "Most people entering the world of work for the first time experience a spasm of culture shock when they learn that mastery of their profession's specific training and skills isn't enough. They trip up time and again on unwritten but strictly observed protocols; like religion, (business) has its mysteries, rituals and rites that must be learned."[1]

To understand this special problem it is helpful to examine a few of the basic differences between the two worlds. The world of the landscape architecture student is highly cloistered. It is a world of long hours, hard work, hard play, and good comaraderie largely confined to a very small and very specific part of the campus community. The demands on time and energy seldom allow for extra curricular activity. The studio teaching concept limits personal contact with students pursuing other professions or business fields.

The specialized nature of landscape architectural instruction, and the social and physical environment necessary to instructional success is seldom dupli-

The good natured commeraderie found in the school studio setting will not likely be duplicated in the work world setting.

cated, however, in the world of work. The only common thread will be hard work and occasional long hours.

The cloistered comfort of the studio concept, with its good-natured competition for grades and peer recognition will, in the world of work, be replaced by highly serious competition for job advancement often requiring willingness to travel, social contact with people outside the profession, political acumen, leadership ability, business acumen, diplomacy, intuition, resiliency, patience, and an instinct for survival. In short, success is no longer based solely on the criteria used to judge advancement in the world of academia.

This does not suggest that competence in the profession's special skills and technical areas is not important. This expertise is, indeed, fundamental to success, but by itself is not sufficient to insure professional success. Far too often the school world fails to emphasize the human skills which are equally important to professional success. The time restraints imposed by the acquisition and understanding of specialized technical knowledge seems to leave the student little room for human skill development. And yet this development is critical, for in the world of work, human skills will be tested on an almost daily basis.

The school world and the work world are vastly different, and those entering the work world for the first time must come to grips with the "new" world, sloughing off the past and acclimating to the future as quickly as possible.

Understanding Yourself

The successful practice of landscape architecture requires a constant interfacing with people. No matter how much one might prefer to work alone, to independently solve a tricky design problem, or to spend the day quietly at a drafting table, the world of work seldom allows this.

In the world of practice it is essential to work with others in the development of client contacts, communicating proposals, making presentations, motivating employees, dealing with regulatory boards and agencies, collaborating with other professionals, directing contractors and otherwise facing a constant onslaught of interpersonal relationships.

All of this is critical to the design professional's success, and yet there seems to be something in the training, interest, habits, and psychological makeup of many design professionals which tends to block effective interpersonal relations.

Studies conducted by Morris Rosenberg at Cornell University showed that the design professional preferred to work with "things" rather than people.[2] Rosenberg's studies showed that the design professional placed high values on tasks which required special technical abilities and low values on tasks requiring social contact or dependency on "faith in people". While certainly, this psychological trait is shared by other highly technical professions, most of them do not share the same level of daily need for cooperation and collaboration which is common to the design professions.

Psychologist John L. Holland suggests six personality types which can be related to job preference.[3] These personality types include Realistic, Intellectual, Social, Conventional, Enterprising, and Artistic. Landscape architects frequently fall in the artistic classification, for certainly this skill has become a traditional measurement standard in the professional training programs. Artistic persons, Holland tells us, see themselves as: "intuitive, liberal, complicated, curious and imaginative". They are less likely to admit, Holland continues, that they are also inclined to be "thin skinned, introverted, more interested in broad concepts than the nuts and bolts of an issue, and are likely to thrive on ambiguity".

Holland's "pigeon-hole" concept does not suggest that the artistic type person has these and only these characteristics, but the profile is a generalization of

Client meetings—Presenting ideas—Finding Potential clients—Directing Field work are all forms of interpersonal relationship skills.

dominant traits which have stood the test of statistical research. As a matter of fact, Holland further suggests that most artistic types share many characteristics in common with the intellectual types. These common traits would include problem solving skills, perserverence when the going gets tough, and often eccentric and anti-social attitudes.

Not every landscape architect fits this tidy mold, but certainly many do. Success in landscape architecture may also depend on other traits and attributes which are common to the realistic, social, conventional, and enterprising personality types. From the "Realist" the traits of practicality, responsibility and hard headedness are often essential to business success (most engineers are realists). From the "Social" type the characteristics of believing in a better world, the desire to lend a helping hand, and the ability to get other people to talk out their problems are of special importance to landscape architecture.

From the "Conventional" personality, landscape architects would benefit from traits of conscientiousness, devotion to duty and a high regard for systematic approaches to problem solving. From the "Enterprising" type, traits which include, industriousness, competitiveness, outgoing attitude about life, and an energy equal to the task at hand, would serve the professional practitioner well.

There are, of course, few people whose psychological profile contains all of the traits just outlined. It is important, however, that every landscape architect understand that a variety of personality attributes are necessary for success. Those traits associated with the artistic direction of the profession will not be enough to insure professional success. It is important that landscape architects learn to assess their personality attributes and understand the areas of weakness. Knowing and understanding oneself is an important first step in developing interpersonal skills. Most interpersonal skills can be learned and developed with effort and practice. By clearly identifying the missing skills a starting point and a check list for the learning effort can be devised.

The Role of Interpersonal Skills in Professional Success

Understanding the role of interpersonal skills in professional success requires a clear picture of how these skills are used on a daily basis. The brief list which follows provides just a few of the areas where interpersonal skills are used in daily professional practice.

- Communicating orally and in writing
- Listening
- Dealing with stress
- Controlling emotion

- Getting along with subordinates, peers and superiors
- Managing people
- Providing leadership
- Resolving conflicts
- Bargaining, negotiating, compromising
- Building networks and teams
- Overcoming resistance to change
- Understanding and dealing with human frailties

The above list identifies only a few of the nontechnical factors which can have a dramatic impact on technical decision making. No technical decision made at a corporate level is accomplished without the application and utilization of human interpersonal skills. Without these skills even the most competent technical person will have little influence on final decisions made in the work world. The absence of these skills along with poor business acumen may well account for the large number of small business failures each year.

While all interpersonal skills are important to professional success, an in-depth discussion of each goes well beyond the scope of this publication. It is possible, however, to single out some of the more important skills and to place others into general categories for discussion purposes.

Behavior Under Stress

All people are equipped to handle some stress. Most people, in fact, produce quite well under tolerable stress levels. This ability is inherent in the human species and can be traced back through human evolution to the days when humans were hunting and hunted creatures. Under certain conditions stress can even be first rate therapy. British researchers discovered, for instance, that anxiety, depression and other symptoms of neurosis virtually disappeared in the population of London during the bombing Blitz of World War II.[4]

It is important to point out, however, that the level of stress which can be tolerated by a cohesive group with clearly defined goals, and that which can be tolerated by an individual or a disorganized group will be greatly different. Tolerance levels and the ability to effectively function in stressful situations rise in proportion to group cohesion, commonality of goals, preparedness and carefully articulated and interrelated responsibilities in task accomplishment.

Stress can be defined in an unscientific way as any threat to the fulfillment of basic needs. Everyone encounters such threats in both their personal and professional lives, almost daily. Emotional happiness, however, seems to be clearly linked to a course which is designed to meet and resolve daily stress situations rather than one which circuitously seeks to avoid stress causing events.

In professional practice, corporate risk taking is essential to success and stress cannot be avoided. It is incumbent then, that those responsible for the success of a professional practice, learn how to deal with stress as a creative force and to develop procedures and techniques designed to eliminate major stress situations.

Several rule of thumb guidelines can be identified for dealing with stress situations in professional practice. These would include:

1. Remain Calm: Remain calm inwardly and especially outwardly. Your outward image during a crisis will have a dramatic impact on those who are dependent on your decisions.

2. Do Not Practice Defensive Avoidance: While some stress causing situations will, in fact, go away if ignored or avoided, most will not. Those that do not go away usually get worse when left unsolved.

3. Document the Facts: Many stress situations are caused by misunderstanding and poor communication. Even real stress situations cannot be solved, however, until they are carefully and accurately documented. The first step in problem solving is a clear articulation of the facts.

4. Seek Outside Help: Frequently close personal involvement in a stress situation makes resolution difficult and often impossible. Discussing the problem with someone with no personal involvement can be very helpful. Many stress situations will also demand the help of an expert professional.

5. Develop Crisis Firedrills: Many crises events and situations are predictable. While no one likes to forecast stress causing events, it is possible to do so, and to develop strategies that can be practiced to insure their successful employment when needed. No one likes to imagine a school building burning, but no one doubts the importance of regular firedrills.

6. Avoid Escalating Stress: Stress caused by crisis events is common to all forms of professional practice. A more serious form of stress which faces the design professional, however, is that which builds up slowly and over a period of time. In most cases this kind of stress is caused by poor business procedures. Getting behind on project delivery schedules, failing to recognize employee discontent, poor billing and collecting practices, inadequate record keeping and a host of other problems can cause an escalating form of stress. In almost every case, real damage can be done before the crisis is clearly defined.

Dealing with stress is an important skill, one which involves the ability to understand and work with people. Building a cohesive working team with clearly articulated assignments and goals takes real skill. Working relationships within a professional practice organization are often complex and even perplexing. Successful practice, however, demands that such diversity and complexity be woven into a cohesive unit if stress is to be dealt with effectively.

Working Relationships

Working relationships in professional practice can be classified as intra-organizational and extra-organizational. The two are uniquely different, and developing skills in both are important. For the new employee, however, it is imperative that the intra-organizational relationship skills be mastered quickly.

The Intra-organizational Environment

Nearly all organizations have policies and traditions which govern protocol, dress, decorum, and a range of other conditions directly affecting interpersonal relations. Most of these policies will be contained in an "Office Policy Manual" and it is wise to learn about them before accepting employment. Other policies may be unwritten or matters of tradition and they must be learned by observation within the first few weeks on the job. Add to all of these, common sense, common courtesy, and a sensitivity to human needs and expectations and you have an excellent foundation for good interpersonal relations with peers, subordinates and superiors.

It would be valuable to list a few common sense dos and don'ts which would apply in nearly all intra-organizational situations:

1. The Territorial Imperative: Every employee in the organization has an area they call their own. Invasion of this area, especially when unoccupied is a definite DON'T. Borrowing equipment without asking, rummaging through papers on someone's desk, even sitting in someone else's chair in the lunchroom or conference room can create irreversable road blocks to effective interpersonal relationships. Respect the territory of others and insist that they respect yours.

2. Eating at Your Desk: Colin Covert suggests: "If God had intended us to eat at our desks, He would not have created the cafeteria".[5] Taking lunch at your desk while reviewing a set of specifications or re-working a construction detail will not impress your employer, or anyone else in the office for that matter. Your employer will be a great deal more impressed if you lunch at Rotary or any other place where a useful business contact might be made.

Don't eat at your desk.

3. Meetings: As a new employee your role at meetings, both in and out of the office, will be that of listener, not orator. Take notes, learn and record as much as you can, but avoid doodling. You can certainly ask questions for clarification, but don't suggest new avenues of discussion unless invited to do so. If you feel that something being said or decided is incorrect, hold your concern for later. Discuss your concern with the person involved in private. It is possible that you were unaware of an overriding issue or a previous decision. If the person was wrong, your stature will increase for not having made that person look bad in the meeting.

Respect the territory of co-workers.

Be a listener at meetings, not a doodler.

4. Recognize Personal Idiosyncrasies: Nearly every person has quirks and idiosyncrasies. Learning those which are associated with moods and predispositions can often forewarn you of conflict situations. The same can be said for human frailties. Everyone has them. Watch for these among your co-workers and avoid words or actions which could offend or be misunderstood.

Understand the moods and dispositions of your co-workers.

5. Constructive Criticism: Learn to accept constructive criticism. Above all don't take criticism personally and don't attempt to shift blame to someone else. Even if you are not at fault, there is little to be gained by over-reaction to constructive criticism and even less to be gained by shifting the blame.

Learn to accept well intended criticism.

Getting along with your co-workers, or the fine art of interpersonal relations within the organizational structure, is essential to success. During your early career these skills will govern your job advancement. In later years they will be critical skills in your role as a leader and a director of people and projects. Without these skills you may well be confined to a position with no growth potential. If you have the ability to combine intra-organizational relationship skills with extra-organizational skills you have many of the tools necessary to lead your own organization or become a top level manager.

The Extra-organizational Environment

In many ways interpersonal relations outside the organization are similar to intra-organization interpersonal relations. Certainly common sense, common courtesy and understanding of human needs and expectations plays a key role in both environments. Beyond this, however, there are unusual differences.

For many people, the extra-organizational environment presents a frightening and inhospitable picture which frequently causes an inertia difficult to overcome. Because the extra-organization world is peopled largely by non-landscape architects, moving within it requires an outgoing nature, an extroversion, that many believe they do not possess.

While many landscape architects are indeed introverts who find it difficult to participate in the extra-organizational world, most can train themselves to function quite well in this environment. The task begins by nurturing a basic liking for people which everyone possesses, and includes developing an affinity for social contact and involvement in the world around us.

A list of dos and don'ts can also be developed for extra-organizational relationships and include:

1. Community Involvement: Getting involved in the activities of your community is a fundamental key to your success. If you find it difficult at first you may have to force yourself. Make no mistake about it, however, community involvement is a must to your professional advancement. Start slowly and coordinate your involvement with the interests of your organization. Pick an area that has appeal to you, however, and volunteer your time and energy. Every community needs responsible volunteers and your offer to help will be gladly accepted. With your first involvement in community life you will begin to develop a network of social and professional contacts that will assist your career for the remainder of your life. Continue to broaden your community involvement and increase the level of responsibility you assume in volunteer roles. Not only will your knowledge and leadership skills grow, the community will quickly learn that you are a responsible person and will believe that because you are good at your volunteer tasks you must also be equally good at your professional tasks.

2. Don't be Defensive or Offensive About Your Profession: Too many landscape architects feel they must be constantly on the defense about their choice of professions. "Everyone thinks we are bush pushers", or "Why can't they say landscape architect instead of landscaper?", are frequently heard defensive comments. This attitude is often changed to an offensive posture in extra-organizational situations. Neither posture helps you, your organization, or your profession. If someone at a party asks you what you do for a living and you are afraid to answer try this; "I'm a landscape architect, what do you do?" Most people really prefer to talk about themselves, it is human nature. When rapport is established you may find it much easier to talk about your own profession.

3. Remember the Proprietary Nature of Your Organization's Work: There are always certain aspects of your organization's work effort which are, or should be, confidential in nature. Maintain this confidentiality. The same caution applies to prospective work of the office. Resist the temptation to brag about work the office is doing or is about to do. Final contracts may not yet be signed and a competitor may be listening.

4. Build a Broad and Diverse Base of Friends and Contacts: School days are behind. No longer can your advancement be assured within the comfort of a social world composed solely of landscape architects. Your social contacts and friendships should be as varied as possible. Through community involvement and work related activities ample opportunities will present themselves to establish solid and lasting friendships with people from many walks of life. Take advantage of these opportunities. These are people who will be really interested in what you do and in your career advancement. They will become missionaries for you and for your profession. This does not suggest that you should shun social contact

with your co-workers, but that your community of friends must be much wider and more diverse.

Build and nurture friendships outside the office.

Interpersonal relationship skills are important to success in any business situation. To landscape architects they take on greater than normal proportions, however. The ability to understand people and to design for peoples' use and enjoyment is considered a fundamental precept of the profession. How can landscape architects understand people well enough to design for them without also being good at interpersonal relationships? To believe that these are two separate issues represents a kind of naivety that can lead to professional stagnation.

The profession, moreover, demands more and better skilled advocates. Those who can speak out with eloquence on behalf of the profession are needed in greater numbers if the profession is to continue to grow. Combining interpersonal skills with technical and design competence is the first step toward leadership.

When landscape architects talk E. F. Hutton listens (a true incident).

Leadership

No discussion about interpersonal relationship skills would be complete without a section on leadership. Motivation, productivity, quality control, bargaining, negotiating, overcoming resistance to change, managing, directing, and a host of other decision making activities are functions of leadership skills. But what makes a leader? Psychologist John Holland again provides some clues.

Holland suggests you look at your personal history. If you fit this personality profile you likely have the promise of leadership ability:

"(Your leadership potential is high) if you completed college in the top third of your graduating class, earned a hefty portion of your college cost yourself, got your first job before you were fifteen years old, have a definite aim in life, and are willing—even actively seek—to have more and more responsibility, you're (on your way to the top). You'll also need above-average intelligence and superior emotional control, the ability to remain unflappable in the most trying situations. You should be a pro at organizing what everyone else has to do and will be good at inspiring them to do it. In meetings, that special sparkle of leadership will come through. But at the same time, you're always aware that you're on a team and that somebody up the line is still the coach. If you're never quite satisfied with where you are, that's good; you should have a strong drive for upward mobility. And in whatever you do, you'll always foresee the outcome and implications before you take the plunge."[6]

While not a classic definition of leadership, Holland's personality profile does identify those traits frequently found in top leadership positions of business and industry. Douglas McGregor in his essays on leadership and motivation suggests, however, that leadership is not so much a matter of personality traits as it is a matter of relationships.[7]

McGregor says leadership is a function of the relationship of four major variables: 1. The characteristics or personality of the leader or potential leader; 2. The attitudes, needs, and other personal characteristics of the followers; 3. The characteristics of the organization, such as its purpose, its structure, the nature of the tasks to be performed, and 4. The social, economic, and political milieu.

Most research studies, according to McGregor, clearly show that nearly all leadership skills can be learned and that very few inherent characteristics or personality traits are required for effective leadership. Certainly ambition and the desire to be a leader are important and may stem from inherent personality traits. The ability to "get along" with people may also be a personality trait. Most personality types, however, do not directly thwart either of these, and the potential pool of effective leaders is great indeed. With all of this information in hand, then, what can people do to enhance their leadership potential and build their necessary leadership skills?

It is possible to identify four aspects of leadership skill which operate in concert with the relationships discussed by McGregor. Every effective leader will have highly developed skills in the following areas:

1. Knowledge of the Industry: An intimate knowledge of the industry, in this case landscape architecture, is paramount to effective leadership. Leadership, of course, functions at lower, middle and upper management levels, and the degree and kind of knowledge required will vary from one level to the next. A project team leader, for instance, must have detailed knowledge about that particular type of project as well as the specifics of the project itself. To be an effective leader that team leader may not need detailed knowledge about the aspects of another team's activity.

An office production manager, on the other hand, will need an intimate knowledge of all the project types and services offered by the organization. At this middle management level, however, knowledge required for effective leadership will shift from the "nuts and bolts" of project detail to broader issues dealing with scheduling, productivity, client concerns, personnel motivation, administration, and coordination of the organization's resources.

At the upper management level of corporate officers and executives, the knowledge requirements shifts to include state-of-the-art and industry wide concerns, marketing management, fiscal management, agency policy, public relations and overall coordination.

At all levels of leadership the knowledge required must be both pragmatic and intellectual. Every effective leader must have total competence in those skills necessary to get "the job" done. Moreover, the effective leader must have the intellectual knowledge and ability to conceptualize, to look ahead and forecast events, a kind of "sixth sense" ability to anticipate problems and head them off, and the ability to understand the role played by the task at hand in the overall mission of the organization.

2. Networking: Networking is the art of building a collection of professional, community, and social contacts which are an ongoing source of information and who can provide access to people and institutions of importance to your professional activities. Networking has three objectives. First a network provides a continual means of staying abreast with the state-of-the-art of the profession, not only on a local level but a national level as well. Most successful leaders will accomplish this through active participation in the professional society or organization which represents their area of interest. Personal contacts made as a part of this participation can provide a wealth of information and insights about the profession which can lead to improved methods of practice.

The second purpose of networking is to build a diverse number of contacts who can provide information on current and potential project activity. This can be accomplished through community involvement, participation in local building organizations, trade shows, public speaking, and so on.

The third purpose of networking is to develop contacts who can supply information of a specific nature, or provide access to other people or institutions. Suppose, for instance, that seeing the governor was important to the mission of your organization. The chances that you or anyone else in your organization has direct access to the governor are slim. A good network, however, would include a contact who could provide this access. A smart networker knows for example, that the governor's office has a patronage chairperson in every city and county. That person knows exactly how to access the governor, and should be a part of the organization's network.

3. Understanding Group Dynamics: Leaders are normally called upon to lead more than one person at a time. Two or more people make a group, and effective leadership requires the skill to direct and motivate groups.

While much is known about group behavior and more is being learned every day, group dynamics remains a mystery to many people.

Effective leaders, however, must understand what

is known and continue to upgrade their skills in this area.

It would be helpful here to briefly look at some known overriding concepts which deal with group dynamics:

- Group consensus can produce changes in individual behavior that will exceed the changes which can be achieved by attempting to modify behavior on an individual basis.
- Groups and individuals within the group require a strong sense of belonging to the overall organization and to the group itself. There must be a high level of cohesion within the group before it can function in a synergistic way.
- A group, to be effective, must have a high level of esteem for itself. It must feel that it is important as a group and that it has an important job to perform.
- A group must feel that its efforts are relevant, not only to the reason for its formation, but to the overall mission of the organization.
- Group decision making is largely a function of information and perception. Groups require a structured situation in order to reach appropriate decisions and will base their perception of information received largely on their structural format. As groups increase in size the requirement for structure increases and the information provided must become more precise.

Group dynamics play an important role in the success of any practice form and managers and leaders must quickly become skilled at dealing with intra and extra-group relationships.

4. Self Image: The image a person presents to subordinates, peers, and superiors will usually be a sign of that person's leadership level. In many professions and business activities the leaders can be easily identified by their appearance. The football coach is easy to spot, the head nurse in a hospital ward is unmistakable, the superintendent on a construction site, the shop foreman, teachers, and many others wear their leadership rank in very visible ways. Sometimes leaders are identified because their appearance is different from those they lead (the football coach is dressed differently than the players). Other leaders are identified by a special badge or symbol (Superintendent printed in large letters on a hard hat, Head Nurse stamped on a name badge).

In most business situations, however, the image of leadership is more subtle but still unmistakeable. The successful leader has a self image which is clearly transmitted to others. This image clearly says here is a leader and may be transmitted in any or all of the following ways:

- **Appearance:** A leader will look like a leader. A trite but true statement. Dress and personal hygiene habits will be completely appropriate to the work situation. Work stations will be neat and orderly. Mannerisms and idiosyncrasies will reflect a calm and collected personality.
- **Confidence:** A leader will exude confidence and certainty about the work to be done and about the methods selected to achieve the work effort. This confidence will spring from a demonstrated competence in the work to be accomplished.
- **A Listener:** A successful leader will be an accomplished listener. Listening to and understanding what others have to say, and taking action as appropriate, is fundamental to mutual trust and respect. A leader's image will clearly reflect an ability as well as the desire to listen to others.
- **Diversity and Relevance:** A leader's image will demonstrate a great diversity of interests and show special concern for the relevance of issues to the mission of the organization.

Not every landscape architect needs to become a leader, but all must master interpersonal skills if they are to survive and advance within the profession. As the demand for these skills receives greater recognition in the formal education programs leaders will emerge to fill the growing number of positions of great responsibility which are available throughout the profession.

Landscape architecture, like all professional endeavors, is not merely the application of technical skills, but the combination of these skills with human skills that ensures the ability to temper theoretical and technical decision making with wisdom and an understanding of human frailties, and to overcome the potential nearsightedness of specialization.

Chapter 7 Notes

1. Colin Covert, "Things Your Alma Mater Never Told You"; *TWA Ambassador*, May 1980
2. Morris Rosenberg, "Occupations and Values", Research Paper, Cornell Univ., 1975
3. Bernadette Doran, "Does Your Job Have Personality?", *TWA Ambassador*, May 1980
4. Editors, *A Collection of Information that will be valuable to Design Professionals in Private Practice Who are interested in reducing Their Professional Liability Exposures*, The Design Professionals Insurance Company, 1974
5. Ibid 1
6. Ibid 4
7. Bennis & Schein, ids., *Leadership and Motivation, Essays of Douglas McGregor*, MIT Press, 1966

Chapter Eight
Making Decisions

Sound decision making is frought with pitfalls and intuitive frailties.

Introduction

The ability to make sound and often immediate business and project specific decisions is an integral part of professional practice. All too frequently, however, business and professional decisions are based on intuitive judgements rather than sound decision making processes. Intuitive decision making can often lead to faulty results. "Good intentions informed by bad judgement still produce bad decisions."[1]

While many successful business and professional people are often quite good at intuitive judgement making, the process is fraught with pitfalls and compromised by a variety of inferential shortcomings. Every person has a set of preconceived ideas or knowledge structures which can form significant roadblocks to successful decision making when based on intuition or judgements alone.

In fact, judgement is not even the same thing as decision making. "Decision implies choosing a particular course of action, while judgement, the raw material of decision making, is simply drawing an inference from data".[2] While intuition can play in important supporting role in the decision making process, it is imperative to consider process itself as the most appropriate way to determine a particular course of action.

This chapter looks, in some detail, at the decision making process. The chapter begins with an exam-

ination of the pitfalls common to inferential judgement making, moves to a discussion of the scientific
approach to decision making and concludes with a
look at a process-oriented approach to decision making in the business and professional world.

Knowledge Structures

Rational, process oriented decision making is often
subjected to subconscious attack by a host of preconceived, often irrelevant and frequently inaccurate information which is stored in the mind from the day
of birth. This collection of abstract beliefs and emotional feelings are known as knowledge structures
and they play an important role in our lives.
Throughout our lives we develop concepts and perceptions as a means of coping with daily living. "Life
would be a buzz of meaningless stimuli without
(these beliefs)."[3] Much of our lives would be incom-
prehensible without the mind's ability to assimilate
and store a multitude of inputs. Regrettably, this assimilation process is unable to differentiate relevant
from irrelevant stimuli. "Objects and events can be
mislabeled and processed through inappropriate
mind channels."[4] When recalled, this mental data
can often lead us greatly astray.

This assimilation, storage and recall of knwoledge
and beliefs represents a function unique to the human mind. This function not only allows us to cope
with daily life, but also forms the basis of abstract
thought and creativity. This same functional ability,
however, can also lead to heuristic judgements, or a
kind of exploratory problem solving based largely on
intuition, which can be woefully misleading. This
intuitive process can often lead to risky assumptions
which can be fatal to business activity.[5]

Nisbett and Ross suggest that our knowledge structures, when called upon to solve problems intuitively, can arouse data which is useless for solving the
problem at hand. They suggest that there are a number of human judgmental frailties that can result from
dependence on our knowledge structures. A few are
presented here to provide a perspective of the danger
involved.

1. Perception: People interpret events and problems according to their perceptions, which may or
may not, be accurate. Perceptions, or personal beliefs, can be greatly influenced by often emotionally
held sexual, racial, ethnic, occupational, and other
forms of stereotypes. These preconceived ideas are
often difficult to recognize and even more difficult to
overcome.

2. Covariance: The human mind frequently fails
to distinguish the covariation between events. People
are often inclined to assume that a probability connection exists between events (cause and effect) be-

cause the outward appearance makes the connection
seem reasonable. To connect a particular clothing
style and voice inflection with homosexuality in
males is an example of the covariance problem.

3. Fundamental Attribution Error: Overestimat-
ing the role of people's pre-disposition as a cause of
their behavior, when in fact situation factors play a
more significant role, is a fundamental attribution
error. To suggest that attorneys who defend accused
murderers condone murder is an example of this human frailty.

4. Discounting Base-rate Data: Making sound predictions about people or events requires a thorough
working knowledge of statistical probability principles which runs counter to intuitional judgment
making. When making intuitive judgments, a great
reliance is placed; on the similarities between the
character of the prediction and the desired outcome,
and too little reliance on the relative frequency of the
outcome in real life. Sound decisions require sufficient base data to insure statistical reliability.

5. Judgmental Perseverance: People are greatly
inclined to persevere in their judgmental decisions
even when the evidence is overwhelming that they
are wrong. Once formed, intuitive judgments become
a mind set and can be totally resistant to subsequent
attempts to change.

Reliance on our knowledge structures in decision
making is human nature and obviously plays an important role in our decision making abilities. Knowledge, after all, is the basis on which all decisions are
ultimately made. But failure to understand the pitfalls of purely intuitive decision making, and failure
to utilize a logical decision making process, will
most certainly lead to business and professional
practice decisions with grievous results.

Landscape architecture, no matter how it is practiced, is a business, and as such requires sound decision making practices. Business decisions cannot
rely solely on the intuitive use of knowledge structures. A more reliable process is required. To better
understand the business decision making process, it
is helpful to look briefly at intuition's opposite ex-
treme; the scientific approach. The business decision
making process does, in fact, lie somewhere between
the two extremes.

An Empirical Question

To the scientific decision maker, the term empirical means founded upon or derived from replicable
experimentation. While the luxury of true scientific
experimentation can seldom be afforded by those
decision makers in the design professions, a process
devised to test the accuracy of business decisions is
possible and imperative. Moreover, it is possible to

borrow from the scientific world certain empirical concepts which can be directly applied to daily decision making.

Fundamental among these concepts of empirical decision making is the development and maintenance of a reliable data base, supported by theory and ability to apply statistical probability to factual evidence. Decision making which relies upon guess work or memory recall can hardly be effective, and will surely lead to incorrect answers. Development of an information resource base, and an appropriate retrieval system is the first step to decision making with a scientific process foundation.

The scientific decision making process provides some helpful guidelines to business decision makers.

The scientific approach to solution finding is, above all, highly process oriented. It begins with a clear statement of the problem. This is followed by a statement of the expected or probably outcomes (hypotheses) and a clearly defined path to proving or disproving the hypothesis. The path from beginning to end includes a carefully designed series of tests and experiments which slowly but surely eliminates alternative answers and narrows the choice of conclusions. While an identical process is difficult to follow in the design professional's world, the business decision making process can, in fact, track the scientific process in many important ways.

It is possible, then, to draw from the scientific decision making process with its empirical emphasis, several useful concepts. Developing and using reliable statistical data and the following of a step by step evaluation process can dramatically improve the business decision making process. Landscape architects, by virtue of their education and training, should be well equipped to translate these scientific concepts to daily decision making. Their special understanding of and the ability to utilize a process-oriented approach to design gives them tools not shared by many in the business world.

The Design/Problem Solving Decision Making Process

The design process, often equated with the problem solving process is well known to landscape architects and is used on a daily basis. The very nature of the design decision making process requires a systematic and methodological approach. While some designers believe intuitive decisions produce the most creative results, few feel comfortable, given the increasing complexity of the profession, with a strictly intuitive approach to design. Intuitive decisions which flow from years of practice experience and countless exposure to the design decision making process serves some designers well, but this enviable status is enjoyed by only a few practitioners.

The argument between intuitive design and process oriented design decision making is really moot. While some design will continue to be created intuitively, the vast majority of good design; that which looks good and works well, both technically and behaviorally, will come from a process which follows a logical progression of evaluative steps and alternatives testing.

Understanding the design process places the design professional in a position to use the business decision making process with equal skill. Regrettably, many design professionals consider the design process and the decision making process to be identical. While similar, the two processes are far from identical, and the distinctions must be understood.

Until the early 1970s, the design process was thought to be a straight line system beginning with a design problem and ending with a design solution and a constructed project. During the late 1960s many professionals began to argue that the process should be circular or reiterative with project evaluation following construction to furnish useful criteria for the next project of a similar nature. During the early 1970s others argued that the design process should explore and respond to social behavioral issues identified throughout the process. User need determinations, pretesting of program criteria, citizen participation, and feedback loops should become integrated into the process from beginning to end. In fact, the process should not end at all but become a constant series of feedback loops. The following charts show the straight line process and one example of the circular design process models. The feedback loop design process model is shown on the subsequent page.

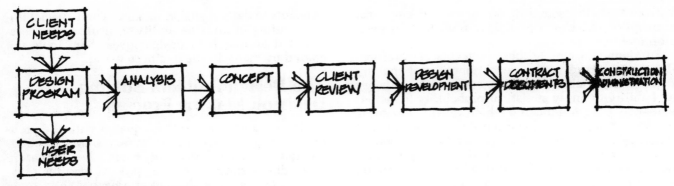

The straight line design process

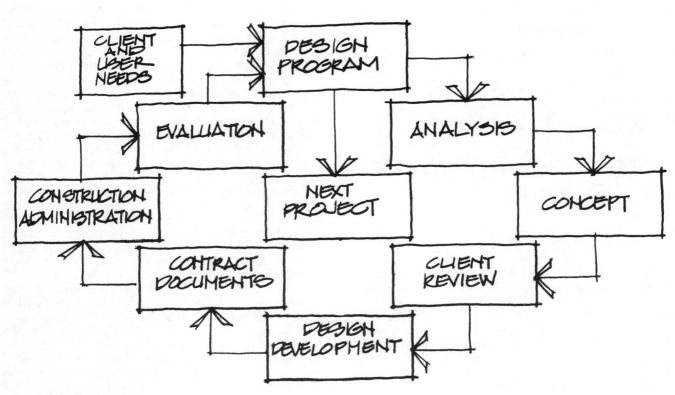

Circular design process

The business decision making process has little similarity to the straight line design process, but does enjoy some commonalities with the circular and feedback loop process. An outline of the business decision making process follows. Understanding the differences and similarities will allow for a more intelligent utilization of both processes.

The Business Decision Making Process

1. **Problem Statement:** Like the design process, the business decision making process begins with a clear and concise statement of the problem. Frequently, however, the problem to be addressed involves human, emotional, or conceptual business issues which

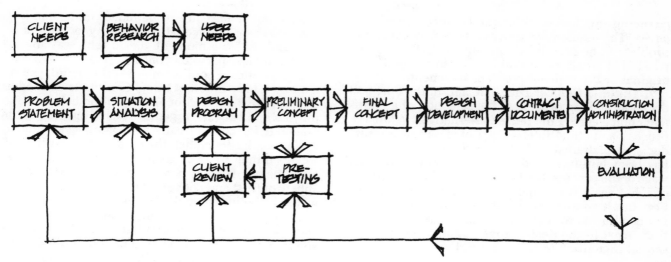

The feedback loop design process

may have little relationship to design or the technical knowledge skills, making a clear statement of the problem difficult for many design professionals. Interpersonal, human and financial resources, and growth forecasting issues are far different from design issues. In developing the problem statement then, the design professional must recognize the need for other forms of knowledge and expertise and utilize them as necessary.

2. Situation Analysis: This step also bears some similarity with the feedback loop design process. Determining the social, political and economic environment within which the decision will be made is the goal of the situation analysis. Under what constraints and circumstances will the decision be made and how will these impact the potential success of the decision? The situation analysis must deal with real facts and information and often involves research and extensive data gathering.

3. Alternative Possibilities: In the business decision making process it is imperative that all alternative solutions be identified and carefully defined. While the design process certainly looks at alternative solutions, it seldom attempts to identify them all. There is an assumption in the design process that "good" design evolves from an assessment and analysis of alternatives, and while there might be an infinite number of alternatives, the number of viable alternative solutions is relatively small. This assumption would be fatal in the business decision making process. All of the alternatives must be identified, including the effects of no decision at all.

Many bad business decisions have been made simply because the best alternative was not identified.

4. Preliminary Assessment of Alternatives: Since the list of alternative choices may be quite long, it is necessary to employ a method of eliminating some very early in the assessment process. This, of course, can be very risky. Many alternatives, if not well articulated, could be overlooked or rejected during this preliminary cut. The preliminary assessment should look for those alternatives with the highest level of unpredictability. If it is impossible or very difficult to predict the outcome of an alternative, it should be dropped from consideration, but not forgotten. It may be necessary to return to it at a later date if other alternatives prove equally unpredictable.

5. Determination of Best Alternatives: With the field of choices narrowed during the preliminary assessment, this step is designed to allow a detailed assessment of the remaining alternatives and rank ordering of these. This assessment would include measuring for each of the best alternatives: the probability of its success, the requirement it places on resources (money, people, materials, time and space), its comparative payoff or benefit, and the latitude it provides for fallback in the event of failure. It is imperative that during this step assessment be based on factual evidence and not intuition. If an alternative cannot be tested, it fails to meet a high enough level of predictable outcome and must be ranked low.

6. Restate the Problem: With the best alternatives determined and ranked it is wise to clearly restate the problem. Frequently problems change as a result of changing practice conditions and other outside influences. The assessment process itself may cause the problem to be seen in a different light. The highest ranking alternatives should be measured against the original or the evolved problem statement.

7. Optimal Choice: The final step in the business decision making process is the selection of an optimal choice among the ranked alternatives. While the process is not infallible, the risk of making the wrong decision is dramatically lessened when the process has been faithfully and honestly followed. By this stage of the process, the best decision should be obvious, but again it is important to guard against intuition. Intuitive warnings should be checked, but must not be allowed to freeze a decision maker into inaction. Trust in the decision making process is an essential ingredient in its successful use.

Resolving Conflict

Most conflicts, even the most serious,

Can be satisfactorily resolved.

Decision making without conflict is rare, indeed. Conflict is a natural state. Conflict is encountered by every person every day in dozens of ways. Fortunately, most personal conflicts are resolved quickly and without serious damage. Most husbands and wives are quick to make up after a fight. Sibling conflicts are soon forgotten. A brief upsetting encounter with a harried public official or a bureaucratic delay will pass with time. Most personal conflict situations are resolved without the need for outside expert help or arbitration. A measure of patience, understanding, and tolerance, coupled with the ability to "step back" and cool off for a moment goes a long way toward resolving most personal conflict.

Organizational conflict, on the other hand, can often be a totally different thing. Conflict is defined as a competitive event. Since competition between employees and between organizations is inevitable, the potential for conflict runs high. Managers and organization leaders must, then, be skilled conflict resolvers if they are to be good decision makers. Moreover, they must know how to create a working atmosphere of trust and cooperation. With this in mind, it would be helpful to look at some simple rules which apply to creating and maintaining trust and cooperation within organizational groups. The rules are simple enough, but their application is often quite subtle and requires great skill.

1. Individual Esteem: All employees must be convinced that they play an important role in the overall effort of the group. They must be convinced that there is no threat to the longevity of their jobs. Employees who feel insecure about their positions within the group are primary sources of conflict.

2. Common Goals: A group must clearly understand organizational goals and recognize their part in the accomplishment of these goals. A group must feel that their role in accomplishing these goals is important and is shared by all members of the group. The efforts of the group must be fully shared by all members of the group. An employee who is uninformed about the group's activity may purposefully create conflict out of anger, jealousy, or frustration, or from ignorance of the facts of an event or situation.

3. Shared Support: Group rapport must be maintained at the highest possible level. All members of a group must be convinced that they have the total and complete support of other group members. The exchange of information between employees is critical to this process. Frequent staff meetings, effective inter-office communications, and encouraging employees to discuss their hopes and aspirations with each other and with management are among the techniques to accomplish this goal.

4. Organizational Policy: Organizational policies can assume either a threatening or trusting tone, and will have a corresponding effect on an organizational group. If employees perceive organizational policy to be unfair or that it is designed to encourage individual effort more than group effort, the result can be severely damaging to synergistic group action.

5. Selective Retention: Finally, an effective organization must practice a conscientious program of selective employee retention. Some people just don't work well in group situations. When these people surface, they must be transferred to a nongroup situation or terminated if no such situation is available.

Moreover, incompetent employees must be quickly spotted and terminated. Employees will quickly spot incompetence in other and mistrust for the organization will slowly but surely smolder if incompetent employees are retained and receive the same rewards as other employees. This is a difficult problem for many organizations. No manager wishes to act quickly or hastily when considering competence, especially in new employees. If this compassionate feeling is allowed to overcome a manager's responsibility to the group, however, the results can be serious conflict.

Fairness and understanding . . .

. . . are critical to conflict resolution.

Skilled managers understand and utilize these simple yet fundamental rules for avoiding conflict in daily business decision making. When applied with fairness and the understanding that all people are different, most conflict situations can be avoided or quickly nipped in the bud. But what happens when conflict cannot be avoided? Again, there are some rules of thumb. To understand these rules, however, it is necessary to understand the three possible strategies which can be adopted by the participants in a conflict situation.

1. Participants may attempt to maximize their own outcome through a conflict situation.
2. Participants may attempt to minimize the outcome of other participants in the conflict situation.

3. One or more participants may attempt to maximize the combined outcome of all parties in the conflict situation.

Obviously, the last strategy would be preferred and it is normally the task of the manager to see that one or more conflict participants adopt this strategy. Maximizing the outcome of all participants in a conflict situation usually requires the ability to expand the parochial view of the participants to a higher and more balanced level. It is also frequently necessary to convince the participants that compromise does not mean defeat.

In complex conflict situations, managers will often utilize role playing techniques where each participant is asked to assume another's point of view. When properly orchestrated, this technique can give all of the participants, including management a better understanding of the issues involved and can greatly ameliorate the conflict. Other techniques to conflict resolution would include the following:

1. **State the Problem:** The event or situation which has caused the conflict must be clearly identified using input from all conflict participants. All too frequently conflicts are caused by simple misunderstanding. It is also important that both sides of the issue or situation be fully articulated. Often a conflict situation can be easily resolved when all participants completely understand each other's real concerns.
2. **The Maximizing Compromise:** Many conflict situations are resolved through compromise, especially one which maximizes the outcome of all participants. Frequently this involves finding a "face saving" device for some participants who recognize their error in the conflict situation but are too embarrassed or fearful of retaliation to back down on their own.
3. **The Larger Issues:** Identifying larger issues will frequently provide conflict participants with a clearer picture of the parochial nature of the original conflict. If the conflict situation poses a real threat to the overall goals of the organization, it may be possible to appeal to the participants sense of loyalty and personal stake in the organization's future. Identification of the larger issues will help keep the conflict situation in proper proportion and reduce its chances of getting out of hand.
4. **Professional Help:** When all else fails it may be necessary to seek outside professional help. Professional mediators and arbitrators are skilled at conflict resolution and can do so without threat of emotional involvement. Any potentially serious conflict should be immediately reported to the organization's legal counsel. While the lawyers may not become directly involved in the conflict resolution, they can offer important guidance along the way and will be better prepared in the event they are needed.

5. Record Keeping: With the exception of routine inter-office conflicts, it is important that all attempts to resolve a conflict along with all pertinent information concerning the conflict situation be carefully and fully documented.

The design professional operates in a complex arena, one which involves a wide variety of individuals and organizations. This arena is not a sterile place, but one which constantly involves the hopes, aspirations, and the frailties of human beings. Conflict which is inevitable need not be a negative force. Understanding this allows the design professional to acquire and constantly improve the skills required to deal with conflict and to build an organizational atmosphere of trust rather than threat.

Decision making, whether it be design, personal, or business-oriented is an essential part of landscape architectural practice. Developing the skills to be an effective decision maker is as important as developing skills in graphics and grading and all the others so commonly associated with the profession. Those who master these essential skills will become the movers and the shakers of the profession.

Chapter Eight Notes

1. Mort LaBrecque, "On Making Sounder Judgments", *Psychology Today*, June 1980

2. Ibid 1

3. Nisbett & Ross, *Human Inference: Strategies and Shortcomings of Social Judgment*, Prentice Hall, N.Y., N.Y. 1980

4. Ibid 3

5. Slovic, Fieschoff & Lichenstenstein, "Risky Assumptions", *Psychology Today*, June 1980

Chapter Nine
Effective Communications

Introduction

Column 1

0. integrated
1. total
2. systematized
3. parallel
4. functional
5. response
6. optional
7. synchronized
8. compatible
9. balanced

Column 2

0. management
1. organizational
2. monitored
3. reciprocal
4. digital
5. logistical
6. transitional
7. incremental
8. third-generation
9. policy

Column 3

0. options
1. flexibility
2. capability
3. mobility
4. programming
5. concept
6. time-phrase
7. projection
8. hardware
9. contingency

The preceeding is the Wordsmanship System Chart. It was developed by a Washington, D.C. civil servant especially for those people who delight in various forms of gobbledygook and jargonese. To use the system simply select at random one digit from columns 1, 2, and 3. 363, for instance, provides the fetchingly meaningful phrase: parallel transitional mobility. No one knows what that means, of course, but therein lies the beauty of the system. Those who recognize the use of the Wordsmanship Chart will say nothing for fear of giving away a highly useful device. Those who don't understand will say nothing for fear of appearing ignorant.

Every profession has its own "buzzwords" which

form a part of the language used to communicate ideas, instructions, feelings and experiences to others on a daily basis. The profession of landscape architecture is not without its own language which can, like all the others, deteriorate to gobbledygook. Consider the following chart adapted from architect R. Jackson Smith's, "Architectural Innovator System".[1]

Column 1	Column 2	Column 3
0. synergistically	0. retro-fitted	0. designs
1. visually	1. interfaced	1. analysis
2. energy	2. systematized	2. land forms
3. computer	3. articulated	3. environments
4. user	4. consumptive	4. projects
5. behavior	5. modulated	5. implementation
6. aesthetically	6. modified	6. communication
7. conceptually	7. relevant	7. inventories
8. resource	8. based	8. planning
9. creatively	9. directed	9. parameters

Try number 809 in your next project presentation. "Our design solution is soundly based on 'resource retro-fitted parameters' ". The variations are nearly endless, and many professionals use the word game with great seriousness and considerable creativity. No matter how creative, word games like these are nothing more than gobbledygook and can be aptly described by number 846.

Communications transmit:

Effective communication is the cornerstone of successful professional practice. Not only is effective communication important to professional success, it is also the principal means of avoiding costly and emotionally debilitating legal actions which frequently stem from misunderstanding, misinformation, or no information at all.

Communications are the complex systems used to transmit ideas, feelings, directions and experiences to others. There is nearly always a desired effect associated with the communications effort. The effect would be to stimulate a response or a change in response by the receiver or recipient of the communication message. "This would include such outcomes as the following: the acquisition of information, the understanding and/or acceptance of an idea or point of view; the motivation to carry out a purpose that the (sender) has in mind; a change in attitude or belief; the creation of a mood or feeling; and enjoyment or emotional satisfaction."[2]

Some communication systems also play another important role in the business world; that of providing a written or recorded historical record of professional and business activity. Written communications forms are discussed in greater detail in a subsequent chapter on Business Procedures. This chapter will deal with communications as an effective tool for directing and motivating the internal organizational business operations and for linking the organization with the external world. The emphasis will be on the skills and techniques required to eliminate gobbledygook and ward off communication failures.

The Basic Skills

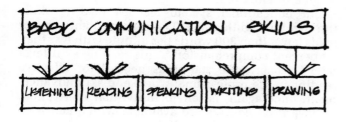

The basic skills needed for effective communications are easily recognized but often acquired with great difficulty. These skills include listening, reading, speaking, and writing ability. In the design professions, graphic communication skills must be added to the list. While all these skills may seem self evident, too few professional degree programs provide specialized skill training in the first four areas. Certainly the importance of these skills is recognized by the educational programs, but very little formal attempt is made to encourage their acquisition. This is usually left to individual motivation and the ability to find class offerings that do not compete with design studio courses.

The communication skills are related and interrelated. Only speaking and writing can be separated from the group as distinct or unrelated skills. This is to say that a good speaker may not also be a good writer, and vice versa, but both will be good listeners and good readers. A closer look at the communication skills follows.

Listening: "If your listening skills are average, 75 percent of the messages you send are not effectively received."[3] This startling fact points to the inexorable link between listening and communicating. Good listeners seem to be rare, indeed. Most people, it would seem, prefer to be either talkers or passive listeners. Few people actually work at developing their listening skills and most fail to recognize the importance of this skill.

Nichols and Stevens, in their book, *Are You Listening?*, make no excuse for the fact that listening is hard work, but fundamental to business and personal success. They propose a number of useful guide lines for improving listening ability. They are quick to point out, however, that good listening begins by overcoming the perils of over-stimulation and under-stimulation in listening situations. Being so "turned-on" or so "turned-off" by the speaker or the subject matter makes rational assessment of the message nearly impossible. "Hold your fire", they suggest. Listen calmly and follow these simple guides:

1. Judge content, not delivery.
2. Focus on central ideas and do not be mislead by characteristic and jargonese language.
3. Take notes only if this helps you. To some it may be distracting.
4. Resist distractions.
5. Maintain an open mind.
6. Be sympathetic, and encourage the speaker to elaborate. Show an interest in the speaker and subject matter.
7. Be patient, most people will sooner or later get to the point.
8. Don't interrupt or enter into debate until you are sure the speaker has had every opportunity to present the intended message.

Overstimulation and understimulation are basic blocks to effective listening.

The guidelines seem like good common sense as well as plain common courtesy, but one marvels at how infrequently they are followed. One needs only to attend a typical local planning commission or similar governmental meeting to see the art of listening abused. When a controversial issue is being considered, both sides of the issue will be represented by people whose emotions are overstimulated. Speakers are often interrupted by boos and groans, and very few really listen to what is being said. The same questions are asked over and over because no one listened to the answers given in the first place. When the meeting is closed, both sides have heard only what they wanted to hear.

The pros and cons take opposite sides and seldom listen to each other.

Effective communication is an art most attorneys practice with great skill. Good lawyers are also the most effective listeners. The next time you attend a meeting, watch the attorneys present when they are scheduled to speak. While others are speaking they are listening intently. They frequently take notes and are mentally organizing their own remarks in rebutal. They are so intent on listening that even gross distractions do not seem to bother them. They understand the link between listening and communicating.

Reading: Being well informed and being a good communicator are also directly linked. Understanding not only your profession, but the world in which you function will play many important roles in your future success, not the least of which will be your

ability to effectively communicate. If you find reading difficult or dull, your communication skills will be greatly impaired.

Our educational system teaches reading skills through the eighth grade. The average eighth grader reads fewer than 300 words per minute with less than 70 percent comprehension.[4] This reading skill level falls far below the standards needed for effective reading in the professional world and skill advancement, once again, is left to individual motivation. College level courses are available which can help improve reading skill levels, but they are seldom encouraged by professional design degree programs. The importance of reading skills must receive greater attention, and all professional aspirants must develop strategies for improving this skill on their own volition.

Speaking: Speaking skills among design professionals would appear to be even more rare than listening and reading skills. Unless you attended an exceptional high school, were active in clubs, organizations, or dramatics or were on the debate team, your speaking experience will be limited and your fears of addressing more than one person at a time will be great. Again, the professional design degree programs do little to help develop these skills. While many programs will utilize stand-up presentation to juries, the infrequency of this activity makes it a poor substitute for effective speaking development. The professional aspirant must be self motivated and develop skill training strategies in this area as well.

Graphic communication skills without speaking and writing skills are not sufficient for successful practice.

Poor readers are likely to be poor communicators.

Learning to stand and think on one's feet is an essential ingredient in almost all forms of professional practice. The ability to motivate, direct, lead, promote and sell, and present design solutions to clients are all directly linked to speaking skills. Development of these skills also sharpens other skills like decision making and interpersonal relationships.

Speaking and writing are the primary communication transmission systems. In the design professions, graphics can also be an effective communication technique, but in the total spectrum of the professional and business world, graphics have only limited value. Sometimes too much importance is placed on graphics as a communication device. While important and unique to the design professions, graphic skills without speaking and writing skills cannot provide the necessary communication power to properly transmit ideas or concepts and your skill level will fall short in those situations where changing the attitudes of others is critical to successful practice.

Writing: The importance of writing skill as a communication transmitter cannot be stressed enough. Inter-office memos, proposals and contracts, daily correspondence, reports and studies, reviews and assessments, and a host of other activities of a written nature compose a large part of the work product of every professional practice form. In a survey conducted of public and private professional offices in 1980, each respondent was asked to estimate the percentage of office time devoted to written products or similar efforts. The private practice firms reported an average of 25 percent of their production time devoted to writing activity, and the public offices reported nearly 50 percent of their time devoted to written products.[5] These figures do not include time devoted to inter-office communication, daily correspondence or writing for publication. The results surprised some private practitioners, but most were quick to point out that writing skills were essential to their practice activity, and that many new projects were generated as a result of their firm's capabilities in this skill area.

The spoken word has great power and a unique ability to influence people. The printed word has even more power. Using this power and influence effectively has not been one of the landscape architect's strengths. Perhaps this is because of the inaccurately perceived power and influence of graphic communication, or perhaps because of a reluctance within the profession to substitute words for pictures when conveying ideas and concepts. Whatever the cause, the profession, as it continues to grow, demands a greater quantity of better writers. As Francis Bacon pointed out, "Reading maketh a full man, but writing maketh an exact man".

Blocks to Effective Communication

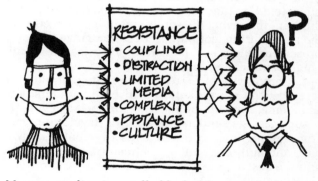

Message sending is usually blocked by some form of resistance.

Communication, like the transmission of radio signals, begins with a sender or transmitter, ends with a receiver or audience, and encounters resistance along the way. If the resistance along the way is great, the signal will be weak and the message easily misunderstood. Moreover, the sender and the receiver must be on the same wave length. The interests and view point, comprehension and interpretive ability of the sender must interlock with those of the receiver. This notion strongly suggests that responsibility for assuring an interlock must rest with the sender.

But, alas, along the message path lies potential resistance which can block even the best interlock. Six potential forms of resistance have been identified which can block effective message understanding:

1. Coupling: Coupling is the connection between sender and receiver. An obvious poor coupling example is a faulty phone connection, or a conversation conducted under very noisy conditions. The use of an intermediary to convey important messages is another example of poor coupling. Failure to schedule an important informational meeting is an example of no coupling at all.

2. Distractions: Distractions, like poor coupling, are insidious to the communication process. Noise, confusion, too many senders at one time, and competition of other sorts are examples of distractions. Less easily spotted, however, are distractions in the receiver's mind. Personal problems, tiredness, fatigue, the effects of depressants and stimulants, illness, and a host of emotional or psychological irritants can cause insurmountable distractions to effective communication.

3. Limitations of Media: It is nearly impossible to transfer thoughts from one mind to another in exact form. The transfer process is modulated by differences in attitudes, viewpoints, perceptions, and levels of experience, and the type of communication used will impact different people in different ways. Even when carefully articulated a message can be interpreted by the receiver to mean something quite different than what the sender intended. Selection of the transmitting techniques must recognize this ever present problem and be carefully devised to eliminate misunderstanding.

4. Complexity of Content: The more complex the message, the more likely it will be misunderstood. The same concern holds true for message length. Many message senders are fond of developing very complex and lengthy messages as a symbol of knowledge and authority. Such practices are often unwise, and the best advice is to keep the message short and simple.

5. Distance: Physical distance can greatly impede communication. Try effectively communicating with a friend across a wide street or large open space. The effort is difficult and the message may require frequent repeating. Even after several tries, neither person is sure the messages were correctly received. Organizations with widely scattered branch offices constantly face this communication problem.

6. Culture: Cultural differences between sender and receiver can also cause great communication difficulty. This works in a variety of ways, some of which are quite subtle. Cultural differences between sender and receiver can set up immediate mental blocks. If the sender attempts to structure the mes-

sage to suit the receivers cultural mode, the receiver may feel that the sender is being condescending or even mocking. If the sender attempts no cultural modification to the message, then he or she may be accused of arrogance, dispassion or even down right rudeness.

Less subtle but of equal concern are the differences in meanings associated with words and phrases resulting from cultural differences. The word "heavy" to some people means weighty or difficult to lift, to others it can mean good or first class. Body language also plays a special role in communications between culturally different peoples. Differences in personal space characteristics, symbolic signs, and gestures will vary greatly from one culture to the next.

When the blocks to effective communications are understood and guarded against, the transmission of messages will be dramatically improved. With the six resistance factors in mind it is possible, then, to develop a model for truly effective communications.

Developing Effective Communications

The art of effective communications revolves around reducing the resistance encountered between sender and receiver. To assist in this effort the Design Professionals Insurance Company recommends the following four point process:[5]

1. Analyze the Receiver: A careful analysis of the message receiver is the first and most important step in developing effective communications. Regrettably, it is also the step most commonly overlooked or improperly executed. The more one knows about the message receiver, the easier it is to develop an appropriate sending strategy, select a proper media technique, and prepare an understandable message. Without good reliable information about the receiver, the ultimate message may be subjected to great misunderstanding.

Learning about the message receiver implies doing a little "homework". The homework techniques will vary, but the results should yield as much information about the receiver as possible. If the receiver is an employee, talk to that person. Learn about that employee's hopes and aspirations, habits, family background, leisure activities, and so on. This is not prying, it is just good business. Most people like to talk about themselves, and will gladly do so if an inquiry is friendly and straightforward. If the receiver is a large audience, the homework technique will change. A small amount of effort can provide information on the group's history, positions on community and national issues, common membership characteristics, and specific information about its current leadership. Taken together, this information can be of great value in message development and transmission.

When properly researched and analyzed the information about the receiver(s) can assure messages which are appropriate to the situation and less likely to be misunderstood. When the research and analysis is not done, or done improperly, the message results can be disasterous. The following is a case in point:

A firm of design professionals was retained to design a six hundred acre planned community to be located in a large but sparsely populated southern state county. The firm's solution was well conceived, developed with sensitivity for the natural landscape, and rendered in a handsome graphic form. The client/developer was delighted with the solution and after carefully exploring the project's economic potential, gave the go ahead for the next step; governmental approvals. The first step in the approval process was to obtain the rezoning needed to accomplish the proposed land use.

The rezoning process began with a presentation to the county planning commission whose recommendation of approval was critical to the rezoning process. The design professionals arrived on the night of the scheduled public hearing to present their client's message. They arrived enmasse, six of them, dressed in three piece suits, and bringing with them a dozen panels of handsome graphics, beautifully bound reports, and a slide presentation.

The design professionals arrive enmasse.

But alas, our professionals had failed to analyze the receivers of their message and the evening was a near disaster. The planning commission was composed of seven men. Four were cattle ranchers, two were citrus farmers, and the seventh man owned the local hardware store. Without exception, the seven men relied largely on native common sense and plain talk to get them through their business and social lives. By meeting time most of them had already completed fourteen hours of hot, dusty, hard work. They attended the meeting in open neck shirts and slacks. Two of them chewed tobacco, and all of them

wished they were at home or at local taverns drinking a beer with their friends. They all took their planning commission job seriously, however, but expected no-nonsense presentations, and greatly disliked those occasional meetings which dragged on until late in the evening. The commissioners were not the least bit sophisticated, but they were fair and open minded, and favored quality growth for their county.

The planning commissioners were ranchers and farmers.

All of this information was readily available. A ten minute conversation with the county planning director would have surfaced most of it. The rest could be easily learned through informal conversations with the planning commissioners themselves. Regrettably, our team of design professionals had not done their homework. Their presentation strategy, media selection, and the message itself was more appropriately suited for a highly sophisticated "big city" planning commission composed mostly of professionals.

Not only was the team poorly prepared, they failed to recognize their mistake. They began their presentation at 9:30 p.m. and ended with the last slide at 11:15 p.m. When the lights were turned on every planning commissioner was startled from a rather sound nap. Without asking a single question a motion was made to deny. Only the quick thinking of the client, who asked for a continuance, saved the

The presentation began at 9:30 p.m. and went on and on and ...

... on, and on!

The planning commission was tired and unimpressed by the presentation.

project from defeat. A classic example of a well conceived project nearly destroyed by a well meaning team of professionals who knew nothing about the ART of effective communication.

2. Determine a Strategy: Once the receiver has been carefully analyzed, determining a message strategy is a relatively simple task. Empathy and common sense must be the principle guides, being certain, however, that the strategy is appropriate to what is known about the receiver. The primary goal of strategy selection is to eliminate defensiveness on the part of the receiver. In the planning commission example, the design professionals, by their numbers, dress, and formality of presentation, put the ranchers and farmers immediately on the defensive.

To eliminate defensiveness, a supportive climate must be created. "This can be accomplished by appealing to the supportive mode of six matched and interactive strategies."[6]

• Shift from Evaluation to Description, provide information not judgements.
• Shift from Control to Problem Identification. Rather than giving orders, establish an atmosphere where all agree to take directions from the situation.

• Shift from Superiority to Equality, minimize individual and group differences.
• Shift from Certainty to Provisionalism, be flexible rather than dogmatic.
• Shift from Neutrality to Empathy, emote warmth and understanding.[7]

3. Selecting the Technique: With the homework done and the strategy selected, a message presentation technique can now be developed. Which of the various communication techniques and media types best suits the selected strategy? In the planning commission example the sleeping commissioners indicates that the use of slides was an incorrect selection of media and presentation technique. Verbal, written, visual, and body signals are the basic techniques available. Frequently several or all of the techniques will be used in concert. Within each technique category there are also dozens of sub-categories, all too numerous to detail. To aid understanding, however, a look at how one category might subdivide would be helpful.

Verbal communication techniques have the advantage of being feedback oriented, and can take a variety of different forms. In the planning commission example, an oral presentation could be given by one professional, or all six taking different parts. The presentation could have been taped in advance and merely played for the commission. An attorney might have been hired to act as a surrogate voice for the professionals and their client.

Simple, face to face presentations are often more effective than complex shows with too many players.

In the planning commission example, a simple face to face oral presentation involving the client and one spokesperson representing the professional design team would have been the most appropriate presentation technique. The presentation should have been short and concise, but informal and relaxed. The client acting as the principal spokesperson could have identified his mutual concern for quality growth in the county, and allowed the commissioners to deal with him on a friendly and personal basis. While graphic panels were helpful, handout information in a simple format would have been of greater value, and the slides would have been better left at the office. The entire presentation should have lasted no more than thirty minutes.

4. Preparing and Sending the Message: This final step addresses the issue of quality. How well the message is prepared and delivered will directly influence how well it is understood. The key element is organization. This implies knowing exactly what is to be sent and exactly in what order.

Simplicity and clarity must always rule, and emphasis should be given to the message's major points. If the message is presented orally, emphasis can be added by voice inflection, pauses, gestures, and repeating the key elements. If written, emphasis can be added by prose style, word selection, underlining, using headings and subheadings, highlighting, special indentations, and capitalization.

Transition from one thought to another must be smooth and understandable. Preparing the receivers in advance of a new thought or subject is also very important.

Once prepared, delivery of the message is also critical to its understanding. If the presentation is to be oral, be sure that the person making the delivery is good at the task. If graphics are to be used, be sure they can be seen and understood. Don't be caught in a situation where a detailed 18" × 24" drawing must be used across a twenty foot space, or where a super graphic or oversized drawing must be spread out on a coffee table.

When delivery of the message requires specialized equipment be sure, in advance, that it is working properly and that it will be available when needed.

When these four steps to effective communications are carefully followed, message sending and receiving will be dramatically improved. Both internal and external message sending will result in more reliable reception of ideas, feelings, directions, and experiences.

A Final Thought

This chapter began with a good natured jab at professional jargon and gobbledygook. It would be appropriate to end the chapter with a serious comment on the same issue.

All professions adopt a language or jargon of their own. Frequently external use of this jargon, whether to impress peers or clients, can have a damaging impact on a profession's image and status. A specialized language usually has a very rational internal justification for professional practice. It usually allows for faster and more efficient communication between professionals in the course of their routine efforts. The specialized language of the space in-

dustry is a case in point. Professionals who serve the general public, however, have no justification to externalize their jargon.

When design professionals speak to their clients, to public gatherings, and even to their out-of-the-office friends about retrofiting and interface and computer modulated parameters, the results can lead to mistrust, resentment, and even outright dislike for the speaker and the profession that person represents. At the very least, professional jargon creates confusion and alters public images in often negative ways.

Landscape architecture can ill afford any potential negative reaction to inappropriate use of jargon. The profession's ethic and its practice neither requires nor is profitted by anything other than plain and straight forward messages given with feeling and stemming from unquestionable competence.

This chapter concludes Part Three: The Human Skills. Interpersonal relations, sound decision making and effective communications are, indeed, human skills and mastering them is critical to professional success. Getting along with others, making reliable and profitable daily business and personal decisions and being clearly understood by business associates and friends is a part of business and personal life. There is no mystique here, just plain common sense.

Chapter Nine Notes

1. Gerre L. Jones, *How to Market Professional Design Services,* McGraw-Hill Book Company, N.Y., N.Y., 1973
2. Benjamin Bloom, ed., *Taxonomy of Educational Objectives,* Longman Co. N.Y., N.Y. 1954
3. Nichols & Stevens, *Are You Listening?,* McGraw-Hill Book Company, N.Y., N.Y., 1957
4. William H. Day, *Maximizing Small Business Profits,* Prentice-Hall, Inc., Englewood, N.J., 1978
5. Lane L. Marshall, Unpublished Questionaire conducted in preparation of this manuscript; 1980
6. Design Professionals Insurance Company, *A Collection of Information That Will Be Valuable To Design Professionals In Private Practice Who Are Interested In Reducing Their Professional Liability Exposure*
7. Jack Gibb, "Defensive Communication", *Journal of Communication,* Vol. XI, No. 3, Sept. 1961

PART FOUR
THE BUSINESS SKILLS

Chapter Ten
Basic Business Principles

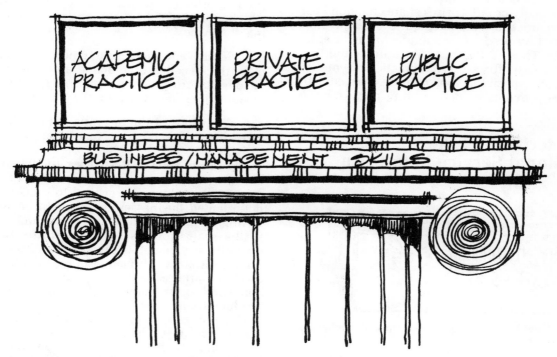

Business and management skills are required by all landscape architectural practice forms.

Introduction

A professional service enterprise includes any organization that essentially sells or renders the knowledge of its people. So defined, such enterprises would include any organization, whether a profit-making commercial business, a non-profit enterprise or institution, public agency, or an operating unit of any of these, whose basic 'product' is the knowledge of some of its people.[1]

The practice of landscape architecture, in all its many and diverse forms, can certainly be classified by this definition as a professional service enterprise. An understanding of the "business" of landscape architecture then, must begin with the recognition that all of the profession's practice forms share common needs for business and managerial skills. No practitioner is immune by virtue of practice form or role from the need to acquire and apply these skills.

The private practice landscape architect has long recognized the importance of business acumen, though not much attention is given to the acquisition of these skills in the professional degree programs. Of greater concern, however, is the number of young landscape architects who aspire to teaching or public practice roles with the assumption that sound business skills are the sole concern of their counterparts who practice in the free enterprise system. This myth has been popularized by professional practice courses in the professional degree programs which devote the vast majority of their time and attention to issues and business procedures peculiar to the functioning of a private practice office. For the most part, the skills being taught could be more appropriately learned during an apprenticeship period following graduation, freeing the professional degree programs to concentrate on development of skills common to all practice forms.

This chapter attempts to deal with broader business issues, and avoids extended discussion of practice specific business concerns. The material covered in this chapter has been selected for its responsiveness to the needs of all professional service enterprises.

Finally, it is equally important to recognize that professional service enterprises share common business characteristics which are quite different from those shared by product or manufacturing-oriented enterprises. These differences are unique and they provide the basis for a service practice orientation that is equally special. A look at these characteristic differences provides a good starting point for this chapter.

Characteristics of the Professional Service Enterprise

Professional service enterprises are in the knowledge selling business.

Most modern day business management practices and procedures are predicated on the growth and experience of commerce and industry during the twentieth century. They are largely oriented to product and manufacturing businesses and frequently have little relationship or relevance to the professional service enterprise. The professional service enterprise that fails to recognize the totally different character of their "business" can easily be trapped into poor quality business decision making. A clear understanding of these special differences becomes the first step toward the development of sound business procedures and techniques in the professional service enterprise.

Robert Sibson, in his book *Managing Professional Service Enterprises*, suggests four specific areas where there are marked differences between product-oriented businesses and service-oriented businesses.[2]

1. Service enterprises sell knowledge, their primary resource is human talent rather than capital or financial assets.

2. Because the "product" is knowledge, service enterprises have unique opportunities for quite different types of selling procedures, product differentiation, choice and change decisions, and pricing policy.

3. Service enterprises are, by comparison to product-oriented business, smaller in scope and have a higher level of "client" involvement in the rendering of service.

4. Service enterprises are typically subject to special ethical codes of practice and regulatory provisions that are quite different from product-oriented organizations. (see Chapter 4)

A closer look at the meaning implied by Sibson's assessment reveals some very interesting business insights.

The Use of Human Resources: In most individual business enterprises one or two facets of operation are usually unique and critical to success. In product-oriented businesses these might be pricing, or styling, or product precision, or research and so on. In the professional service enterprise, the critical operational element is always the effective use of human resources. Human resources are the principal asset of a professional service enterprise and can be compared to the financial assets and inventory of a product-oriented business.

This not so startling fact suggests the need for special skills and understanding, not only of coordinating human effort, but also of how to employ the correct number of people with the right skills and expertise to accomplish the service mission. These human resources must be viewed as the service enterprise's "stock-in-trade" and must be dealt with as skillfully as an accountant totals a balance sheet.

The human resource orientation of the professional service enterprise creates a relatively low requirement for capital investment. Salaries and employee benefits comprise the primary operational costs and together can amount to as much as 70 percent of annual capital needs.[3] While this fact of business life makes starting a professional service enterprise relatively easy, it does present special problems. Without the requirement for a substantive capital resource base many professional service enterprises tread a narrow line between financial success and failure, and their growth potential is greatly limited. Business growth requires capital resources and financial protection during slow activity periods and is also dependent on an accessible capital resource base. These relatively low capitalization requirement may also be responsible for the low opinion some landscape architects hold for financial management skill development.

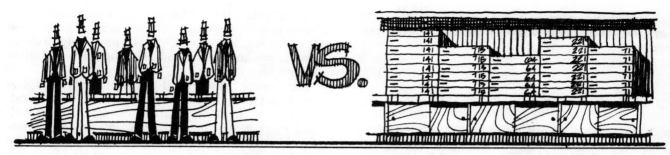

Professional service enterprise: principal asset is people.   *Product enterprise: principal asset is money and inventory.*

The Selling of Confidence: The purchaser of a professional service enterprise's "knowledge" is essentially buying confidence. The typical buyer will have little or no understanding of the quality of the service being offered. There is no way to "test-drive" the product of a professional service enterprise, or to return it if not "completely satisfied". This is a fundamental difference between service and product-oriented enterprise and it has a dramatic impact on business strategies and management.

The techniques used to promote an appliance or a breakfast cereal are of little use to the professional service enterprise. Traditional business strategies common to product-oriented business, like channel distribution, packaging, styling, shelf position, test marketing, and others have no real meaning to the service-oriented enterprise and directly impacts how a professional service enterprise conceives and implements marketing strategy, product development activities and quality control. Marketing management, along with other specialized areas dealing with the selling and promoting of confidence, are discussed in more detail in Chapter Eleven.

There is no way to test-drive or provide a money back guarantee when professional services are being sold.

Product Differentiation: Unlike the product-oriented business where competitor's products usually have great similarity, the opportunities to differen-

tiate "products" in professional service enterprises are great. The differences between two brands of appliance are likely to be little more than a matter of styling. Human abilities, interest, enthusiasm, and focus, however, vary greatly and so will the service offerings within any particular professional firm or agency. The highly creative nature of the design professions adds further to the potential differentiation of services.

Most product-oriented enterprises work constantly to differentiate their product from those of their competitors: The results are largely superficial and can never match the variety of product differentiation found in the service professions. Successful professional service organizations will recognize the value of highly differentiated services and use these differences to their advantage.

Choice and Change: Product-oriented enterprises have little opportunity to choose and to change business activity. New product development is a slow and costly process and decision errors on new products can be financially disastrous. The service professions, however, are not bound by these same formidable constraints. Service enterprises can change directions and add new service offerings quickly and with relatively low capital risk, and a correspondingly high potential for reward. All that is normally required is a recognized market and the acquisition of the necessary knowledge to supply services to that market. While, certainly, choice and change decisions must be carefully made, the ability to move quickly when appropriate, is unique to the professional service enterprise.

Regrettably, there are two major obstacles that seem to prevent maximization of this unique feature of the service professions. The first is resistance to change. Landscape architecture's rather slow acceptance of the computer as an important business and design aid is a good example of this resistance. The second and more difficult obstacle to overcome is the inability of most design professionals to predict change and forecast future professional or business directions. The design professional's generally low opinion of the value of business acumen seems to carry with it an equally low opinion of futures forecasting.

Many "Designers" have been slow to accept the computer as a business aid.

Professional service organizations who can overcome the two choice and change obstacles have a unique opportunity to develop a real competitive edge in the business world.

Customer Participation: A characteristic totally unique to the professional service enterprise is the exceptionally high level of involvement by the customer (client) in the providing of service offerings. In most cases the success of the service offering itself is a direct function of client involvement. This fact of business life frequently requires that the professional service enterprise be able to modulate the differences between a service offering that is technically or aesthetically correct and one that is the most appropriate or best for the client.

The ability to coordinate client involvement in the service offering becomes critical to business success and represents a procedure seldom found in product-oriented enterprises. This management function includes developing trust, demonstrating concern and support for client needs, providing timely actions, keeping commitments, and insuring ongoing follow up activities.

The unique features and characteristics of professional service enterprises differ widely from product-oriented business principles. Practices developed to serve product-oriented enterprises, consequently, are of small value. Unfortunately, there are very few other business standards available. It becomes necessary, then, to adapt and redesign those product-oriented business practices which are success tested to fit the particular characteristics of the service professions. To start this adaptive process five basic business principles are addressed in the closing part of this chapter. Each business principle is viewed in the context of those unique business aspects of the professional service enterprise.

Planning

Landscape architects spend their professional careers planning. Preparation of master plans, schedules, programs, and cost estimates are among those planning functions that landscape architects do very well. And yet, many landscape architects have difficulty doing for themselves what they do so successfully for their clients. In this regard, landscape architects are not alone. Most business people have some reluctance to indulge in serious business planning. Perhaps because planning, by its very nature, requires dealing with the future rather than the present, suspicion of the unpredictable causes an emotional block to the planning process. Moreover, most design professionals have never been taught how to plan in any idiom other than design and they have no real notion of how to begin or carry forward the business planning process.

For whatever reason, business planning is often regarded with only minimal seriousness by many professional service organizations. The resulting day to day business processes are often aimless and uncoordinated.

Sibson suggests that professional service organizations undertake three types of planning functions: Strategic, Opportunity, and Operational.[4]

Strategic Planning: This form of business planning looks to the future. It considers new services, markets, operations, personnel, and activities which could change the character of the enterprise. Strategic planning requires careful assessment of the organization's resources, the practice environment, the special interests and preferences of the principals and staff, and projects these facts into future growth plans.

Many landscape architects have difficulty doing for themselves what they do so well for their clients.

Opportunity Planning: Akin to strategic planning, opportunity planning is the process of organizing for and anticipating unforeseen business opportunities. Unlike strategic planning, which attempts to predict future events, opportunity planning recognizes that many unexpected events can, in fact, be partially predicted. A reaction plan designed to assess and evaluate these events immediately is critical to successful operations. The opportunity plan must be designed to evaluate not only the positive but the negative aspects of the unexpected. A professional service organization, by virtue of its great choice and change freedoms, has almost unlimited opportunity to take advantage of the unexpected, and can ill afford to miss a business opportunity. Neither can it afford to go chasing wildly after a scheme that could be a business failure.

Operational Planning: The professional service enterprises' operational plan deals with the immediate future. It is not open ended like the strategic plan, but attempts to put the organization's current resources to optimum use. In most professional service organizations, the operational planning period is six to twelve months, and requires a formalized periodic updating which is keyed to strategic planning.

Chapter Eleven discusses the business planning process as an integral part of a service organization's marketing management program. While the process is discussed in some detail in Chapter Eleven, it would be helpful, at this point, to review the business planning process in skeleton form. The actual undertaking of the process will vary from one organization to the next, and the amount and sophistication of planning required will increase as operation size increases. Even the smallest of service organizations, however, require some formalized planning effort. The basic planning process divides itself into two functional phases: preliminary and final planning.

The planning process begins by asking questions.

Preliminary Planning (A Plan to Plan): This planning phase applies specifically to new organizations and those who have never planned before. The procedures are in constant use, however, by successful professional service organizations of all sizes and degrees of sophistication. The preliminary planning steps include:

1. Clearly establish the organization's reason for being. What are the purposes for the organization's existence?

2. Within this framework, determine the organization's planning needs. What kind of plans are

needed? What are the time frames for short and long range plans?

3. Determine planning responsibilities. What person(s) within the organization will conduct the planning function? What methods of reporting goals and objectives will be used? What role will other members of the organization play in the planning process?

4. Set target dates for the completion of the planning function and activation of the plan(s).

5. Develop a control system for monitoring the plan's operation and for regular updating.

Final Planning: With a "Plan to Plan" in hand, preparation of strategic, opportunity and operational plans for the short, middle and long range periods can begin. The Design Professional Insurance Company recommends the following steps:[5]

1. Identify Issues: Issues in this sense are those aspects of an organization which could benefit from planned change. These would include the strengths and weaknesses of personnel, physical plant, marketing approach, personal contact selling, and so on. Questions concerning the capitalization of strengths and the correcting of weaknesses should receive primary attention.

2. Establish Planning Families: Organizational issues should be grouped functionally into logical categories. For example; recruitment, apprenticeship program, employee turnover controls, continuing education, and employee training could be grouped together under the planning family of Personnel Development.

3. Assess and Evaluate the Issues: When the issues have been grouped into planning and functional family categories it is possible to collect hard data relevant to each area, to assess this data, and to evaluate a number of alternative approaches to optimizing organizational growth in each area. The assessment and evaluation process depends largely on research and homework activities which will lead to reliable forecasting of expected futures. Intuitive guesswork is of little value to this process except in the area of opportunity planning.

4. Develop Goals: The assessment and evaluation step will lead to an array of alternatives for organizational growth. These alternatives can now be measured against the organization's mission. Those which most clearly reflect and advance the mission can be translated into organizational goals which can be used to direct policy emphasis and ongoing decision making. The goals must be reasonable and attainable, and be flexible enough to accomodate changing conditions as the planning process goes forward.

5. Develop Objectives and Strategies: When goals have been defined, a linked set of objectives or strategies for accomplishing the goals can be formulated and given to the appropriate functional division and/ or personnel of the organization. The interdependence of these strategies must be clearly identified and every individual and decision maker within the organization must fully understand the overall strategy as well as their special role in attaining the goal.

The most common starting point in determining a final business strategy is the establishment of a goal for market position. Too few professional service organizations, however, understand the need for a marketing strategy. This is especially true for the public and institutional service enterprises. All professional services enterprises must plan in order to survive, and their planning activities must be conducted within the framework of a marketing strategy. The importance of a marketing strategy cannot be stressed enough, and the matter is discussed in much greater detail in Chapter Eleven.

Organizational Theory

Sound organizational structure increases in importance, just as the planning function does, as a service enterprise increases in size and complexity. Since the vast majority of professional service organizations start their life cycle as small (frequently involving only one or two persons) and uncomplicated entities, organizational structure is seldom viewed as critical to business success. The truth, of course, is that when success depends upon growth in size and complexity, organizational structure which is both manageable and efficient is a prerequisite.

For many years, courses in professional practice have suggested that staff organization was either horizontal, vertical, or a combination of the two in character. While not technically incorrect, the two organizational structures have failed to relate to more modern organizational theory. They will be discussed briefly, however, as a starting point and to provide a basis for understanding the more modern matrix team building approach to organizational structure.

Horizontal Organization is oriented toward specialty skills within the staff. The staff is divided into groups which perform a specific role and only that role in the overall service offering of the enterprise. A complex project would pass from one group to another, each group performing its specialized and specific task. This type of organizational structure relates closely to the traditional approach used by product-oriented enterprises (an auto assembly line for example).

Vertical Organization, on the other hand, relies on generalists who have the capabilities to perform a number of different functions and who are largely capable of providing all required service skills for a

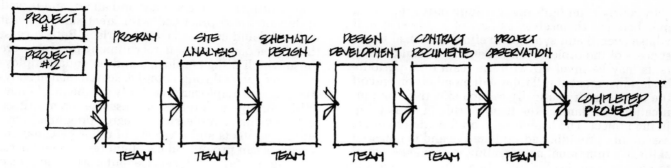

Horizontal organization chart

project from beginning to end. In larger organizations the vertical approach has lead to the formation of Project teams. Each team would be headed by a generalist, but could include several specialists members. This approach, of course, is a combination of both the horizontal and vertical structures.

At this point traditional teaching of organizational structure has stopped, and overriding management issues have been largely ignored. Managing a professional service organization, as discussed in this chapter, is distinctly different from managing a product-oriented enterprise. It is imperative, then, that the distinction and its impact on organizational theory be understood.

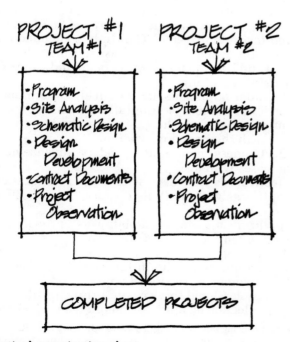

Vertical organization chart

From the Bottom Up: The traditional method of dividing and allocating operational duties downward from the top employed by product-oriented enterprise does not work for the professional service organization. The top down method organizes staff by operational functions such as personnel, finance, administration, and production. Because the professional service enterprise's "stock-in-trade" is people with specialized knowledge, structural organization must be from the bottom up. The product-oriented top down organizational approach concentrates decision making at the middle to upper management levels and assigns very few decision making opportunities to the lower levels. This approach cannot work for organizations whose daily decisions are reached in reaction to situations rather than directives. In the professional service organization top management must result from organizational team groupings at the bottom.

While large professional service enterprises may well have top management people providing specialized top-down functional services, these people normally act in an advisory capacity and have no "on line" service decision making responsibilities.

Matrix Organization and Team Building: Modern organizational theory suggests that the best approach for the professional service enterprise is one based on both organizational function and project type. Knowledge teams are assembled for each specific project. The team leader and the team members are selected on the basis of their functional skill and the specific emphasis of the project. Under this approach, nearly all staff members of the enterprise have the potential to be a team leader, and may, in fact, be both a team leader on one project while being a team member on other projects. It is also possible that the team leadership may change as the project moves from one functional phase to the next. The matrix team building approach, however, does depend on maintaining the remainder of the team composition intact throughout the course of the project.

In matrix team building it is imperative that team members see themselves as part of a cohesive unit whose overall and synergistic effort is critical to the success of the project. While certain special consultants may be involved with the team on a periodic basis, movement of full time staff members on and off the team can dramatically reduce effective communication and damage the team's pride of authorship in the project. The team leader, on the other hand, is essentially providing administrative and managerial skills of a functional nature, allowing some potential to change team leadership when appropriate to the project's functional phase.

Matrix organization and team building, then, allows for staff to serve in both a functional and a project specific way. A large multi-disciplinary firm might, for example, organize itself functionally into architectural, engineering and landscape architectural divisions. The members of each division, however, would frequently find themselves on teams containing members from all three divisions. The team leader might be either architect, engineer, or landscape architect depending on the project's phase of activity. The individual members of the team would be selected for the contribution they could make to the overall effort required, and would remain team members until the projects completion.

Staffing

Building an efficient and productive staff is a fundamental ingredient of professional service enterprise success. In contrast to the product-oriented enterprise, professional service employees below the management levels are more highly paid, more expensive to train and less easily replaced. Because their work is highly creative and less dependent on operational guidelines and standard procedures, the staff of a professional service enterprise is of special importance, and becomes one of management's primary operational concerns.

Building, maintaining, and strengthening the staff of a professional service organization is a five part management process which includes: recruiting, selecting, training, selective retention, and motivation. A brief look at each of these activities follows:

1. Recruiting: All too frequently, recruiting new employees is left purely to chance. When a job position becomes available a hasty advertisement is prepared, a few phone calls are made, and the decision to hire becomes a matter of guess work and chance rather than strategy and goal accomplishment. Even when firms take some pains to investigate potential new employees, their recruitment skills are so poor that the potential job candidates frequently fall far short of expectations and needs.

Recruiting is both a science and an art, and is well understood and practiced with great skill by most industrial and commercial enterprises. Both suggest that the most successful recruitment programs are those which bring employers and potential employees into contact through non-job search related activities. As one employer repeatedly comments, "I never hire strangers". Professional association meetings, lecture visits to professional degree programs, community contacts and a variety of other personal approaches can provide an excellent recruitment base.

Many professional service enterprises are also rather casual when defining the job position which needs filling. More often than not these same enterprises fail to relate job skills to organizational goals and objectives. Good recruitment begins with a concise and clear statement about who is really needed to advance the goals and objectives of the organization, and ends with a systematic search designed to find exactly that specific person.

2. Selection: Most design professionals have found resumés and even portfolios to be a poor method of selecting new employees. Many prefer to rely on personal interviews for evaluating a job applicant. This approach, however, has also proven highly fallible.

One of the most effective means for screening potential employees is the reference check, yet its use seems rare indeed. The head of a major program in landscape architecture, for instance, reports fewer than a dozen calls a year from prospective employers about the program's most recent graduates.

Some additional selection criteria is provided by the results of a study conducted by the Stanford Research Institute in 1966.[6] The study concluded that grade point average was the least reliable selection criteria and lists the following as better indicators for successful recruiting:

- The older applicants are less likely to terminate.
- The fewer number of prior full time jobs the applicants have held, the longer they can be expected to stay with the new organization.
- Effectiveness, measured by salary advancement, increases with age.
- Effectiveness increases with level of education. Applicants with multiple degrees are more effective.
- Applicants manifesting ambition as a primary motivation tend to be more effective.
- Married applicants tend to be more effective than single applicants, who in turn are more effective than divorced or separated applicants.*

Each professional service enterprise must develop its own selection techniques. Keeping careful records

*Changing social values during the years following the SRI study casts some suspicion on the validity of this finding today. (author's note)

of selection procedures compared to applicant success within the organization may help define those techniques which work best. Above all, however, the selection process must be organized and systematic, and conducted with the same level of professionalism used in the enterprises' service offering.

3. Training: Chapter Five of this book discussed the educational continuum and the apprenticeship concept in considerable detail. Maintaining a competent staff and advancing the skills of that staff is a primary function of management. Those professional service enterprises which overlook or pay only minimal attention to this requirement have set a dangerous course. They will experience costly staff turnover and attrition, and they will quickly fall behind their competition.

4. Selective Retention: Selective retention simply suggests management must recognize that some staff turn over and job mobility is a fact of life. Turning this obvious fact to the enterprise's advantage is the goal of selective retention. The practice of this management function has two elements, both predicated on a clear and concise understanding of staff members and nurturing advancement potential among all employees as the first element. Knowing when an employee has reached the limit of his or her potential is the second element. Both require considerable human understanding and the latter requires the ability to make difficult decisions about termination of employees unable to move ahead. The elimination of "dead-wood" is not a pleasant task but is a business necessity.

5. Motivation: Staff motivation is a pervasive aspect of every successful organization. The full concept of motivation goes well beyond the scope of this book, but many of the motivation techniques available have been discussed earlier in these pages. It is most important to understand, however, that motivation of staff must be designed into every decision of the professional service enterprise. When dealing with human knowledge services, personal motivation is the only means of increasing productivity of the enterprise. While new technology and automation may have a dramatic impact on the productivity of product-oriented enterprises of the future, the overall impact on the service professions will be marginal. People are and will continue to be the primary producers in the service enterprise.

Directing

When properly motivated the methods for effectively directing a staff are communications and leadership. Both skills have been discussed in some detail in this book. The skills and techniques of effective communication and sound leadership, however,

must be employed within a framework or structure of policies and procedures which provide guidance and set directional courses consistent with organizational goals. Office procedures, personnel policies, written communication guides, quality control procedures and a variety of operational standards are fundamental aspects of staff directing. Many of these will be discussed in Chapter Twelve. There are no substitutes, however, for sound managerial leadership and a cohesive staff totally committed to the overall goals of an organization.

Effective directing requires sound technical, human, and business skills.

In summary, the nature of the professional service enterprise emphasizes human knowledge not a "hands-on" product. Directing the professional service enterprise is not merely a job of moving people along a specified course, it is a task of managing an organization's principal resource. With the traditionally low capital requirements common to the professional service enterprise, staff direction takes on significant meaning. A poorly directed staff can spell disaster, quickly and decisively, to a professional service enterprise.

Financial Planning

Financial planning is the fifth and final basic business principle to be considered here. Of all the basic principles, budgeting and financial planning seem to be the least understood by landscape architects. Like so many other aspects of professional practice, little is contributed to the development of these skills during the years of formal education. More often than not graduates go into the world of business without even the most rudimentary skills in accounting, budgeting, or financial management. Moreover, these new graduates are likely to find that their first job position provides little access to skill development during the apprentice years.

This dilemma is further confounded by the popular belief among students and some practitioners that financial planning skills are not essential for those landscape architects who wish to teach or to enter public practice. Regrettably, nothing could be further from the truth.

Budgeting and financial planning skills are critical to all forms of landscape architectural practice. They are the principal means for forecasting and measuring achievement of goals. Without them any professional service enterprise commits itself to a no-growth posture, or at the very least, a course without direction.

Making a profit (or avoiding operational loss) should be a primary goal of every professional service enterprise. Private practice firms budget for operating profits. Public agencies and educational programs must be operated within set financial constraints, avoiding financial loss and constantly justifying ongoing and expanding operational funding. Managers of all practice forms utilize financial planning skills on a daily basis.

All professional service enterprises, even the non-profit types, run on money, and a systematized approach to money management is essential to them all. Financial management is accomplished through the utilization of accounting procedures selected to reflect the particular needs of an organization. There are a variety of accounting procedures available, but they all share the common goal of systematically tracking the operational costs and income of the business endeavor. Cost and income information provides the necessary data to measure achievement, and a closer look at their meaning is important.

Costs: Costs are normally divided into three functional categories: direct costs, payroll burden, and overhead or indirect costs.[7]

1. Direct Costs: These costs refer to any expense directly associated with the delivery of the organization's service. They would include salary, project related travel, printing and reproduction expenses, phone calls, and out-of-pocket expenses. Firms dealing mostly with projects will organize these costs and report them on a project by project basis. Educational programs may organize these costs on a course-by-course or research project basis. Public agencies may allocate direct costs to functional divisions or specific service related programs.

2. Payroll Burden: These costs include vacation, holiday, sick leave, group insurance, workmen's compensation, pension plan, social security contribution and other employee benefit expenses. They are mostly related to payroll costs and some organizations may allocate them to the direct costs category. This is an acceptable practice, but it is important that these costs be accounted for separately. Employee benefit packages are important to staff morale and motivation, but they can also get out of hand, growing disproportionately to the value received.

3. Overhead: The final cost category includes all those expenses which cannot be specifically allocated to a project, a direct service, or a functional activity, but which apply to all aspects of business operation. Rent, utilities, interest on borrowed money, bad debt expenses, general office supplies, and promotional costs fall in this category. Some organizations will pro-rate these costs into their project or service program activities. Prorata formulas vary, but they all attempt to provide the organization with a comprehensive means of measuring achievement on a service delivery basis.

Income: Income would appear to be easy to define. In reality, however, it can take a great number of different forms and will vary greatly from one practice form to the next. In public agencies and educational programs, income is that money allocated on an annual basis for the performance of the organization's mission. While the final amount allocated is normally determined by some higher body or governing group, the approval process includes budget requests and justification presentations. Public agencies and educational programs fight for their income in much the same way as private firms. They will also attempt to supplement their annual income allocation through grants, special contributions, consulting activities, and other "outside" legitimate sources.

In the private practice area, income is divided between those monies received for services provided and those received for direct service related reimbursable expenses. This latter income reflects those costs discussed under direct costs.

In all practice forms accounting and budgeting are linked functions. Budgeting is a predictive process and accounting is a record keeping and tracking process. Together they provide the primary means of measuring practice achievement on a periodic basis. The measurement results must be linked to the goals and objectives of the organization mentioned earlier in this chapter.

Financial planning looks to the future and sets a defined and measurable economic path. It equates growth to probably costs and income, defines the probability of financial success or loss, and determines the most appropriate means to capitalize growth costs. Financial planning must be viewed as a critical aspect of professional practice, and acquisition of these specialized skills is equally critical to the success of individual practitioners and their organizations.

The professional service "business" may be unique, but is and always will be a business. The uniqueness of the professional service enterprise must never be allowed to confound the importance of skillful utilization of essential business principles and techniques. The basic principles described in this chapter provide a solid foundation for understanding the realm of business skills employed in the practice of landscape architecture. The following chapters look at a host of other and more specific business skills required. Chapter Eleven looks at the commonly misunderstood issue of marketing management and its importance to all forms of landscape architectural practice.

Chapter Ten Notes

1. Robert E. Sibson, *Managing Professional Service Enterprises*, Pitman Publishing Corporation, N.Y., N.Y., 1971

2. Ibid 1

3. Ibid 1

4. Ibid 1

5. The Design Professionals Insurance Company, *A Collection of Information That Will Be Valuable to Design Professionals In Private Practice Who Are Interested in Reducing Their Professional Liability Exposures*, 1974

6. Stanford Research Institute, "Hiring Criteria", Journal No. 9, March 1966, Palo Alto, Cal.

7. The American Institute of Architects, "The Architects Office", Chp. 6, *Architect's Handbook of Professional Practice*, 1971

Chapter Eleven
Marketing Management

Introduction

Landscape architects, like most design professionals, equate the term "marketing" primarily with promotion or public relations. They believe that to market one's services or skills is merely a selling job. As a result of this attitude, professionals in public and academic practice areas tend to disregard marketing altogether, believing that there is no need to market their particular form of services. They are not, after all, selling anything in the free enterprise marketplace.

These design professional's beliefs about marketing are far from accurate. While promotion and public relations are, indeed, embraced by the marketing concept, marketing management is a great deal more and has important applications to all practice areas. Understanding the marketing concept and applying its precepts is an essential business skill, and serves the professional service enterprise in the same way it serves the product-oriented business enterprises.

Marketing is a pervasive business concept which embraces three essential ingredients: User Orientation, Coordinated Effort, and Profitability. All business forms, product and service alike, must operate within these essential marketing parameters. Business managers must then understand and become skilled in the utilization of the marketing concept on a daily basis. This chapter has been designed to look more closely at the tools and techniques of marketing management and the marketing concept as it applies to the practice of landscape architecture in all of its forms.

The Marketing Concept

Marketing, as a concept, must be a pervasive business practice. In other words, it must permeate an organization's effort and decision making processes at all levels. The marketing concept must be intrinsic in an organization's mission statement, goals and objectives, policies and routine problem solving. Its application to an organization's successful mission accomplishment must be understood by all staff levels, practiced in every department, and monitored throughout the delivery of the organization's service product. To better understand the marketing concept, a closer look at its three essential components is necessary.

User Orientation: "The function of marketing is to study and interpret (user) needs and behavior and to guide all business activity to the end of (user) satisfaction."[1] This statement strongly suggests that all business activity is predicated on the conceptual mission of satisfying user demands, and that business success will be directly tied to how well this is accomplished. This concept carries with it two fundamental precepts. First, a business must determine what the users want or need (demand), and second a business must determine how well its product or service satisfies that demand.

This all seems like simple business common sense. Design professionals, however, are presented with a complex set of problems when attempting to determine user needs and their ability to satisfy these needs. More often than not, those who pay design professionals for their services are not the ultimate user of those services. In many situations services may pass through several parties before reaching the ultimate user. A private practice landscape architect, for example, may design a master plan for a large housing project for a land developer. The developer in turn may sell off parcels to builders, who may construct speculative homes. The ultimate home buyer is three times removed from the original design professional. In this example, the ultimate users are those people who eventually buy a home in the project. The initial service user, however, was the land developer. Because the ultimate user is not directly involved in paying for those initial services, it is difficult for them to project their daily needs and behaviors into the design process other than via their buying habits.

The landscape architect's services may pass through several intermediaries before reaching the ultimate user.

Moreover, because the ultimate user is not directly paying the bill, the landscape architectural firm seldom sees them as a part of the marketing process. It is the project instigator or interim user who captures the marketing attention of the firm, not the ultimate user. This two and three fold insulation between service vendor and the ultimate service user is not confined to the private practice sector. Consider the number of interim users lying between a State Park Department and a park's ultimate users. There is the State Legislature, which provided funds to build the park, the General Services Department which administrates park construction and distributes the funds, and a host of State agencies who must be pleased with the park's design, function, operation, maintenance cost, and development.

Consider also those professionals who teach. Are they responsible to their students or to the industry which they are training those students to serve? Are the teacher's clients the students, the industry, the university who pays their salary, the parents who provided the students, or the general public who will eventually be users of the students efforts?

As one can readily see, user orientation in the professional service enterprise can be a complex issue and can involve a confusing hierarchy of users, many of whom have no fiscal control over the service offering. This unique aspect of the professional service enterprise frequently leads to the mistaken belief that marketing can be directed more specifically toward those at the instigating (paying) end of the hierarchy. On the surface this appears to make sense. A successful professional service enterprise, however, learns very early on that the user orientation precept of the marketing concepts includes all users along the hierarchy, and devotes energies and resources to coordinate the needs of all into the service effort of the firm. This includes determining a complex and diverse set of user needs and expectations and developing systems designed to monitor and report user satisfaction of services delivered. All users of the professional service enterprise, from instigator to final user, must become a part of the service offering. This is often difficult to do, but is always essential to practice success.

Coordinated Effort: The second component of the marketing concept is total coordinated effort of the professional service enterprise to the accomplishment of organizational goals and objectives. The coordinated effort must strive for a synergestic effect. Synergism as defined by Webster is, "cooperative action of discrete agencies such that the total effect is greater than the sum of the effects taken independently".[2] All individuals, project teams, departments, divisions, and other subgroups within an organization must coordinate their activities to produce this synergistic result. The principal elements in successful marketing coordination are research, planning, goal setting, and communication. A breakdown in any one of these areas can have a devastating impact on coordinated effort. The role of the academic, public or private practice manager in this coordinated effort process has already been discussed in Chapter Ten, along with the elements of coordination described above. It is not necessary to cover this same ground again. It is, however, important to underscore the role of coordinated effort as an element of an organization's marketing concept.

Accomplishment of goals and objectives must be a coordinated effort.

Profitability: Coordinated effort implies productivity, which in turn implies profits. Make no mistake about it, all forms of landscape architectureal practice rely on some form of financial reward for survival. While this reward will certainly take a variety of forms, the incentive to secure it is identical throughout the profession. To a landscape architectural education program profit may take the form of achieved prestige which can attract research grants, better qualified teachers, higher salaries, greater status on the campus, or more students.

The same comparison can be made for public practice where profit may be measured in increased recognition and budgets, higher salaries, greater responsibility for more numerous and/or important activities, increased participation in agency objective setting and so forth. In both public and academic practice, however, these rewards are not often perceived as profit and are seldom built into the organization's marketing strategies. Management strategies in all practice forms must include goals of productivity and financial reward. In public and academic practice areas, the alternative means of measuring profit must be determined and strategies devised to ensure productive efforts to attain these goals.

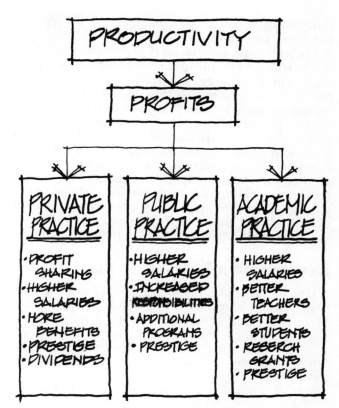

Profits, while measured differently by the various practice forms are the reward for productive effort.

Peter Drucker suggests that productivity in this country, as in all developed countries, is on the decline.[3] We have been lulled into believing that the opposite is true, however, by outdated accounting measures which are incorrectly showing annual gains in Gross National Product. These accounting practices fail to consider the cost of replacing operating and growth capital as a business expense. The U.S. steel and automobile industries failed to understand this problem over 25 years ago and are suffering financial decline prompted by lack of user orientation and their inability to replace operating capital. Throughout this entire 25 year period, however, both industries showed annual profits while productivity was going down. This, says Drucker, can spell disaster over the long haul, and the economic future will be more directly keyed to productivity increases than ever before.

What this means to landscape architects is the compelling need for the profession to see itself as an active and interactive member of the marketing community. All practice forms must adopt a profit motive based on increasing productivity, and understand and prepare to meet the demands for replacement and growth capital.

All landscape architectural practice forms, in order to survive and prosper in the years ahead, must know where they are going and how they are going to get there. To accomplish this they must develop a marketing plan; a plan that is consistent with the overall mission and goals of the organization, and which charts a course that will produce the greatest profit and ensure the continued advancement of the mission. Such a marketing concept, which consists of user orientation, coordinated effort and profitability, must become a comprehensive statement of strategy about the future of the organization and its directions. The elements of a marketing plan and the procedures for developing such a plan follow.

Developing a Marketing Plan

Development of a marketing plan begins with research designed to clearly articulate the needs of the user. This information leads to the formulation of strategies and goals which will become the ingredients of a marketing plan. The marketing plan provides guidelines and procedures which are used to determine strategies about service offerings, market segments, promotional programs, and follow up activities.

A marketing plan has three distinct elements; a situation analysis, a problems and opportunity statement, and a statement of marketing strategy. In many ways the parts of the design process resemble the parts of a marketing plan and should make design professionals comfortable with the development process.

Situation Analysis: This step is designed to determine the business environment in which marketing will take place. It involves an assessment of current conditions as well as trend situations, with emphasis placed on forecasting and determining future events and business conditions. In landscape architectural practice this assessment would include a close up look at the following concerns:

1. Demand: This assessment would include investigation of both the nature and extent of user demand for services and skills. How are services sought out or "purchased"? Who makes the purchase decision? What kinds of information influences these decision makers? How often do they purchase? These are the kinds of questions that must be answered along with the most important question of all: for what level of quality are the purchasers looking? The academic practitioner, for example, must know everything possible about those firms and organizations who are potential employers of the program's graduates. The public practitioner must un-

A marketing plan contains three important elements.

derstand the expectations and idiosyncrasies of the voters and the governing body to which their agency is answerable. The public practitioner must be able to determine demands created by such issues as the environmental movement, the decentralization of government, the tax revolts and other socio-economic trends. These questions deal with the nature of demand, but it is also imperative to know the extent of demand. The academic practitioner must have a good idea about how many jobs may be available for the type of graduate turned out by the program. If the program is designed to provide specialized skills, there should be some assurance that those specialized skills are in demand. The demand segment of the situation analysis must constantly look ahead. What happened last year or the trend over the last ten years may be helpful but is not sufficient for accurate predictions about the future. Developing forecasting skills is essential to business management, and critical to predicting the nature and extent of demand for services.

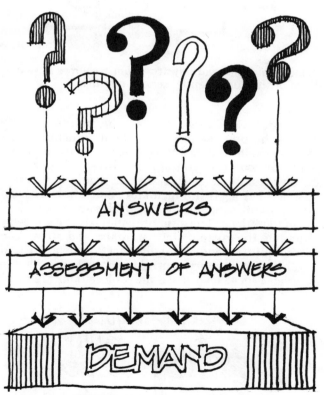

Questions about the nature and extent of service demand require accurate answers.

2. Competition: Knowing exactly what the competition is doing at any given point in time is the second important assessment element of the situation analysis. In some industries this information is so critical that competitors resort to espionage and other criminal activity to secure it. Landscape architecture, fortunately, does not fall into this category. Most landscape architects are very open and very giving. They are usually willing to share information and ideas, and are often unafraid to discuss what they are doing at the moment. Many landscape architects find annual professional society meetings along with other trade and professional meetings to be a fundamental source of information about the competition. It is especially important to know the number of competitors in the marketplace, their share of the market, their skill resources, and their marketing strengths and strategies.

Annual society meetings provide many informal opportunities to learn what the competition is doing.

3. Business Climate: Landscape architecture is practiced in a marketplace which is dramatically and constantly affected by changing social, economic, political, and technological forces. To practice without understanding these influences, or attempting to assess and forecast the impact of these changes is pure folly. Changing demographics, increasing leisure time, government decentralization, energy shortages, and technological innovations, to name only a few of the more obvious forces of change, may vastly alter markets for the profession in the years ahead. All practice forms must recognize the changing business climate and provide data relevant to changing conditions as a part of the overall situation analysis.

Social, economic, political and technological change has a direct impact on business climate and opportunity.

4. Stage of Service Life Cycle: All professional services and skills have a life cycle or a period of time during which they are appropriate in the marketplace. Most services, particularly the specialized ones, have a life span which can be be predicted and must consequently be updated, revised, or even dropped when they have outlived their marketability. The situation analysis, then, requires a comprehensive look at service offerings and their life cycle. A private practice firm with a principal specialty in school site planning should recognize, for instance, that changing demographics and an aging population, coupled with tightening public funds may cause these specialized skills and the corresponding service offering to have completed their life cycle. As a result this firm should begin to look for alternative ways to utilize those skills, or find new skills and services to market.

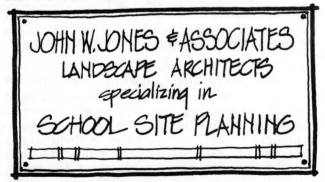

Some service specialities are life-cycle limited by the changing business climate.

5. Resources of the Firm: The situation analysis must also take a careful look at the organization's resources. Two issues must be addressed in this assessment. First, does the firm have the human, financial, and physical plant resources to compete in future markets? Second, does the organization's resources compare favorably with the competition? This assessment must determine what current resources are no longer needed, and what new resources will be needed, and when. Resources should be viewed principally as people and their knowledge, but should also include physical plant, specialized equipment, support facilities, and of course, capital.

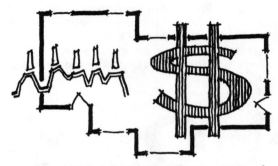

Human, financial and physical plant resources have a direct bearing on potential service offerings.

6. Legal Constraints: Legal constraints directly impact the practice of landscape architecture in all its forms with increasing regularity. Antitrust laws, pollution control, zoning, building codes, subdivision regulations, special district regulations, and a host of other legal and regulatory considerations can play a significant role in the profession's access to the marketplace. The situation analysis must clearly articulate the current state of affairs and attempt to predict future trends. What impact, for instance, will the shift of regulatory control from the Federal to the State and local level have on professional practice?

Landscape architecture is practiced within a maze of legal constraints.

How will this decentralization affect a professional service enterprise with multi-state offices? The laws of this nation and its fifty states are constantly changing. The situation analysis must recognize this and develop a predictive mechanism for assessing the influence these changes will have on the organization's practice opportunities.

Problems and Opportunities: This second part of a marketing plan, like the design process, requires an assessment and evaluation of the collected data and the translation of data into criteria for the guidance of organizational decision making. While the problems and opportunities step does not add new data, it summarizes the information learned from the situation analysis, listing on one hand the problems identified, and on the other hand the opportunities. Special attention is given to those issues which appear to be borderline between a problem and an opportunity.

Frequently, problems are, in reality, opportunities. With careful thought and assessment a problem may be turned around and used as an effective stimulus to the development of new marketing opportunities. Listerine Mouth Wash, for instance, tastes particularly bad. To many people this would present a serious marketing problem. The manufacturers of Listerine, however, turned this problem into an opportunity. "How could anything that tastes good really be effective at killing germs?" Listerine convinced everyone that in order to work mouthwash had to taste bad.[4]

The Marketing Strategy: Translating the collected data and converting the problems and opportunities statement into a marketing strategy is the third and final step in the development of a marketing plan. This step is complex and involves two very important sub-steps. The first is a careful definition of marketing objectives, and the second concerns developing a comprehensive mix of service offerings which serve the marketing objectives. Developing a marketing strategy is a singularly important business process and deserves a more detailed investigation.

A Close Up Look at Marketing Strategy

Defining Objectives: Program decisions about an organization's marketing strategies must be based on the overall goals and objectives of the organization. Marketing objectives must be defined as supportive of overall goals and must be based on a thorough assessment of the data collected during the situation analysis. The marketing objectives will normally include three sets of specific concerns.

1. Target Market: Specific identification of the market potential for an organization's skills and services must form the basis for all ongoing marketing decisions. Determining market potential requires the establishment of a target market, or that group of most likely users of the organization's services. In marketing terms these target markets can be classified as undifferentiated, differentiated, or segmented.

In an undifferentiated target market, an organization will attempt to attract as many users to their service as possible from the entire mass market. This approach involves the offering of a single or basic service and concentrates on a single marketing strategy. Normally competition is not very intense, and the market mass is quite diverse.

In areas where competition is stiffer, organizations will frequently attempt to gain a competitive advantage by employing a marketing strategy of service differentiation. In this strategy emphasis is placed on service differences between the offering firm and the competition. The differences may be either real or imagined. Marketing activities are specifically geared to identify and heighten the marketplace perception of these differences. A design-built firm, for instance, might attempt to emphasize its ability to offer a unique level of quality control in project development. While all other aspects of its service offering are much the same as the non-design build competition, the design-build firm would look to markets where quality control is of special concern (residential, certain types of commercial and service operations like financial institutions, funeral homes, etc.) and develop their promotional activities to mesh their service offering differences with service need differences in the marketplace itself.

Most professional service enterprises recognize, however, that the marketplace is not a homogeneous mass of prospects, but rather a variety of sub-markets, each requiring a specialized marketing approach. Defining each of these sub-markets and developing a strategy to reach it is known as market segmentation, and is the approach most commonly used by landscape architectural professional service organizations. This approach requires the careful identification of the many sub-markets and their purchasing habits, service needs, and special idiocyncrasies in relation to the organization's skills and abilities, or the potential development of same. Marketing strategies can then be developed to concentrate on these segmented market areas.

Frequently, professional service enterprises will identify their service offerings first and then seek out markets which match these offerings. Most product-oriented enterprises do just the opposite. They will determine what the market place is looking for and then attempt to provide that product. In this case the professional service enterprise can learn much from the product-oriented enterprises. All too often professional service organizations fail to recognize that their service offerings need changing and updating, just as toasters, cars and clothes do. The professional service enterprise would be wise to look more often to the marketplace for ideas as to what services they should be offering.

2. Volume: The second concern which must be addressed when developing marketing objectives is the volume of service demand which can be expected. How much demand actually exists within the market defined and what portion of that can the organization expect to capture for itself? Objectives, then, must relate this information to staff size, skills, productivity, and availability, as well as support facilities, physical plant, capital requirements and special needs. All of these factors must then be compared to what is known about the competition, the practice environment, and the proposed marketing activity. Does, for instance, the predictable volume of service demand which can be captured by the organization warrant the hiring of new personnel, expansion of operational facilities, and the development of a promotional program? Can the volume even be predicted at all? These are critical questions and have a significant bearing on the development of a marketing strategy.

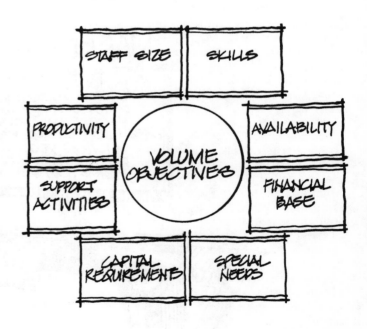

3. Profit Analysis: Private practice landscape architects have no difficulty recognizing the importance of profit objectives when formulating organizational goals. Academic and public practice, however, are often viewed as not-for-profit modes of practice, and those young professionals aspiring to these practice areas will frequently underrate the need for economic and business skills as a result. This misconception about academic and public practice fosters a kind of naivety which must be corrected. All practice forms function under "profit" motivation. While the academic or public practice profit may not be measured in dividends paid to stock holders, it can surely be measured by increased annual budgets, higher salaries, greater prestige, and more agency "clout."

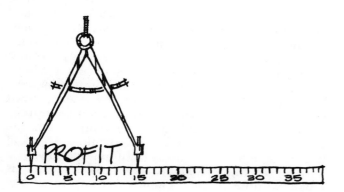

However it may be measured, profit is the measurement of the achievements of the efforts of a professional service enterprise, and a marketing strategy must carefully assess potential expectation. Does the target market and the expected volume yield a profitable excess of income over expenses? What must the volume be in order for the service effort to be profitable? How strong must the target market be in order to assure a profitable volume? These are the types of questions which must be answered, and they can be translated into the vernacular of each practice area.

Service Mix/Program Decisions: When the marketing objectives have been clearly defined, the next step in developing a marketing strategy is the development of programs and services aimed at the accomplishment of the objectives. This process also involves three separate activities:

1. Service Decisions: With the market objectives defined, a careful assessment of the organization's human and professional skills and current service mix is necessary. This begins with an evaluation of current service offerings in relation to market demand. Services which have no relationship to demand may need to be dropped, while others may need to be developed. Still others may only require modification to more closely conform to demand. The objective here is to match service offerings as closely as possible with market demand. It is far eas-

ier to alter service offerings than to change the nature of service demands. Service decisions at this level, however, can be only as good as the information about market demand is accurate. While the professional service enterprise has great choice and change freedom, it can not afford casual investigation of market demand.

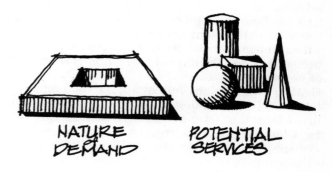

2. Distribution Decisions: Service offerings, like products, must be available where they are needed. Like products stored in a warehouse, services listed in a brochure are of little real value, and may, in fact, be a liability until purchased. For the professional service enterprise, most distribution decisions are locational in nature. Can, for instance, a multi-state regional market be served from a single location or will branch offices be required? Is one city better than another city for serving a regional or even a smaller market area? Is a downtown location preferable over a suburban location? There are literally dozens of variations involved with distribution decision making, but more often than not the distribution strategy is decided on the basis of chance and the habits established by tradition. Organizations often put more emphasis on locational image than on access to market demand, and make very inappropriate decisions about distribution strategy as a result. This is an important marketing decision area and must receive the same studied assessment and evaluation that goes into any of the other steps.

3. Promotion Decisions: The final set of decisions involves promotion of the service offering. What is the most effective way of letting the largest number of potential service users know about the availability of the service offering? Of equal importance, what is the most effective way to stimulate these potential users to actually purchase the service offering? Most landscape architects agree that satisfied clients and personal contacts provide the most effective promotional tools. There is certainly no substitute for the word-of-mouth promotion gained from a happy client, or the value of personal selling. There are, however, a number of additional promotional techniques and the development of a marketing strategy should include consideration of all that are applicable.

In the mid 1970s most of the design professions abolished prohibitions against advertising and many professional design service enterprises use the media in highly effective ways. Even if paid advertising is not employed, every organization has a variety of free media promotional opportunities. Through "press releases" an organization can keep the public informed about their professional awards, special accomplishments, completed projects, community involvement and other activities, along with personnel promotions, the addition of new employees and other newsworthy events.

Many organizations employ special field representatives, called "bird-dogs", whose sole job is to move throughout the target market area making user contacts and promoting the organization on a daily basis. The subject of "bird-dogging" and an outline of other valuable promotional tools is discussed in more detail in Chapter Twelve. In making promotion decisions all of the techniques and tools should be considered. The final decision may employ several of the techniques in a comprehensive promotional effort.

When service offering mix, distribution and promotional decisions are reached and meshed into a comprehensive organization effort, a marketing strategy has been developed. Like all business goals and objectives, the marketing strategy must be attainable, and should be flexible enough to allow for periodic and systematic reevaluation and updating. All of the

marketing strategy decisions, in initial strategy development and updating, must be based on accurate and current information. The importance of this data gathering process has been stressed throughout the discussion, and to a large extent must rely on market research methodology. Few design professionals understand research methodology, let alone that which deals with marketing issues. For this reason it would be appropriate to look briefly at market research as a closing element of this chapter.

Market Research

Information is power, but the information must be accurate and current or power turns to weakness and inevitably leads to poor decision making. The marketing concept is dependent on the ability to translate information into decisions concerning programs, operations, and strategies designed to benefit a business enterprise. To be effective the information must be qualitative, objective, accurate, and timely. It must also be provable via some form of empirical testing. Market research techniques have evolved over the years to provide this kind of information. A look at the more important of these techniques follows.

Types of Market Research: Market research is much like other forms of empirical research with one significant exception. Frequently market decision making cannot afford the luxury of great blocks of time devoted to in-depth scholarly and scientific research. To overcome this problem, and at the same

time provide reliable market information, most organizations will conduct market research on an ongoing basis in order to expand lead time and increase the reliability of research results. Moreover, the various types of market research are carefully designed to identify their level of reliability. When research is exploratory in nature and the results less easily tested it is clearly labeled that way. Marketing research generally falls into three categories; exploratory, specific, and routine feedback.

1. Exploratory Research: This kind of market research can best be described as probes into the market in search of data and information which could provide insight to new market opportunities. The research itself might include the use of questionnaires or interviews which solicit user attitudes of a very general nature in hopes of turning up a specific market surprise or hitherto undiscovered piece of useful market data. A landscape architectural firm, for instance, might send a survey to all its past clients exploring their feelings about other services the firm might offer. The results could be useful in identifying the organization's weaknesses and might even produce a very specific and helpful clue to new market opportunity.

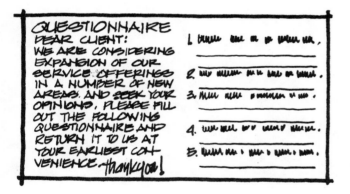

2. Specific Research: Specific research is utilized to provide data about a specific concern. If exploratory research indicated some potential for a new service offering, specific research could then be designed to investigate the specific issues of that opportunity. The research design would be tailored to the specific informational needs. It could also include the use of attitude surveys, interviews and questionnaires, and might employ some form of test marketing procedure.

3. Routine Feedback: This type of research suggests an ongoing review and assessment of business operational feedback information. It requires both quantitative and qualitative operational record keeping and tracking procedures. When properly kept, stored and systematically analyzed, an organization's ongoing business records can provide a wealth of marketing information. Business journals, professional society publications, and a variety of marketing research organizations also provide a regular assessment of business and industry trends and feedback data. Again, the feedback data may point to a potential new market, and allow for the development of specific research into the potential of that new market.

The primary purpose of market research is to aid in demand forecasting. What will the demand for service by, what will be the extent of that demand, how can it best be accessed, and what new skills will be required to supply the services, are basic questions to be answered. Intuitive answers will not suffice. Marketing strategy decisions must be based on objective data not subjective guesswork, and the role of market research is critical to this process.

Marketing is an all-pervasive concept which must guide and direct the mission of all professional service organizations. Its pervasiveness is as important to landscape architecture as it is to any product-oriented business. Moreover, marketing plays an equally important role in all of landscape architecture's many practice forms. It must not be perceived only as an issue to the private practice firm. All of the practice forms must adopt a market orientation to the performance of their service mission. They must develop the specialized marketing management skills necessary to formulate and follow a marketing strategy and maintain the highest possible level of marketing orientation.

Without a high level of marketing orientation all of the business principles and management techniques which are discussed in the following chapters will not be sufficient to insure an organization's success.

Chapter Eleven Notes:

1. Rewoldt, Scott, Warslaw, *Introduction to Marketing Management*, Richard D. Irwin, Inc. N.Y., N.Y. 1977
2. Editors, *Webster's Eighth New Collegiate Dictionary*, G & C Merriam Co., Springfield, Mass. 1974
3. Peter F. Drucker, *Managing in Turbulent Times*, Harper & Row, N.Y., N.Y., 1980
4. Ibid 1

Chapter Twelve
Business Administration and Office Procedures

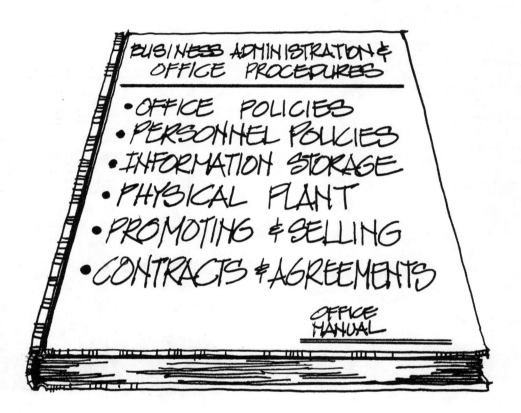

Introduction

A vital component of human rationality which distinguishes humankind from the beast, is the faculty for making order out of chaos. Human beings must organize innumerable pieces of knowledge into usable wholes in order to function effectively in their environment. Organizing involves arranging, classifying, and systematizing, as well as thinking and planning.

Irving Burstinger[1]

With the basic business principles and the marketing concept firmly in hand, it is time to turn to the organizing, classifying, and systematizing aspects of professional practice. Remember that effective use of human resources and individualized knowledge is the fundamental management goal in a professional

service enterprise. This chapter takes a closeup look at those administrative and office procedures which form the core of business management.

While there are special differences between product-oriented and service-oriented enterprises, sound administrative procedures are nearly universal and there are very few dissimilarities in application between the two types of enterprises. The differences which do exist stem mainly from disparities in scale of operation and methods of selling.

It can also be noted that, with the exception of promotion and selling, the administrative and office procedures discussed in this chapter are equally applicable to all forms of landscape architectural practice. What will vary, obviously, is the level of sophistication required by organizations of varying size, service offering, location, and practice form. These differences will alter the complexity of an organization's operation and correspondingly alter the level of sophistication needed to manage business operations.

Office Procedures and Policies

Many office procedures and policies need to be formally defined.

Staff efficiency can be greatly increased when certain standard procedures are developed to act as guidelines for routine business activities. Most organizations will standardize procedures and policies in the following areas: clerical and central storage systems, time utilization, security and housekeeping, and inter-office communications. The precise policy or policies adopted in each of these four areas will vary according to the special needs of each organization, with the more complex requiring more policy direction and a greater level of sophistication. A closer look at the kinds of procedures and policies which might be considered in each area follows:

1. Clerical and Central Systems: Procedures and policies in this area would deal with routine administrative functions such as:

- Preparation, compilation, and maintenance of employee time records.
- Use, disbursement and record maintenance of petty cash expenditures including non project specific travel and expense reimbursement.

- Routing and handling of incoming and outgoing mail.
- Assignment of secretarial time to staff members.
- Organizational system, daily handling and maintenance procedures for central filing of business and project specific files and their retrieval.
- The use, maintenance, and record keeping of office equipment and hardware.
- Telephone answering and message taking procedures.

Central filing systems should be kept and arranged in an easily understandable order.

2. Time Utilization: In this administrative area, procedures and policies are designed to increase productivity through the employment of effective time management systems which might include:

- Office hours, including policies on flex-time, core hours, and overtime activities.
- Establishment of a specified "quiet time", usually a period during the work day when telephone usage, visitor activity and employee visiting is held to a minimum.
- Procedures on schedules and deadlines.
- Inter-office socializing and break time.

3. Security and Housekeeping: The delicate nature of the "work product" of the landscape architectural office places a special importance on security and housekeeping procedures and policies. The neatness and appearance of the office also tells a great deal about the professional attitude and the work habits of the organization. For these reasons most organizations will adopt very specific procedures and policies which would deal with the following activities:

- Processing of visitors by receptionist, controlling visitor access to production areas and to staff.
- Storage and security arrangements for original drawings and other documents.
- Distribution and use of office keys and locks.
- Appearance, personalization and maintenance of work stations.
- After hours use of the office and personal use of office space and equipment.
- Use of library and book lending policy.
- Daily clean-up and custodial duties.
- Proprietary and confidential nature of project information.

4. Inter-Office Communication: This final office procedure and policy area is designed to serve the proceeding three areas as well as the overall managerial function of the organization. Communications

are linked to time saving and record establishing procedures which commonly use standardized forms and/or set policies which might include;

- Inter-office memorandums.
- Information transmittal forms.
- Telephone message forms.
- Information routing procedures.
- Regular staff meetings.
- Chain of command re: complaint and grievance problems.

In smaller organizations, office procedures and policies may be unwritten and constantly evolving to meet changing conditions. Adherence to them is by mutual consent and is reactive as daily situations and events dictate. In larger organizations, however, office procedures and policies are more likely to be formalized and maintained in a written document called an office manual.

Whatever form or level of sophistication they may take, office procedures and policies provide a much needed structure and systematic organization to business operations. When properly conceived and consistently applied, office procedures and policies can reduce the burden of routine but necessary activities and free human resources for more creative effort.

Personnel Policies

All employees have the right to know what is expected of them and what they may expect in return for their loyal and productive effort.

Appropriate, fair, and clearly stated policies dealing with the rights, privileges, and responsibilities of employees can be the cornerstone for maintenance of a productive and happy staff. Every staff person should be apprised of the "rules of the game". Every employee needs to know what is expected of them and what they may expect in return for their productive and dedicated effort. An organization's statement of personnel policies is designed to provide answers to these types of questions. The policy statement is usually divided into four sections; A Mission Statement, Conditions of Employment, Compensation and Benefits, and Professional Development.[3]

- **Initial Employment**
  - Hiring policy
  - Part Time/Full Time employment
  - Equal Opportunity Policy
  - Introductory/Apprenticeship Period
- **Advancement Opportunities**
  - Promotion Policy
  - Performance Evaluation Policy
  - Selective Retention Policy
- **Termination Conditions**
  - Retirement Policy
  - Grounds for Dismissal
  - Resignation and Reinstatement Policy

"REASON FOR BEING"

1. Mission Statement: An organization's mission statement has been discussed before in this book. It is an important aspect of business and plays a special role in the area of personnel policies. The firm's philosophy and "reason for being" must be clearly understood by all employees. It is imperative that employees identify with the goals and objectives of the organization, and it is one of the responsibilities of the mission statement to provide this identity. The mission statement should include at least the following information:
- Philosophy of the organization.
- Organizational goals and objectives along with short and long range strategies for their attainment and the methods used to measure achievement.
- Exact nature of the organization's service offering or work product.
- Organizational structure, including an organizational chart, names and addresses for officers and key personnel, and job descriptions for all employees.

While the mission statement is not itself a policy, it does provide the framework for all personnel policy positions. It provides the rationale for employee conformance with personnel policies and if not properly conceived or unclearly stated, great damage can be caused to the morale and effectiveness of an organization's staff.

2. Conditions of Employment: Four areas of employment conditions are addressed in this section of an organization's policy. They include:

- **Performance and Appearance Standards**
  - Personal Appearance and Dress Code
  - Language and Office Decorum Policy
  - Moonlighting (work out-of-office) Policy
  - Community Involvement Policy
  - Confidential Information Policy

3. Compensation and Benefits: Policies concerning basic salaries, fringe benefits, and compensation related payments are obviously of great concern to employees. As such, they must be carefully devised and clearly stated. Among the wide range of policies which might be considered in this category, the following would be the most important:

- **Basic Compensation:**
  - Pay Period
  - Overtime Pay Policy
  - Distinction Between Salaried and Hourly Employees
  - Statutory Withholdings
- **Fringe Benefits**
  - Time Off Policy to include Vacations, Holidays
  - Sick Leave, Maternity Leave, Emergencies, etc.
  - Payment in Lieu of Vacation
  - Group Insurance Benefits and Qualifications
  - Pension and Profit Sharing Plans
  - Incentive and Bonus Conditions
  - Expense Reimbursement Policy
  - Personal Use of Company's Purchasing Power
  - Stock Options

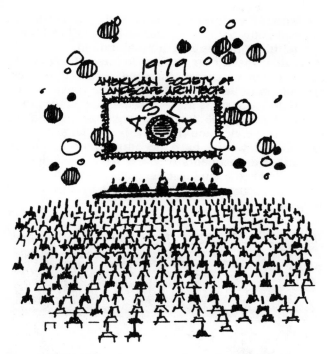

Professional development for all employees must be a conscious policy of every service enterprise.

4. Professional Development: The ongoing professional development and education of a professional service enterprise's staff is of critical importance to organizational success. Some firms and organizations view professional development activities as a fring benefit given as a reward for loyal service. Others don't even consider professional development in their annual operating budgets. Both situations are dangerous to the professional service enterprise where human skills are the principal resource. A wise and successful organization recognizes the great importance of ongoing professional development for its staff and designs its organizational policies accordingly. A good policy package in this category might include:

- **Professional Organization Membership**
  - Annual dues payment policy
  - Time off for meetings, committee work and other forms of professional involvement
  - Meeting registration fees, travel and per-diem reimbursement policy in connection with meeting participation, and other forms of professional involvement
- **Personal Development**
  - Continuing Education Policy
  - Lecturing and Teaching Assignment policy
  - Publication policy
- **Community Involvement**
  - Civic and Service Organization Memberships and involvement policy

- Governmental and Public Interest Activities policy
- Political Campaigning and Endorsements policy

Like office procedures and policies, personnel policies may vary greatly from one organization to the next. In whatever form they may take, however, they play a major role in maintenance of a productive staff, and are also directly linked to staff recruitment and retention. An in-depth discussion of the specific detail of the policy areas outlined goes beyond the scope of this book. For more detailed information the document, *Guidelines For Personnel Management,* American Society of Landscape Architects, 1977, is highly recommended.

It is also important to note that personnel policies, like office procedures and policies, must be subject to evolutionary change. Personnel policies must track current business procedures and industry standards, as well as changing social codes and mores. Moreover, to be really effective, personnel policies must be subject to periodic employee input and modification. When employees feel that the organization's personnel policies are fair and in their best interest, these policies will be more likely followed.

Information Storage and Retrival

The need for a properly designed and efficiently operated information storage and retrieval system is directly linked to staff productivity in a professional service enterprise. The storage and retrieval of general business records, project records, product information and state-of-the-art resource data is a fundamental business concern. When one considers the almost limitless amount of information which can accumulate in the process of providing a professional service, it is easy to see how human time resources could be dramatically wasted by poor information storage and retrieval systems. Time is money, and the need for systematic information storage and retrieval is clear indeed.

While surely simplier than the problems faced by complex product-oriented enterprises with their inventory, distribution, and warehousing concerns, the operations of a professional service enterprise can be equally hampered when an information and retrival system breaks down. A misplaced project file or a lost drawing can cause costly delays. Page by page searches through stacks of magazines for that remembered article dealing with the exact problem at hand can be time consuming, frustrating and expensive, and may not even turn up the information needed.

In a recent survey of landscape architectural private practice firms one practitioner reported a complete set of original working drawings missing for more than a year. The documents finally turned up, misfiled in the wrong storage tube. In the interim period, however, the firm went through the costly process of creating new originals photographically from a set of constructions prints retained by the general contractor.

The list of horror stories generated by breakdowns in information storage and retrieval systems is long and frightening, but provides a very dramatic lesson. To avoid adding to the list a few simple suggestions are offered.

Record Keeping: The official records of a professional service enterprise are not only important for historic purposes, they are in fact, the "product" of the organization's service effort. If lost or destroyed, the service effort may be lost forever.

Record keeping must be systematic and contain a variety of backup procedures. In professional service enterprise operations, record keeping can be divided into general business activities and project or service related activities.

The computer can offer a high speed and very efficient means of record storage and retrival.

General Business Records: This category includes all of those records which relate to the overall administration and management of the organization. It would include financial records, personnel records, general correspondence, promotional data, and similar information. These are normally maintained by a single administrative person or division, or may be divided among functional divisions in larger organizations. The financial records in larger organizations, for instance, would be kept and maintained by the accounting department, the personnel records by the personnel department, and so on.

The keys to successful storage and retrieval of general business records are simple: Know what records are being kept, know where they are being kept, and know how they are ordered or arranged. In addition to these three simple rules, good record keeping will also include backup systems. Many organizations, for example, will keep a secretaries' log or typing log for backup purposes. As each piece of information is

produced an additional copy is made and is filed in a chronologically ordered master file, while all other normal filing procedures are maintained.

Service Specific or Project Related Records: As Chapter Ten discussed in some detail, a service-oriented enterprise is not likely to be organized by functional divisions in the same way a product-oriented enterprise tends to organize around its project or service activities. Only the largest of organizations would have accounting departments, personnel departments or other functional departments. Even the smallest agency or firm, however, needs to keep and maintain service specific record keeping systems.

Storage of plans and other drawings is a very real problem for most offices.

This requirement is further enforced by the peculiar nature inherent to the design professions which allows for the continued ownership and maintenance of all original drawings, and other service documents. The volume and physical dimension of this material alone presents complex storage and retrieval problems not faced by many other businesses. Not only is storage and retrieval of these records a problem, developing records backup systems is even more complex. Some organizations will photograph all original material and maintain a negative file as backup. Others may produce an extra set of prints of all material and store these in a separate location.

Storage of drawings can be handled in a variety of different ways. Most organizations prefer to store drawings in flat files, but space limitations frequently limit this storage to current work only. Inactive project drawings may be stored in vaults, tubes, packing cases, plan racks, and many other ways. Each organization will devise its own storage and retrieval system based on volume, demand, space limitations, drawing sizes and other variables. Whatever the methods used, however, some simple rules apply in all situations:

- Tracings or original drawings should be refiled in their proper location as soon as they are no longer needed. Many organizations insist on refiling all drawings at the end of each work day.
- A single person should be responsible for the storage and retrieval of all drawings not associated with current project activity.
- Neatness and orderliness in the work area is an absolute must, and will avoid unnecessary loss or damage to original documents. Food and beverages should be confined to the employee lounge and not allowed in the work area.
- If cleaning and custodial services are performed by an outside firm, the crews must be carefully instructed about what to throw away and what not to throw away.

If not properly informed, custodial people will have no idea what to throw away and what to keep.

Project or service specific job files also require special consideration. The information they contain is critical to the project as well as the organization's continuity. Normally the "job" file is maintained by the project team leader or manager. It is wise, however, to store the job file in a central location, rather than in the team leader or manager's office. The contents of the file must be available to all members of the team and to the organization's management people. It is also wise not to take the job file into the field. Field conditions, including foul weather, construction activities, rugged terrain and other unusual conditions can play havoc with the contents of a job file. Most organizations will maintain a separate job file for field use. This file contains only duplicated material with no original documents.

In addition to the secretaries' log or typing log a project job file may require other backup systems. Duplicate copies of project contracts are often kept in a contract log, and certain key pieces of client communication might also be kept in duplicate backup systems.

Larger and more complex projects or service activities will require a comprehensive set of job files. This set of files would begin with an index or administrative file containing the project or service contract, a list of all the participants involved with the activity (and their phone numbers and responsibilities), general project information, and an index to all other job files. Additional files will be organized to fit the particular needs of the project, but should always have a table of contents inside the front cover. Chapter Fourteen discusses project management in some detail and provides an organizational approach for job filing systems.

A final word on record keeping. Neatness definitely counts. Sloppy files can lead to trouble and normally reflects a casual attitude on the part of the person maintaining the files. Together this can lead to many serious problems.

Libraries: Collection and maintenance of product and state-of-the-art information is of special importance to the professional service enterprise. Maintaining a current and complete collection of professional information is most important and is matched in importance by the need to be able to readily access the information on hand. Knowing that somewhere in the library is an article that would help solve a pressing current problem is of little value if the article can't be found.

Material maintained in the library should, at the very least, be cataloged and tracked by a subject index system. As new publications are received, the general subject matter can be noted and recorded on

index cards along with the exact name, date and other reference pertinent to the publication. A cross reference system could be added without great difficulty and would provide simple, but useful, retrieval potential. More complicated systems are obviously available, but the utilizaiton of some approach is most important.

The library is the knowledge resource base for a professional service enterprise, and its continued growth and maintenance should be carefully planned. Acquisition of new library materials should be a line item in an organization's operational budget. Selection of material should be aimed at expanding the organization's knowledge base and increasing opportunities for professional development of the staff.

A routing system should be utilized to insure that all employees are aware of new material and new acquisitions upon arrival and that appropriate employees have immediate access to specialized information of a functional value to their operational mission.

Lending policies and a checkout system must be developed to insure the library's efficiency. A separate library location is usually preferred over the scattering of materials throughout the office. A conference room or employee lounge might double as library space but, it would be desirable to maintain the indexing and card cataloging system in a more controlled area where unintentional disruption would not be caused to the system. An organization's library is its learning resource center, and it should be treated with great respect. There are many who believe that an organization's true competence is reflected in the quantity and quality of its library.

The Computer: Increased capability and greatly reduced cost has made the computer and the vast array of other micro-electronic hardware most useful tools for the professional service enterprise. Many excellent computer systems can be purchased for about the price of a good copying machine and the equipment cost goes down each year. A basic hardware package could handle an organization's accounting and billing activities, most record keeping and information retrieval systems, intra and extra-office communications, engineering functions, and provide visualization aids. The computer also can provide a backup system to nearly all business functions.

The computer holds great potential for the professional service enterprise. The computer can take over a large number of routine business functions and perform them at incredible speed. The result is more time available for human resource activity in more creative areas. To an industry whose stock-in-trade is human resources, this freed up time must be considered as a potential new source of income. While many design professionals are slow to accept the computer, it may, in fact, be the single most important new tool to the profession since the blue-print machine.

Physical Plant

Physical plant requirements for professional service enterprises will vary greatly. It is appropriate to suggest, however, that an attractive and comfortable working environment is not only important to staff productivity, but is also a reflection on the organization's philosophy and professional competence.

In the most general of terms, the physical plant requirements of the landscape architectural organization can be divided into four functional areas with the following use concerns:
- **Administration**
  — Entry, reception, and waiting area
  — Principal's and key managerial offices
  — Conference room
  — Library
  — Secretarial, bookkeeping, and other administrative areas
  — Active filing and storage areas
- **Production**
  — Work space for staff and other support personnel
  — Storage for current project documents and drawings
  — Space for printing, reproduction, report binding and similar activities
  — Area for special equipment such as computers, type setters, etc.
  — Shop area for model making or similar activities
  — Dark room
  — Layout and project review areas
- **Storage**
  — Vault space
  — Dead storage for drawings and project files
  — Storage for general materials and supplies
- **Service**
  — Staff lounge
  — Rest rooms
  — Janitorial space
  — Parking

Every organization will have specialized needs and space requirements in addition to those described. The American Institute of Architects suggests, however, that these functional requirements translate into an average area requirement of 140 gross square feet per full time employee for most design firms.[5] A recent survey of landscape architectural offices, both public and private, suggests that a figure closer to 200 gross square feet per full time employee is more reasonable.[6]

Promotion and Selling

Promoting and selling the knowledge of the professional service enterprise is an important management function and properly belongs in this chapter on business administration and procedures. The task is an ongoing function and as such demands carefully defined procedures and policies.

The notion of promotion and selling may seem a remote concern for those professional landscape architects who aspire to academic or public practice. As Chapter Eleven points out, and all those who practice in the public or academic area will attest to, marketing and its task of promotion and sales are issues which cut across the profession. They are not, as some might assume, issues only of concern to the private practice landscape architect. To be sure, the different practice forms are promoting and selling different services to different markets, but the bottom line remains the same for all; fiscal survival.

The director of an academic program, for instance, has the responsibility to promote and sell the program's value to the College's Dean and other campus leaders in order to secure budget increases, promotion and tenure for staff, and required physical space and equipment. At the same time, the program director must sell the program's graduates to the profession at large, helping them secure the best possible positions. Concurrently the program director must promote and sell the program's value to potential students, hoping to attract the best possible, and to insure the qualitative and quantatative growth of the program. To the academic practitioner these promotion and selling functions are just as critical as finding new paying clients is to the private practice landscape architect.

The public practitioner has equally compelling promotion and selling concerns. Agency budget and the attendent benefits, organizational power, more meaningful program activities, and even job security are all tied to promotion and selling skills and activities.

Promotional Tools: A wide variety of specialized and general tools are available to assist the professional practitioner with promotion activities. Business promotion has two basic goals: name recognition and dissemination of pertinent information concerning the organization's service offering. The best promotional tools are designed to directly serve one or both of these goals.

While direct media advertising is no longer considered unethical by most professional landscape architects, it remains their least effective promotional tool. Nearly all landscape architects would agree that effective selling requires direct personal contact and that the cost-benefit ratio for media advertising is low indeed. For this reason the promotional tools selected for review were chosen for their usefulness as support and backup to direct personal selling.

1. Brochures: Creative and professional quality handout material which documents an organization's skills, competence and service offering can be very useful. When well developed, they can be used for both indirect (mailouts) and direct (in person) selling and promotion. A word of caution, however. An organizational brochure is a very direct statement about competence and skills, and a poorly designed or "cheaply" produced brochure can do more harm than good. For more specific information on how to prepare a quality brochure, The American Society of Landscape Architect's publication, *Developing Your Brochure, A Comprehensive Guide for the Landscape Architect,* is highly recommended.

2. News or Press Release: Information about the activities, successes, and accomplishments of an organization and its individual members is often considered "newsworthy" by the press. News or press releases prepared by the organization or its agent should be sent to all representative media within the organization's market area. The chances are excellent that the information will be printed, and may even stimulate a special feature story.

3. Clipping Services: Many organizations will retain clipping service companies and/or specialized reporting services to watch for and report on business activities of particular interest within the organization's market area. This information can provide useful leads to future projects and to potential clients who can be promoted by direct contact. Really efficient organizations will also use clipping services to report on the business and social activities of all past and current clients within their market area. When a client's son or daughter gets married they will know about it and send an appropriate message. When a

The opportunities for promotion through community involvement and public speaking efforts are limitless.

client's spouse is ill, flowers can be sent. When done with tact and sensitivity, this promotional technique can be very effective.

4. Public Speaking: Garden clubs, civic and fraternal groups; business associations, and many other community minded and public spirited groups are constantly seeking program speakers. Addressing these groups provides an excellent opportunity to indirectly and directly promote one's professional organization. This is, in fact, one of the best promotional tools available, especially to the young and aspiring professional who has not yet become so much in demand that a free lunch is no longer considered sufficient pay for a little information.

5. Satisfied Customers: The best promotional tool is a stable of satisfied and happy clients. The value of their word-of-mouth promotion on your behalf cannot be replicated by any other means. Not only will they come back to avail themselves of the organization's services again, they will encourage their friends and business associates to do the same.

Bird-Dogging: The subject of bird-dogging was raised in Chapter Ten and deserves a closer look under the general topic of promotion and selling. Just as the Irish Setter (among other breeds) seeks out and points a bird, organizational bird-dogs seek out and point a potential customer. This concept is easy enough to visualize in the private practice arena, but conceptual difficulties make it no less important to the other practice forms. In academic practice, for instance, a single faculty person may have the bird-dog responsibility for career guidance activities at the high school level, looking for the sharpest and most promising potential program candidates to receive special promotional and selling attention.

In the public practice agency, the bird-dog might be a single staff person responsible to attend all of the community organization meetings in search of future community leaders who should be sold now on the agency's long term worth to the community. In nearly all cases the organization's bird-dog is only a

The opportunities for promotion through community involvement and public speaking efforts are limitless.

searcher and pointer. Follow-up and closing the deal is often done by someone else. The bird-dog's principal responsibility is to make initial contact, stimulate interest, and report findings back to the organization, where appropriate action is initiated as a result of standing policy, or where strategies for closing the deal can be developed and carried out by the most skilled people. Every organization utilizes this bird-dogging technique but not all of them know they do, or admit to it. Bird-dogging is a perfectly legitimate promotion and selling technique, and when it is employed in a comprehensive and coordinated manner, it can be very successful.

Closing the Deal: The final act of promotion and selling is closing the deal and it will be uniquely different in each of the practice areas. For the private practice enterprise a consumated deal is a signed contract to perform a specified service. To a professional education program it may be a significant increase in the number of the National Merit Scholars enrolling in the program each year. To the public practitioner it may be widespread public support for an agency program.

As a result of this great diversity, the techniques used to close the deal will also vary greatly. The private practitioner will frequently rely on the preparation and presentation of service and fee proposals and in-person presentation of credentials and professional service competency. ASLA's publication; *Presentations and Proposals for Private Practice Landscape Architectural Firms,* is recommended for those with a specific interest in this area.

The academic practitioner may use career guidance days and specialized contact with high school guidance counselors or meetings with parents as a means of closing their selling deals. The public practitioner may rely on citizen participation and neighborhood association or store front activities as a method of closing a deal. While the techniques in this area are quite varied, the bottom line is identical; professional survival. If these deals and dozens of

others are not consumated with great regularity, no professional service enterprise can long survive.

Contracts and Agreements

The subject of contracts and agreements is of special interest to the private and public practitioner, and has an obvious practical interest to the academic practitioner. Contracts and agreements are of great importance to the profession and deserve discussion in this chapter.

Those who rely on hand-shake deals may someday regret such a casual approach to business.

General Considerations: It has been said that any contract is only as good as the parties who sign it. Those who believe this myth, and avoid, as a result, formalized contracts and agreements are doing their part to keep the legal profession rich. There is no substitute for a properly conceived and well written contract. Letter forms of agreement and the so-called "short-form" agreements may be appropriate on very small service efforts but should normally be avoided. Many organizations will avoid letter and short-form agreements for any kind of work effort. A contract's ultimate goal is the avoidance of misunderstanding between the contracting parties through a clear statement of the mutual relationships and obligations of both parties and otherwise meets the following criteria:[7]

- There must be a real agreement or a "meeting of the minds".
- The services offered must be lawful.
- There must be a valid consideration. (something of value must be given in exchange for that which is received)
- The parties must be legally competent to enter into a contract.
- The contract must comply with the provisions of the law with regard to form.

A few other simple guidelines should also be considered:

- A contract should be two directional and be obviously fair to both parties.
- A contract should use precise language. Jargon, and ambiguous terms should always be avoided.
- A contract should be as specific as possible and clearly identify exactly what is being purchased and for how much.
- When in doubt seek qualified legal help. The advice of an attorney can save endless grief and many dollars.

Types of Contracts: The design professions generally recognize three types of contracts, each distinguished by the method of determining the consideration or payment procedure. These three basic contract types are described below:

1. Percentage of Cost Agreement: In this type of contract, professional compensation is based on an agreed upon percentage of construction cost. The percentage of cost approach has the advantage of allowing compensation for services rendered to track cost inflation. Many service purchasers, however, will insist that the compensation percentage be tied to construction estimates rather than actual construction costs. This allows compensation to keep pace with inflation through the preliminary phases of design services but not through the construction phases.

2. Multiple of Direct Personnel Expense Agreement: Compensation under this form of agreement is determined by multiplying direct personnel expenses (ie; salary and payroll burden) by an agreed upon factor or multiplier, usually a figure between 2.5 and 3.5.[8] Direct personnel expenses are usually agreed upon in advance and will normally allow for inflation related pay raises when the contract covers long periods of time. This contract approach does require careful and accurate accounting and auditing procedures and includes client access to the service organization's time and financial records. Hourly compensation contracts are a simplification of this contract form and state an agreed upon hourly rate which includes direct costs and profit without the multiplier factor.

3. Flat Fee Agreement: The flat fee approach to determining compensation appears to be the most simple form of agreement, but in fact, requires complex record keeping of historical data in order to avoid costly guess work mistakes when determining compensation. Many clients seem to prefer this contract approach. Clients who must budget project costs in advance, and hold to these estimates, find that flat fee contracts are essential to the process. The conceptual nature of many types of landscape architectural projects also tends to rule out percentage of cost contracts, and the uncertain nature of determining the time required to complete the service offering will frighten clients away from the multiplier and hourly fee approach. While the flat fee approach is considered the least preferred contract approach, many landscape architectural firms find it to be the most acceptable method to their clients.

Service organizations who face this type of contract approach on a regular basis find that cost accounting procedures for their project and service offering activities are of special importance. Without good accounting procedures which can be used to determine hourly operational costs and help equate project type to historical production data, educated guesses about compensation on a flat fee basis can prove disastrous.

Not only do flat fee contracts require reliable methods of estimating time to complete the service effort, they also require the ability to precisely state the service effort to be rendered for the flat fee. Incomplete statements about the services to be provided can lead to trouble and lost profits.

Parts of the Contract: The format for a good contract will not vary greatly between the three types of contracts described. The differences will occur mainly in the method of compensation section as might be expected. The following outline identifies those parts of a contract that will be found in all standard agreements.

1. Preamble Section
   a. **Date:** The effective date of agreement.
   b. **Parties:** The accurate and full names of the parties to the contract.
   c. **Project Designation:** A careful description of the project, its location, size, shape and other unique characteristics of the site along with the activity or use being contemplated should be identified.
   d. **Compensation:** This section clearly identifies the exact compensation or the precise method of determining the exact compensation for basic services.

2. Basic Services:
   a. **Services to be Provided:** A clear and concise statement of the exact services to be performed for the compensation described.
   b. **Services not Included:** Organizations who offer a variety of services must clearly state those

other service offerings which are not included. When not stated these other services may be construed as being part of the basic service offering.

3. **Additional Services:**
   a. **Consultants:** Professional fees and costs associated with other consultant activities on a project should be an addition to the basic service costs. The prime consultant should also accept no liability responsibility for the work effort of other consultants.
   b. **Other Services:** This provision should be designed to allow for contract expansion to include services not originally contemplated in the basic service section, and to identify the method of determining compensation for these additional services.

4. **Owner's Responsibility:**
   a. **Access to Information:** The owner is responsible for providing the service vendor with all pertinent and necessary data and information concerning the project or activity. This would include market studies, topographical and boundary surveys, legal descriptions, aerial photography, soil data and special tests, and a variety of other information consistent with the scope and character of activity and the site. The owner is also responsible for insuring the consultant access to the project site.
   b. **Additional Information Needed:** This section should identify all additional information needed by the service enterprise to complete its agreed-upon activity. When these items are not specifically known this section should provide for the means of determining these needs and identify compensation provisions.

5. **Reimbursable Expenses:** This section should clearly identify that all direct job related expenses are reimbursable at actual cost. In some cases the service offering firm will provide some reimbursable items at no additional charge (the first three sets of prints are often included in the basic service package with all others being a reimbursable expense). Such provisions should be clearly stated.

6. **Method of Payment:** This section describes how and when earned compensation and expenses are to be paid. Most design professional firms prefer monthly payments of fees and expenses, rather than payment tied to direct delivery of parts of the service package. In this way the compensation is determined by pro-rating the percentage of work completed each month into the total amount of contract compensation.

7. **Conclusion:**
   a. **Termination Clause:** This clause identifies the rights of both parties to terminate the contract and stipulates the procedures involved. Written notice is almost always required and all fees earned up to the receipt of written termination notice must be paid.
   b. **Ownership of Drawings:** This provision stipulates that all original drawings, tracings, and other documents shall remain the property of the professional service enterprise.
   c. **Limitation of Liability:** This clause links the service enterprises' professional liability to a specific top limit usually not exceeding the total amount of professional compensation for the work effort. (see Chapter Fifteen for further discussion of limitation of liability.)
   d. **Successors and Assigns:** This section defines the conditions under which the contract may be transferred to another party, and binds all parties, heirs, successors and assigns to fulfullment of the terms of the agreement.

8. **Signature Section:** The concluding section contains the signature blocks of both parties, and they should match exactly the names shown in the preamble section of the contract. Spaces for signatures of witnesses and a Notray Public are also frequently provided.

A good contract is indispensable to a good project. A good contract protects the rights of everyone involved and no one should be offended by a request to sign a fair and binding agreement. Many professional design organizations seem to fear contracts and formalized agreements and will profess to conduct a vast majority of their work effort by word-of-mouth and hand shake agreements. The truth of the matter is, however, that very few firms can really operate this way, and most find that even the smallest project or service offering demands a good and reliable contract.

Business administration and office procedures represent a very important aspect of landscape architectural practice. It must not be relegated to a second class position behind design or sensitivity for the land or any other aspect of the profession. The business of business must be seen as the bond which holds professional practice together. Without its strength and adhesive power the rest would soon fall apart.

The following two chapters also deal with business issues. Up to this point, however, the business issues discussed have been largely applicable to any professional service enterprise. The material which follows will deal with matters of a nature specific to the profession of landscape architecture.

Chapter Twelve Notes:

1. Irving Burstinger, *The Small Business Handbook*, Prentice-Hall, Inc., Englewood Cliffs, N.J., 1979
2. Robert H. Mortensen, ed., *Guidelines for Personnel Management*, ASLA, Washington, D.C., 1977
3. Ibid 2
4. American Institute of Architects "The Architects Office", Chapter 6, *Architects Handbook of Professional Practice*, AIA, Washington, D.C., 1971
5. Ibid 4
6. Lane L. Marshall, "*Survey of Landscape Architectural Firms*", 1980, produced as a part of the research in the preparation of this publication, unpublished.
7. Robert W. Abbett, *Engineering Contracts and Specifications*, 2nd edition, John Wiley and Sons, Inc., N.Y., N.Y., 1949
8. American Institute of Architects, "Owner-Architect Agreements", Chapter 9, *Architects Handbook of Professional Practice*, AIA, Washington, D.C., 1970

Chapter Thirteen
Construction Documents

Introduction

Professional landscape architectural service enterprises render an unusual variety of services. Frequently these services will be program and policy oriented and will affect the built environment in ways quite different from project-oriented types of services. The great variety of project-oriented service offerings, coupled with the high frequency of program and policy service offerings sets landscape architecture somewhat apart from the other design professions. Both architecture and engineering are highly project-oriented professions, with fewer of their numbers proportionally serving in government policy and non-design oriented roles.

Landscape architecture does find it roots, however, in design and project implementation activities, and such activities have become an important element of the profession's diverse practice. The design and implementation of built projects requires a special set of business skills normally associated with the de-

sign professional service enterprises. Among these very specific skills is the preparation and utilization of construction documents, or the finite translation of design ideas into drawings and instructions which will allow for and insure the final translation of ideas into a built project. The preparation and utilization of these documents is unique to the design professions and deserves careful attention.

Understanding these special business tools and their proper use is important to all landscape architects regardless of practice area. While some may use this information more frequently than others, a large percentage of landscape architects will, at one time or another, become involved in a built design project. Many public practitioners are called upon to coordinate construction efforts on behalf of their agency or to review and approve construction drawings and specifications submitted by private consultants to their agency.

Teachers need these skills in order to teach them. An obvious statement, but teachers also have many opportunities to act as private consultants which require the use of these skills. It would appear that few landscape architects can pursue a professional career without the knowledge and skills necessary to prepare and utilize construction documents and specifications, and for this reason Chapter Thirteen is devoted to a closer look at this subject.

This is not, however, a "how to do it" chapter. The chapter cannot provide the kind of information needed to actually prepare a detailed set of construction documents. For those seeking this kind of data, the *Construction Specifications Handbook,* Hans W. Meier, Prentice-Hall, Inc., 1978, is strongly recommended. There are also several other outstanding publications available on the subject from the Construction Specifications Institute, 1150 17th Street, N.W., Suite 300, Washington, D.C. 20036.

This chapter does, however, take a comprehensive look at the rationale and organization of construction documents and provides guidelines and criteria for their preparation and use. This look logically begins by posing and answering the question; "What are construction documents?" Historically, in the design professions, construction documents have been defined as plans and specifications. In recognition of the fact that these documents, in reality, contain a variety of information that is neither a plan nor a specification, current thought substitutes the terms "drawings" and "project manual".[1] Together, the drawings and the project manual make up the construction documents necessary to translate ideas into a built project. With this in mind a close-up look at both terms is in order.

The Drawings

"The role of drawings in a construction contract today is to define the physical relationships of materials upon which the contract is based."[2] The construction drawing is a key part of the construction document package. It is a pictorial view of how the materials selected fit together, are joined and relate to each other and to the whole. The construction drawings, also known as working drawings, must be clear, complete, accurate, and properly dimensioned. They must also be prepared at a scale which will facilitate accurate cost estimating.[3] In indicating materials and their use, nationally ccepted standard symbols should be employed. Construction sections and large scale details should be used to correlate all parts of the project and to explain the more complex elements of the drawings. The drawings should be organized functionally, and when possible should directly correspond to the contract divisions contained in the project manual.

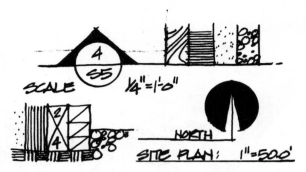

The use of standard symbols makes the drawings more easily understood.

It is important to understand that construction drawings are only a part of the construction documents package. The drawings by themselves, no matter how well prepared, are not a substitute for construction specifications and instructions. The reverse of that statement is equally true. When seen as a part of the whole package, the drawings take on the functional role of providing visual instructions about how the project will go togehter and no more. This fact raises an important issue of concern to the proper meshing of drawings and project manual. The issue is redundancy or the repeating of instructions on the drawings and in the project manual. A closer look at this problem is important.

Redundancy: When seen in the light of their functional role, the construction drawings must seek to avoid confusion and misunderstanding by eliminating the unnecessary repetition of information. Such redundancy is time consuming, confusing, expensive, and can often lead to great misunderstanding about what is actually being asked for.

To help avoid redundancy, many design professionals have adopted the principle of "single statement".[4] This principle stipulates that information should be given once and only once, that it should be given in the most logical place, and referred to as necessary but not repeated. This, of course, raises the issue of what goes where. Should the information be given in the drawings or in the project manual? A simple rule of thumb is offered in answer to this question. If the information deals with the physical relationship of materials it should be shown a single time on the drawings. If the information deals with quality and types of materials or with methods of installing or expected results, then it should be given a single time in the appropriate specification section of the project manual. In this way the drawings and the specifications are performing different but complementary functions.

The Project Manual

A project manual contains two distinct parts; the bidding requirements and the contract documents, and together with the drawings constitute the construction documents used to build a project and act as a contract between "owner" and "contractor". The American Institute of Architects recommends the following project manual outline:[5]

Bidding Requirements:

1. Invitation to Bid
- Project Title and Location
- Name and Address of Owner
- Name and Address of (Designer)
- Place and Time for Receipt of Bids
- Type of Bid Opening
- Short Description of Project Scope and Type of Construction
- Type of Owner-Contractor Agreement to be Employed
- Place Where Bidding Documents May be Examined
- Bid Security Requirements
- Time When Bidding Documents will be Available
- Procedures for Obtaining Bid Documents and Amount of Deposit
- Statement on Time to Complete the Project and Liquidated Damages

2. Instruction To Bidders
- Addenda (changes to drawings and specifications after their completion and prior to bid taking)
- Bidder's Representation
- Bidding Procedures
- Submission of Bids
- Execution of Bids
- Examination of Bid Documents
- Clarification of Bidder's Questions
- Substitutions
- Qualification of Bidders
- Rejection of Bids
- Submission of Post Bid Information
- Performance Bond, and Labor and Material Payment Bond
- Other instructions peculiar to the Project or the Owner

3. Sample Forms
- Owner-Contractor Agreement
- Bid Format
- Bid Bond
- Power of Attorney
- Contractors Qualification Statement
- Performance Bond, and Labor and Materials Payment Bond
- Consent of Surety to Reduction in or Partial Release of Retainage Funds
- Non-Collusion Affidavit
- Application and Certificate for Payment
- Certificate of Insurance
- Others peculiar to the Project

Contract Documents:
1. Owner-Contractor Agreement
2. Conditions of the Contract
- General Conditions
- Supplementary Conditions
3. Schedule of Drawings
4. Specifications

In spite of the length of the outline for a project manual, the vast majority of its contents are found in the conditions of the contract and the specifications sections. Together these two sections will comprise as much as 95% of the project manual. Because of their importance, they will be studied in greater detail in the following sections of this chapter.

Conditions of the Contract

General Conditions: The General Conditions of the project manual are the "fine print" which describes the relationships and procedures connected with the project.[6] The relationship between the owner and the contractor and how the project will be administered is very carefully defined in the general conditions. These relationships seldom change from one project to the next and the general conditions have been standardized throughout most of the design professions. Frequently referred to as "boilerplate", they are usually printed in volume for insertion in each new project manual.

AIA Document A 201 suggests the following outline of articles for inclusion in the general conditions:

Article 1. Contract Documents
2. The Architect
3. The Owner
4. The Contractor

Each article of the general conditions carefully spells out the exact requirements and procedures for dealing with the subject of concern. The exact wording and the conditions defined in each article have slowly evolved into an industry standard with roots which can be traced back to the adoption of the first Uniform Building Code in 1888 by the City of New York. The evolutionary process still continues as new construction technology and construction law is developed. For the reader who wishes to persue this area in more detail, Chapter 13, "General Conditions of the Contract for Construction", *Architects Handbook of Professional Practice,* is recommended.

Supplementary Conditions: The standardization of the general conditions creates the need for a supplementary section designed to deal with relationships peculiar to the project and/or the owner. Every project is uniquely different, and it is impossible for standardized general conditions to anticipate every possible condition of the work. The supplementary conditions, then, are those conditions which are specific to each individual project and reflect those aspects of the general conditions which require modification.

Specifications

Formats and Systems: The construction specifications for a construction project will vary greatly from one project to the next and it is consequently impossible to standardize them in the same way as the general conditions. In order to insure, however, industry wide consistency in the preparation and utilization of construction specifications it was necessary to develop a uniform system for organizing and presenting them within the contract documents. The Construction Specifications Institute (CSI) and the American Institute of Architects (AIA) largely share the credit for development of a standard specification format. CSI refers to its system as the CSI Format and AIA calls their's the Uniform System. Both formats are nearly identical, with the differences not being worthy of note in this book. Both utilize a 16 Division concept with each division further divided into sections. Over the years both CSI and AIA have defined and improved their systems and today offer highly sophisticated computer operations dealing with very specific construction issues and concerns.

In the early 1970s AIA established the Production System for Architects and Engineers (PSAE). This specialized group is composed of professionals from both professions whose function is to collect and collate date on specifications and their use. The group has produced a computerized master specification system known as MASTERSPEC. "The MASTERSPEC program enables a central facility to receive, maintain, evaluate, and transmit by mail, specification information in concise form."[7] The computer is utilzied to continually update the data based on a constant inflow of information concerning new technology, construction methods, practical experience and legal concerns. Using a MASTERSPEC catalog, a practitioner can request and receive the most current data available on specification writing and utilization.

The CSI maintains an even more sophisticated computer information service to its subscribers. Known as "Spec-Data II", this system utilizes a microfilmed catalog system of current specification data. CSI has also developed a computer-aided word processing system known as COMSPEC which is in daily use and accessible via telecommunications across the country.[8]

Divisions and Sections: Both the CSI Format and the AIA Uniform System employ the use of 16 divisions and the subdivision of these into sections. The divisions which are identical in both systems include:

Division 1. General Requirements
2. Site Work
3. Concrete
4. Masonry
5. Metals
6. Wood and Plastics
7. Thermal and Moisture Protection
8. Doors and Windows
9. Finishes

10. Specialities
11. Equipment
12. Furnishings
13. Special Construction
14. Conveying Systems
15. Mechanical
16. Electrical

In landscape architectural practice, all 16 divisions are seldom used. Many landscape architectural firms, however, have modeled their own specifications after the CSI format which may incorporate specific parts of division 2, Site Work. The larger landscape architectural firms may find the scope of their projects often suited to utilization of the entire system.

In general terms a specification division is a grouping of major areas of related activity. A division section, on the other hand represents a basic unit of work. In many cases a section will represent the work and activities performed by a specific subcontractor or specialized trade.

A section of a specification division would normally be organized in a manner similar to the one presented here:

General Provisions
- Scope of the Section
  — Work to be Furnished and Installed
  — Work Furnished but not Installed
  — Work Installed but Furnished by Others
- Notes
- Quality Control
  — Prior Approval
  — Industry Standards
- Submissions
  — Samples
  — Shop Drawings
  — Test Reports
  — Maintenance and Operating Instructions
- Delivery and Storage of Materials
- Protection and Cleaning of the site

Materials
- Acceptable Manufacturers
- Substitutions
- Material Specifications

Performance
- Fabrication
- Installation
- Schedules
- Guarantees and Warranties
- Close-out

Alternates
- When Allowed
- Form of Submission

The Uniform System and the CSI Format have also assigned a standardized numbering system to sections for each numbered division. Division 2—Site Work, for instance, includes the following numbered sections:

02010 Subsurface Exploration
02220 Excavation, Filling and Grading
02550 Site Drainage
02612 Asphaltic Concrete Paving
02750 Irrigation Systems
02800 Planting

In this section numbering system the first two digits represent the division number. The next three digits are available for an array of sections from 001 to 999. The CSI Format and Uniform System have already assigned some of these numbers, as shown above, but many unassigned numbers are available for use by organizations in response to their own project needs.

The section numbering system also allows for the collection of a wide variety of sections dealing with similar construction situations, thus allowing for the use of a section which best meets the particular needs of the project. The introduction of word processing and computer retrieval systems has dramatically expanded the applicability of the uniform section approach. Manufacturers and materials suppliers have also standardized their literature and product specifications to the section numbering system as well. Many offices and agencies are also using the numbering system for product information filing. All of this allows for a much simpler and more efficient approach to compiling specifications. The days of writing a completely new set of specifications for each new project are gone forever.

The use of divisions and sections coupled with a systemized numbering approach means more than convenience to the specifications writer. The approach makes the specifications themselves more easily understood and more comprehensive in nature. All of this facilitates the construction process, insures better competitive bidding and helps to eliminate duplicated effort.

Language: Contract documents are legal instruments and the language used is of critical concern to proper understanding and the enforceability of the documents' stated requirements. The document writer's task is to communicate information and instructions clearly and concisely, without jargon, complexity or understatement. Legal terminology is best left to the attorneys. Quasi-legal terms should be avoided. Remember that specifications are written for a known audience, the construction contractor. Use the contractor's language not the attorney's language. The document writer must know the current terminology common to the construction industry, and know when industry language is no longer in common use.

The specifications should avoid the use of trite or easily misunderstood words and phrases.

Avoid trite, cute or fancy words. If you wish to say everywhere do so, don't say ubiquitous. Watch out for obsolete and coined words, and keep sentence structure simple and direct.

Legal Concerns: The mounting number of law suits against design professionals which arise from poorly prepared contract documents is a cause for great concern. The growing number of precedent cases is having a dramatic effect on the rights and responsibilities of design professionals, owners, suppliers, contractors and subcontractors.

Design professionals are rarely also lawyers, and their understanding of the growing body of construction law is negligible. Yet, all too frequently, design professionals fail to seek qualified legal advice when preparing contract documents and specifications.

Construction law is complex and covers a broad area of legal concern. Those lawyers who specialize in construction law are not going to have a book shelf labeled construction law, but rather a library from floor to ceiling and wall to wall filling an entire room with books on subjects from aesthetics to stress dynamics. The astute design professional service enterprises will seek out a construction law specialist and will consult with this person frequently. These firms will submit their standard documents annually for review and updating. They will submit new sections and substanative changes before final printing and will coordinate their errors and ommission insurance coverage on the advise of their legal counsel.

Design professionals are frequently disturbed when people fail to see the wisdom of their retention

Seek legal help when changing or undertaking a specification section or division.

as consultants. It is sad to see how often these same design professionals fail to recognize the wisdom of retaining a legal specialist when preparing documents of such obvious legal concern. The constantly increasing number of law suits being brought against design professionals are largely the result of poor contracts and even poorer contract documents. A surprisingly small number result from poorly prepared drawings. Design professionals know how to draw, they just do not know how to write contracts and contract documents. With this fact so very evident, one must wonder why it is so difficult to get design professionals to seek legal advice. Seek legal help whenever legal matters become an expressed or implied part of a professional service offering. This is the best advice this chapter can offer.

Awarding Contracts

There are two basic methods of selecting contractors and awarding construction contracts: competitive bidding, and direct selection with negotiation. Both methods should employ the use of construction drawings and project manuals. Awarding a construction contract is a vital part of the process of translating ideas into reality and deserves some attention in this chapter.

Competitive Bidding: This selection procedure is employed in an effort to secure the best possible price for the work to be completed from a representative number of reliable contractors. The procedure requires fully detailed construction drawings and a fully complete project manual. Anything less will not suffice.

AWARD

The competitive bid process also presumes that the completed work will be equally well done regardless of who the low bidder may be. To facilitate this presumption, bidders are often prequalified or screened by the Consultant or Owner for competence and ability to perform the work. Prequalification procedures can take a variety of forms, but at the very least would include assurance that the contractor had past experience with similar construction projects. Private clients will usually reserve the right, in the bid documents, to reject any and all bids and to not be bound to accept or hire the low bidder. Most public clients, on the other hand, are bound by law to accept the lowest responsible bid or reject all bids. This condition associated with most public work places special importance on the use of prequalification procedures.

In the landscape construction industry, competitive bidding can frequently produce rather large cost or bid price difference between the low and high bidder. This is especially true when a significant portion of the project cost is associated with the supplying and installation of plant material. Plant materials are difficult to standardize and cost associated with their growing, supplying and installation will vary widely between competing firms.

The cost disparity in competitive bidding presents both problems and opportunities to the landscape architectural firm. On the plus side, competitive bidding becomes an excellent tool to identify which of all the qualified contractors is best able to perform

the required work at any specific point in time. This can result in the completion of a truly good project for the best possible price. On the problem side, the difficulty in standardizing plant material places special pressure on the development of precise yet flexible specifications. The specifications must describe exactly what is required and expected while at the same time recognize that precision in plant materials is impossible to find. Dealing with these two dichotomous concerns within the same set of specifications is an art that takes many years of field experience to learn.

Most private practice firms feel that competitive bidding offers the best method of determining which contractor should perform the construction effort. Some firms prefer, however, to directly select a contractor and to negotiate a contract price for the work. Every firm will find situations, it must also be pointed out, when direct selection and negotiation is in the best interest of the client and the project.

Direct Selection and Negotiation: This procedure involves the selection of a single contractor, usually one who is known and trusted by the client/owner or the designer, and through negotiation arrive at a contract price acceptable to both owner and contractor.

While there is no competitive incentive in the process, it does have some distinct advantages. One of the principal advantages of direct selection is the ability to start contract negotiation prior to final completion of the drawings and project manual. This can dramatically reduce the amount of time necessary to begin construction and allows the contractor to suggest alternative materials and construction methods before the documents are fixed. Both of these factors can reduce the overall project costs.

Direct negotiation may also allow a project to be built with less detailed construction drawings and will also allow the construction process to start before the drawings are actually finished.

The procedure does, however, put an extra burden on the designer. The designer is placed in the role of cost arbitrator, carefully monitoring the negotiations and acting as the owner's agent while at the same time attempting to be fair to the contractor. This can be a difficult and time consuming process, and if either owner or contractor become unhappy, the designer is quickly blamed. Because of the extra time associated with contract negotiation it is important for the designer to determine, prior to contracting to provide professional services, which selection procedure the owner/client wishes to follow. If this is not known at the outset, then the designer should allow for the extra time required as an extra service provision in the service contract. Most design professional private practice firms will employ both selection procedures, using the one most appropriate to the circumstances of the project and the best interest of the owner. Only experience can be the judge of when one procedure is better than the other, but most firms prefer the competitive bidding procedure when circumstances allow, and most public owner/clients are bound by law to bid all work over a certain price (normally a few thousand dollars).

Construction drawings and project manuals are often thought of as a design firm's "product". They are the only record of a connection between a design idea and a finished project. They prove that a completed project was, in fact, the creation of a particular designer or group of designers. As a service "product" the contract documents take on a very important role in the activity of a design professional service enterprise, and account for why original drawings and tracings and other documents must remain the property of the designer or design firm. If the designer or the design firm is to accept legal responsibility for the accuracy of these documents, they must not be subject to change by anyone other than the parties responsible for their original preparation.

With construction documents complete, the contractor selected and a contract signed, the design professional firm is ready to embark on a new service venture, that of construction project management and contract administration. Chapter Fourteen looks at this activity.

Chapter Thirteen Notes:

1. Hans W. Meier, *Construction Specifications Handbook*, Prentice-Hall, Inc., Englewood Cliffs, N.J. 1978
2. Ibid 1
3. Editors, *"Bidding Procedures and Contract Awards*, The American Institute of Arthitects and the Associated General Contractors of American, 1969
4. Ibid 1
5. Editors, "Construction Documents-Specifications", Ch. 14, *Architects Handbook of Professional Practice*, American Institute of Architects, Washington, D.C. 1972
6. Ibid 1
7. Ibid 5
8. Ibid 1
9. Ibid 5

Chapter Fourteen
Project Management

In most professional service enterprises, project management is very sophisticated work. Some firms even specialize in it as a service offering.

Introduction

Project management is a business procedure of special importance to the landscape architectural professional service enterprise. It involves the use of planning and scheduling techniques, monitoring procedures and record keeping, contract administration, project observation, effective communication, problem identification, leadership skills, and a host of other business practices necessary to coordinating and implementing a project efficiently and successfully from inception to completion.

While project management is most often thought of in connection with the coordination of a project during the construction phases, it is by no means exclusive to these activities. Project management begins the moment a project becomes the responsibility of the service enterprise, and continues until that responsibility has been discharged. The procedures of sound project management are applicable to all pro-

fessional service activities, from the design and implementation of a large construction project to the preparation of a written report. While the degree of sophistication and level of application intensity will vary according to project scope, the steps necessary to good project management will be the same for all activities.

Comprehensive project management will include at least four and frequently five steps or procedures:

1. Planning and Scheduling
2. Resource Allocation
3. Controlling and Updating
4. Running the Construction Project
5. Completing the Project

The fourth step, Running the Project, is really a specialized part of step five, Completing the Project. In many types of service activities completion of the project is a relatively simple procedure and is easily accomplished. When the service activity does not involve construction, completion is usually an in-office procedure and seldom requires the same skills associated with construction management. Because many landscape architectural services do involve construction activities, however, this chapter looks closely at the specialized problems associated with running a construction project, along with the other elements of project management.

Planning and Scheduling

Planning and scheduling is the first, and perhaps most important, aspect of project management. A poorly planned and scheduled project can surely fail even when skillfully controlled and administered in all other ways.

The planning and scheduling process begins by breaking down the entire project into its basic activity components or events. These activities or events are the actual step-by-step occurances from a project's inception to its completion. The activities can be described in very general terms such as, "Construction of lower plaza area", or more specifically, "install water distribution lines in lower plaza area". The degree of detail given to the activity description will vary, and will depend on the scope and complexity of the project. The intent of describing the activities is to determine and define their chronological order and their interrelationships. In the plaza example a more detailed, albeit key word phrase, outline might be described as follows:

Lower Plaza Construction
  Grading and Drainage
  Underground Utilities and Irrigation Lines
  Construction Forming
  Foundations and Footers
  Concrete Base Work
  Planters and Walls
  Large Tree Planting
  Fill Material for Planters
  Concrete Finish Work
  Complete Irrigation System
  Install Electrical Fixtures
  Install Site Furniture
  Clean Up

Each of these activities may be further broken down into sub-work descriptions, to logistical areas within the plaza, or in response to specific construction techniques, or sub-contractor responsibility. It is of paramount importance, however, that the proper chronological order of activities be clearly established. Moreover, this chronology must identify the linkage between activities. Which events must occur before the next can be started? Which events can go forward simultaneously? Which events can be skipped if delays occur? These are linkage concerns and the planning and scheduling process must accurately define them.

Project scheduling must be a collaborative effort between all participants involved with the work effort.

Once the project activities have been defined and broken down into discrete parts and ordered chronologically, time frames to complete each event can be determined and calendar dates attached to the progression of events. This is the scheduling part of the process. While planning may be accomplished unilaterally, scheduling must involve all parties concerned with the overall project. Collaboration is essential to the preparation of a workable project schedule. This suggests that designer, contractor, subcontractors, materials suppliers, owner's agents and any other participants in the project activity must participate in the preparation of project schedules. A difficult task, indeed, and one which distinguishes the good from the mediocre project planners.

To assist in project planning and scheduling a number of specialized techniques have been developed over the years. The Critical Path Method (CPM), Program Evaluation and Review (PERT), and the Precedence Method are the most commonly used of these techniques.[1] Of the three, CPM is the most widely used by design professionals and deserves a closer investigation here.

Critical Path Method (CPM): CPM is a diagramatic technique for showing the chronology and interrelationships of project activities. Its use can be applied to all types of professional service activities, and is not confined to construction projects. The process begins by carefully defining the events or activities associated with the project as outlined earlier under planning and scheduling.

In the diagramming process an activity or event is depicted by an arrow moving left to right with the activity description written slightly above the arrow.

The beginning and end of an activity is called a node and is shown by circles.

When more than one activity is involved in the progression from beginning to end, a logic statement is required to define the relationships of the activities. If activity A must be completed before activity B can be started, then the relationship is clear.

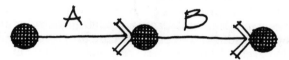

If activity A must be completed before activity B and C can be started but C can progress concurrently with B, the diagram looks like this:

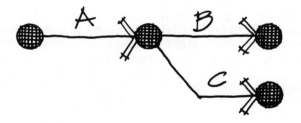

To expand the CPM diagram further, consider the following logic statements:

Activity A must preceed B,C
Activities B,C must preceed E
Activity B must preceed D
Activities D,E, must preceed F

To further clarify the interrelationships of these activities, the nodes may be numbered, moving to the right and down in sequence.

In the example above, the dash line from node 2 to node 3 is called a "dummy" and indicates that event D is restrained by event E. While the two events can happen concurrently, they must both be completed before event F can begin.

To add scheduling to this planning diagram, each numbered node can be given a completion date, or the diagram itself can be superimposed on a scaled calendar as shown here.

This fundamental presentation of the CPM process has been offered only to identify the basic concept. Those interested in a more detailed explanation of CPM are referred to Faulkner's, *Project Management with CPM*.

There are also several other systems for diagramatically demonstrating the chronological movement and interrelationship of activities. Frequently called "flow diagrams", the systems use horizontal or vertical graphs to plot activities on a scheduling calendar. With the increased use of computers in the professional service enterprise, the utilization of more sophisticated, and more easily amendable planning and scheduling procedures holds great promise for better and more profitably managed service activities.

Resource Allocation

One of the principal benefits of good planning and scheduling techniques is the ability to very accurately assess the human, financial, material, and other support resources necessary and available to complete each project activity or event. A project manager must be able to accurately determine the resources needed to complete each activity and com-

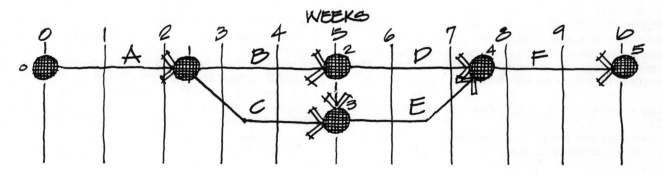

pare this information against the resources available. When resources needed are not currently available, it is imperative that this be known well in advance of need, allowing sufficient lead time to secure the proper support.

In the case of human resources, the project manager must not only determine whether the appropriate personnel are currently on staff or available as special consultants, but also whether they will be available during the specific time frames outlined by the project schedule. What other projects within the office, for example, will be competing for the necessary key personnel? What is the current workload of outside consultants needed for the project, and is their service delivery history good or poor?

Financial resource allocation is of special concern when the project is construction-oriented. Event order and scheduling must be directly linked to the availability of construction funds. This requires answering questions which deal with methods of payment: Are payments to be event-oriented or periodic? Does scheduling need to be keyed to timing of subcontractor's payments?

Professionals, owners and contractors must thoroughly understand the project schedule and the scope of resources needed to follow it.

The resources needed to successfully complete a project must be carefully identified and committed as early in the overall process as possible. All involved parties in the process must be clearly informed of their role and understand why, when and where their activity takes place. Resource competition problems must be satisfactorily settled in advance, and not left to chance or last minute dispute. Resource allocation is a fundamental aspect of sound project management and is directly tied to the planning and scheduling process.

Controlling and Updating

The planning and scheduling process is a means of estimating future project activity. If thoughtfully and skillfully designed, a project schedule can serve as a most useful management tool. It would be inappropriate, however, to consider an activity schedule as an inflexible instrument. Planners are fallible, and unexpected events do happen. For whatever reason project schedules often change, and a good project manager will know how to accomodate this probability. A project manager must maintain a systematic process for gathering, reviewing, and assessing ongoing project data and for updating project schedules accordingly.

This process is nothing more than sound administrative procedure and would include a number of specific techniques:

Record Keeping: All project records must be kept current on a daily basis and stored for easy retrival and review. All persons involved with the project should have access to the project files and should be kept constantly informed of incoming and outgoing communications concerning the project. Moreover, project records should clearly record this information accessing process.

The importance of maintaining written records of all project activities cannot be stressed enough. Word-of-mouth instructions should be avoided and oral communications must be backed up in written form. The written record provides a true historical review of a project and forms the base for reliable project control and proper updating of schedules. (see Chapter Fifteen on legal concerns)

Progress Reports: All responsible persons involved with a project must be required to file regular activity progress reports. The level of detail and the frequency of these reports will depend on the project scope and complexity, but concise weekly progress reports is a minimum expectation. It is important, however, that progress reports be scheduled at regular intervals and with a predetermined and known frequency. The progress reports themselves should clearly indicate current project status, compare this to stated project schedules and identify potential scheduling difficulties. All persons involved with the project should receive copies of the progress reports.

Team and Construction Meetings: Since written communications are not always read or understood, regular face to face project progress meetings are important. Again the frequency and formality of these meetings will depend on the project itself, but even the most simple of projects should utilize such meetings. All project participants should be asked to review the progress of their area of responsibility. All comments and reports should be recorded in the form of minutes, and these should be distributed to all participants.

A project manager's job is to constantly monitor this ongoing flow of project progress information and assess its impact on project schedules. If properly designed, the control and updating process will identify scheduling problems far enough in advance to allow for creative remedial action, not requiring rescheduling.

When remedial action is impossible the project manager will need to modify the project schedule. Even this necessity, however, is less traumatic when sufficient notice is given to all project participants.

Running the Construction Project*

1. **Administration and Project Observation:**
   a. **Verbal Orders and Advice**: All verbal orders given to the contractor should be given by the owner's job inspector or in cases where a job inspector is not used, by the landscape architect. Any verbal orders given should be followed up by a written confirmation or memorandum of the order given to the contractor. All orders to be given to sub-contractors should be given to the contractor's superintendent. Giving of advice to the contractor, sub-contractors or workmen should be done with care. The contractor alone is responsible for quality of materials and workmanship. If the landscape architect or owner tells him how to do his job and if it affects his cost of construction, he would have reason to request an extra charge for such change in his method of doing the project work.
   b. **Written Orders and Advice**: Whenever possible, give all orders or advice to the contractor in writing. The landscape architect should first evaluate the impact of the order on the contractor's work to determine possibility of change in contract price. If a potential price change is likely the written order should request a quotation for any change in price

and not be effective until the contractor has submitted this price quotation and it is accepted or rejected.

2. **Interpretations, Directives and Approvals:**
   The construction documents should clearly establish the right of the landscape architect to interpret the plans and specifications and to have the right to issue directives and approvals, to maintain the quality of the construction as specified in the contract documents. Interpretation of plans, details, specifications or other facets of the construction documents requested by the contractor should be promptly given. Directives should be given with sound judgment and in time to avoid costly delays or expensive changes. In some cases where the contractor has not complied with the contract requirements it is necessary to give a stop order directive or to stop portions of the work until a condition is corrected before the rest of the work can proceed. Staged approvals for segments of the work should be stipulated, and the work inspected before additional portions of the project can continue. Any such approvals prerequisite to continuation of contract work should be given in letter or memorandum form.

3. **Clarifications and Revisions:**
   Clarification of contract documents should be the responsibility of the landscape architect to assure integrity with contract specifications, plans, and the intent of the design. Every clarification should be reviewed for possible change in contract amount. Clarifications should be given in writing. Where necessary to provide additional plan information or to revise plan details, revision drawings should be issued to the contractor in advance of the construction work that is to be done to avoid unnecessary delays and extra costs.

4. **Field Orders and Change Orders:**
   Field orders are used to give directives for minor changes to the contractor to expedite the work, usually in minor amounts. Frequently the owner's job inspector, in addition to the landscape architect, is authorized to issue field orders. A dollar limit should be placed on the amount of the field order, and should be agreed on with the owner before the work commences. A field order may be given verbally, supported with some written document, (either a letter, a memorandum, or a standard field order form) usually prepared by the landscape architect. Field orders are usually sequentially numbered and are incorporated in to a change order at a later time, the change order to be included in the contract documents. A change order is a written document which becomes an official part of the construc-

---

*The following portions of this chapter are reproduced with minor modification from the *Landscape Architects Handbook of Professional Practice*[2]

tion documents. Change orders are usually prepared on a standard form (frequently already prepared by the owner or a government agency or a larger business firm). The landscape architect may want to have his own form to use for the project. Change orders should be numbered sequentially and should state the description of the work change either in the materials or construction operations, changes in the contract time period and changes in the contract amount. The change order form should be signed by the contractor and the owner. Change orders may be written for additions or deletions to the contract time period and amount, or to approve material substitutions, that occur during the course of the work. It becomes a binding legal document supplemental to the actual base contract.

5. **Request for Estimate or Price Quotation:**
Prospective changes in the contract scope which influence the amount of the contract should be preceded by a request for estimate or a request for a price quotation from the contractor. Some landscape architecture offices use a standard form for requesting these price quotations during construction work after award of contract. They become the basis of issuing a field order or change order to the contract. These requests should clearly state the desired change and should be supported by any revision drawings or other necessary instruments to convey the intent of the change being requested. For larger projects sequential numbering of requests for estimates or price quotations is desirable.

6. **Scheduled Job Meetings and Visits:**
For more lengthy and complex construction projects it is advisable to schedule observation visits to the job site and to hold meetings at the site as felt desirable for communication purposes with the contractor. The nature of the construction work will influence the frequency of job visits or meetings. Usually weekly meetings are desirable. The minutes of the job meetings and memoranda of job observation visits are essential to properly administer a landscape construction project. These generally are prepared by the landscape architect, although they may be prepared by the owner's job inspector or another designated party. They can serve as a valuable history of the project in the event dispute, arbitration or litigation arise. Job observation visits by the landscape architect are usually set at a frequency to assure that the construction work is being performed to the quality and conditions stipulated in the contract documents. It is advisable to make regular visits to the site even though an inspection crew is on the job on a daily basis.

The landscape architect should be available, also, for visits to the site or special meetings in the event of problems arising during construction or for other unforeseen circumstances that need attention.

7. **Materials and Samples Submittals and Approvals:**
Contract specifications should indicate types of materials and products that must be submitted for approval prior to delivery to the project site and use in construction. All materials and samples should be submitted by the contractor or supplier well in advance of use in the construction work to avoid delays and to allow time for testing as deemed appropriate by the landscape architect or the owner. It is advisable to get no less than two samples or portions of materials to be used and to properly label one approved for delivery to the contractor, usually at the job site. Samples of construction work such as concrete sidewalks should be prepared prior to the actual construction work on the job. However it is sometimes advantageous for the contractor to install a small portion of the items to be approved on the site in lieu of preparing samples in advance. In this case it must be understood that the work, if not acceptable for quality or other reasons, must be removed and another sample prepared for approval before proceeding with additional work. Some materials and products may, at the option of the landscape architect, be approved at the source of supply prior to delivery to the job, but should be subject to approval or rejection at the job site after delivery. The specifications should stipulate this procedure.

8. **Substitutions and/or Equals:**
The landscape architect should by stipulation in the contract documents, reserve the exclusive right to allow or disallow substitutions and to determine equals to products indicated in the contract documents. Requests by the contractor for substitutions should be carefully evaluated for changes in quality or changes in the contract cost. Where changes are to the owner's advantage they should be reviewed with the owner before a decision on acceptance of the requested substitutions is made. All substitutions and changes in materials or products should be properly recorded in job meetings and change orders to avoid later dispute or demand for removal of equipment or construction work.

9. **Shop Drawings:**
For certain types of construction fabrication techniques, it is advisable to request preparation of shop drawings by the contractor, subcontractor, or material suppliers. These should be

submitted to the landscape architect in sufficient quantity to allow the return copies to the contractor and the owner for approval. The shop drawings then become an official part of contract documents as a supplement to the plans and specifications prepared by the landscape architect.

10. **Time Delays and Extensions:**
Unforeseen conditions arise in almost every construction project that can result in a need for a change in contract time period. Weather delays, indecision by the landscape architect or the owner, or their failure to act promptly may cause the contractor delays. Other construction work being done that influences the contractor's work should be reviewed for legitimacy to extend the contract time period. All delays of this nature should be included in a change order extension of the contract time and officially recorded with the final contract documents.

11. **Payment Requests and Certificates of Payment:**
For larger projects a regular payment procedure is established in the contract documents for periodic payments to the contractor as work progresses. The standard practice is for the contractor to initiate a payment request on a form that has been agreed upon by the owner, landscape architect and contractor and which is submitted to the landscape architect for approval and issuance of a certificate of payment. Both documents are submitted to the owner or owner's representative for payment to the contractor. These payment requests are usually monthly and represent 100% of the work completed during the payment period less a retention amount, usually 10%. The final 10% retention payment is usually made at the end of the maintenance period or at the end of the mechanic's lien period established by local statutes. The certificate of payment is a certification by the landscape architect that the amount of work done to that point by the contractor has been done and that the contractor is entitled to that amount of payment. The landscape architect should have reasonable assurance that the work has been accomplished for the amount stipulated in the payment request before issuing a certificate of payment.

12. **Verification of Construction Quality and Quantity:**
a. **Preventive Observation:** The landscape architect may elect to periodically check the construction operation for both quality and quantity and advise the contractor where the job might better be done following certain procedures. In cases where the quality or quantity of the work is unacceptable to the landscape architect the choice of either stopping the work, getting it changed at that time or to delay until the request for final acceptance by the contractor can be made. A landscape architect with a good knowledge of construction can be a great assistance to the contractor by preventive observation and inspection of the work rather than the corrective approach to it in which the contractor proceeds with all of the work before being advised that it is not acceptable.

b. **Corrective Observation:** Under certain circumstances the contractor will install work and materials where the quality or the quantity is not in compliance with contract requirements. The landscape architect or the inspector may advise the contractor at that time of such inadequacy instead of waiting until request for final acceptance in order to avoid costly removal and reinstallation of work by the contractor or delays in completion of the project. The landscape architect should use good judgment in ordering corrective work before proceeding or in stopping the work until a portion that is unacceptable has been corrected by the contractor. Close communication with the job inspector is most important for the landscape architect to assure that both quality and quantity comply with the contract requirements. The contract documents should stipulate that work may be stopped or unacceptable work must be removed during the course of the work rather than to wait until the final approval request.

c. **Tests:** Many types of tests may be required for a landscape or site improvement project depending on the nature of the materials and construction techniques to be incorporated in the work. These may range from agricultural soil tests, pipe pressure tests, concrete compression tests, asphalt viscosity tests, and performance tests of the installation after completion such as sprinkler coverage tests or water system tests to assure against leakage. All required tests either for the benefit of the landscape architect or as required by the owner, government agencies and others should be specified in the contract documents, and procedures established for obtaining and accepting all of the required tests. Records of all tests should be delivered to the landscape architect as a part of his knowledge of the contract requirements to certify completion of the project as specified.

13. **Rejections and Shut-Downs:**
Construction documents should include a provision for the landscape architect or delegated agent, usually the inspector, to reject any and all

parts of the work or materials, before or after delivery to the site, and manufactured products on delivery or after installation. Unacceptable work may be rejected at the time it is observed by due notification to the contractor or construction superintendent. In the event of failure of the contractor to correct the work promptly and before proceeding with additional work that may be affected by unacceptable portions, it may be advisable to shut down the construction job until the problem has been corrected. In some cases inspections required by government agencies relating to building permits, etc., will result in rejection and shut down of the construction work. Landscape architects must be sure of their rights and responsibilities with respect to the construction documents before acting on rejections. Repeated rejections of work or project shut down can result in removal of the contractor or termination of the contract. In such case, it must be clearly evident that the contractor has failed to comply with the plans and specifications in a timely manner, as required.

14. As-Built Record Enforcement:
For larger projects it is imperative that daily records be kept for project construction as it is built ... particularly work that is placed underground such as utility lines and irrigation lines. The job inspector and the landscape architect should insist on regular recording of this as-built information as the project is being constructed.

15. Project Records:
a. **Meeting Minutes:** Regularly held meetings at the construction site or elsewhere should include preparation of minutes indicating the time, date, place, those attending, and points discussed and decided on in the course of the meeting. The minutes thus prepared and signed by the landscape architect or the authorized preparer of the minutes becomes an official part of the contract record and history. The meeting minutes serve a useful function as the written communication device for clarification of plans, notifications for changes in work procedures or conditions that do not affect the contract amount or other primary provisions of the documents.
b. **Inspection Reports:** If an inspector is working for the landscape architect or the owner on a regular basis, an inspection report should be sent to the interested parties so that all will be advised of observations for that particular portion of the construction. The inspection report can include records of the amount of personnel and equipment the contractor has at the site at any time, weather conditions, and delays in the construction operation due to the inclement weather conditions or adverse site conditions, records of materials and products delivered to the site, and a memorandum of any instructions received from the landscape architect for conveyance to the contractor and vice versa. These become valuable historical documents for the contract during its progress.
c. **Test Reports:** All test reports required for the construction work, materials or products delivered for the construction should be made a part of the construction contract records. Test reports validate the contractor's obligations for quality of materials, and assure the landscape architect and owner that the materials received are in compliance with the requirements. Test reports also indicate products not acceptable, which are to be rejected.

16. Unauthorized Contract Changes:
All changes in the scope, quality or quantity of the contract work that result in a change in contract amount must be negotiated and agreed on prior to directing the contractor to make the change. Too frequently minor changes and occasionally major changes are authorized that are not supported by written change orders or the equivalent. These informal authorized changes in the contract can result in confusion, excessive cost, and either arbitration or, occasionally law suits to determine the amount the contractor should be due for changes that result from unauthorized instructions. Enforce a clear line of authority for the person responsible for making changes in the contract and enforce administration of a contract so that the contractor is not in a position to make claims for extras which are not authorized. No good contractor will accept a verbal authorization making a change in the contract amount.

Closing Out the Project

1. Advance Notices:
The contract documents should provide for ample advance notice to the landscape architect and all other parties by the contractor that final acceptance of the complete work (or of particular parts of it that have been designed for acceptance) will be requested. Normally seven days written notice is required in the contract documents in advance of final acceptance. The contractor should also, by advance notice, advise the landscape architect, inspectors and others, particularly the owner, when systems and materials included in the contract are to be checked out for performance. The landscape architect should enforce the contract provisions for these advance

notices so that every one who should attend has ample prior warning to be available.

2. Pre-final Observation and Punch Lists:

Prior to final acceptance of the construction work or the end of the maintenance period it is common practice to conduct a pre-final observation trip to check all completed elements of the construction operation and prepare a 'punch list' or a list of items to be corrected before the work can be accepted. This serves as advance warning to the contractor of those things considered unacceptable prior to the date of final acceptance inspection. This inspection and preparation of punch lists is an assist to the contractor primarily to avoid unnecessary delay in completion and assures more efficient final acceptance when scheduled. Copies of the list should be given to the contractor and the subcontractors. A copy to the landscape architect and a copy to the owner and inspectors of the works should also be provided.

3. Construction Completion Inspection:

a. **Conditional Acceptance:** Theoretically, on the date requested by the contractor for final acceptance of work all of the construction should be completed and in acceptable condition for delivery to the owner. This does not always occur and consequently a conditional acceptance is sometimes granted where it is in the best interest of the owner to take delivery of the site and begin occupancy or use of the facilities. The work should not be accepted unless corrective items are of minor nature and do not conflict with the intended use of the facilities. The landscape architect should exercise judgment in determining whether a conditional acceptance is appropriate in view of the client's need for the site and the likelihood for the contractor following up promptly with corrective work that would be required as a condition of acceptance. A definite time limit should be set for completion of corrective work if a conditional acceptance is granted. All corrective work items should be indicated in a punch list similar to the pre-final punch list that was been prepared earlier.

b. **Final Acceptance:** Final acceptance of the work should be granted when all of the construction work has been fully completed in an acceptable manner. The date of this should be recorded officially and all parties notified. This becomes the terminal date for the contract period and the commencement of the lein period where that is in effect. It should also be the terminal date for any change orders to the contract either in amount or additional work as far as the contractor's responsibilities are concerned with respect to the original contract. Final acceptance of the contract may be granted at the end of all construction work and the beginning of the maintenance period if such is designated, or a maintenance period may overlap a portion of the completion of construction work and run beyond the final acceptance date. Alternatively, the final acceptance may not be granted until completion of the maintenance period.

The procedure for final acceptance under one of these three terms should be clearly stated in the contract documents.

4. Maintenance Period:

Landscape and site development projects involving substantial amounts of plant material installations including grass, ground cover, trees and shrubbery should include a maintenance period which, in effect, is an establishment period for determining plant survival. The length of the maintenance period will vary depending on the locality, the client's desires and the time of year as it relates to establishment of the various types of plants. The landscape architect should exercise judgment in determining and specifying the length of the maintenance period, taking into consideration when the work is most likely to be completed. Compensation for the maintenance period may be included in the contract amount or it may be set up in the contract documents as a separate item either for a fixed period at a fixed price or on a time interval basis. In some cases it might be desirable to stipulate certain operations that are to be done during the maintenance period on a time and material of a cost plus fixed fee basis. A construction contract may be set up for the contractor to assume all risks and liabilities regardless of weather conditions or other factors for a stipulated period of time. The landscape architect and owner might also elect to have specific tasks done at a fair and equitable price depending on variable weather conditions and other factors that would change the required maintenance needs for manpower, materials, etc., need for a suitable plant establishment period. In some cases where the owner is not prepared to assume the maintenance operation due to a shortage of manpower or a lack of budget the contract may have the contractor continue maintenance for a longer than normal period of time, until the owner's funds or manpower are available.

5. **Notice of Final Acceptance and Recording:**
Immediately following the date of final acceptance of the contract a written notice of final acceptance should be sent to the contractor, to the owner, and other interested parties such as the bonding company, insurance underwriters, etc., relating to the construction operation. Contract documents may stipulate that the landscape architect will be the party responsible for final acceptance; in cases where the owner reserves the right of final acceptance, however, it is usually granted upon the advice and recommendation of the landscape architect. The written notice of final acceptance should be recorded with the county recorder, or equivalent, for contracts that have been recorded to establish beginning and termination date of the contract period. This serves as public notification for commencement of the mechanic's lien period also.

6. **Certifications of Compliance:**
A variety of certifications for compliance with contract document provisions and government jurisdiction statutes and requirements may be needed for final acceptance of the contract. All certificates of compliance required for a particular project should be predetermined and included in the construction documents so that the contractor and others are aware of what will be required for final acceptance. These certifications may include such things as use of all-American products only, compliance with state and federal labor laws, compliance with water quality controls, compliance with building code requirements, etc. Quality of some materials is required under certain contract conditions, particularly for government agencies. This may include certificates of compliance with design mixes for concrete, A.S.T.M. specifications or other accepted testing procedures for materials, plant material inspection and quarantine requirements of local governing agencies, etc. Procedures for obtaining certifications, delivery to acceptance parties and distribution of copies should be pre-established and made routine during the course of the construction operation.

7. **Mechanics Lien Statutes and Releases:**
Most states have statutes that provide protection for material suppliers and sub-contractors to assure that they received monies due for delivery of materials and providing of services for a contractor on a specific project. The party having a claim against the contractor can file a lien against the owner of the subject property in order to recover the amounts due each individual that may file a claim. By state statute there is usually a limitation on the period in which a sub-contractor or supplier may file such a lien ranging from thirty to ninety days after acceptance of the construction contract. Usually 10 percent of the total contract amount is held back for this lien period to assure funds available for paying any liens that may be filed against the contract, any such amounts being deducted from the contractor's final amount due. A common practice is to demand that the general contractor obtain mechanic's lien releases from all material suppliers and subcontractors prior to final acceptance and payment of his final withheld amount. A standard lien release form is used by many government agencies and large private business firms. If a landscape architect is to prepare and use an in-office mechanics lien release form it should be prepared with assistance of legal counsel to be sure it complies with the prevailing statutes.

8. **Withheld Funds:**
a. **Retention:** As stated earlier approximately 10 percent of the total payment should be withheld from final payment until assured that the contractor has paid all bills and satisfied all possible claimants for monies due under the contract. This should be normal procedure for even the smallest contract at least during the length of time of the statutory lein period.
b. **Unsatisfactory Work:** At the time of final inspection any portions of the work considered unacceptable would not be eligible for payment. In such cases a reasonable amount, equivalent to the cost of construction, should

be withheld until the work has been installed satisfactorily. In some cases the necessary funds may be used to retain another contractor to satisfactorily complete the work. A good set of contract documents should clearly specify that the landscape architect and/or owner has the right to have portions or all of the work installed in this manner if the contractor fails to perform satisfactorily.

c. **Damaged Property:** Construction sites having some improvments already in place and some natural valuable conditions such as mature trees, shrubbery, etc., that may be damaged during the course of construction by the contractor may require withholding of funds to assure correction of the damaged work. In the event of damage it is advisable to withhold the amount of repair from the next payment period for the contractor as leverage to get prompt repair work done. In some cases where the type of damage repair is beyond the scope of the contractor's capability, the funds should be withdrawn from the contract amount so that other qualified specialists may perform the repair work. In this case the cost of the construction repair should be deducted from the final contract amount unless the contractor's property damage insurance covers the cost of the repair work and is paid for under this method prior to final acceptance and payment to the contractor.

d. **Failure to Perform:** If a contractor voluntarily fails to perform any or all portions of the construction work, deliver certain materials, or supplies, required under contract conditions, or for other reasons does not meet the contractual obligations, the landscape architect and owner shall determine a fair and equitable amount to deduct from the contract price to have some other contractor do the work. In this condition it is advisable to release and remove the contractor from the site before having another contractor perform the work. This may include lengthy delays for a contractor wrapping up a project where certain incidental work that is supposed to be done is not performed promptly requiring reduction of his final contract amount in order to have the pick-up work done.

9. **Bonding Company Responsibility and Rights:**
A bonding company, usually an insurance surety firm, guarantees to the owner or buyer that the contract will be performed as required in the contract documents for the amount stated, and that in the event of failure of the contractor will provide funds for another to complete the construction work under the contract requirements.

In the event of failure of the contractor to perform it becomes the responsibility of the bonding company to have the work completed by others or to compensate the owner for the amount of the improvements that were not performed by the contractor. Frequently this will include reasonable damages to the owner and possible extra services that may be required of the landscape architect and consultants for another contractor to complete the work as provided under the contract. In providing such a guarantee the bonding company has certain rights as a part of this contractural obligation. The owner's rights should be clearly established in the construction documents to avoid unnecessary delays in completion of the construction work in the event of the contractor's failure to perfrom. The types of bonds required under the contract are usually included in the body of the construction documents in sample form. This would include the faithful performance of labor and material bonds. If the surety company is allowed to write their own type of bonds of these two types they will generally be written in favor of the surety company instead of the owner. It is advisable, therefore, for the landscape architect, with advice of counsel, to establish an acceptable bond form as needed for the construction project. The contract documents should stipulate that the bonding company has the right to remove a contractor from the project and to substitute one acceptable to the owner and landscape architect to complete the work. There should be a time limit established which may be the same as that established for the initial contractor, subjecting the bonding company to damages provisions stipulated in the contract documents as though they were the original contractor. In fairness to the bonding company holding this type of guarantee it is common practice to regularly advise them of the progress of the construction work, and upon completion and acceptance of the contract. A suitable bond form should include a continuing guarantee for the life of any required guarantees on materials, products, or workmanship as specified in construction documents to assure repair or replacement during the guarantee period in the event the contractor fails to act promptly or guarantee provisions.

10. **Penalties and Bonuses—Contract Period:**
Most construction contracts are based on prompt execution of the work-i.e. "Time is of the essence". Failure of the contractor to perform in a timely manner may be handled two ways: either by stipulating a stated amount for damages on a daily basis that would be deducted from the contractor or paid to the buyer/owner by the con-

tractor, or to include a provision for daily penalties for failure to perform by the terminal contract date, with a provision for bonuses for completion of the work in advance of the contract termination date. (Some states have statutes which make it mandatory in utilizing the penalty approach that a bonus be given for completion ahead of construction deadlines.) Be aware of local legal requirements in using either of these types of leverage for getting prompt execution of the work. Be aware, also, that enforcement of damages provisions or penalties must be strongly founded to be effective and to avoid follow-up arbitration or potential lawsuit. There must be clear cut evidence that there were no outside influences on the contractor's operations or ability to perform in order to properly invoke either damages or penalty provisions. It is very important, in this respect, to carefully evaluate and grant time extensions for any change orders during the course of the project. It is important, also, to have accurate records for inclement weather days that may affect contract operations, including days where portions of the contract crew were able to operate and those where the contractor was fully shut down due to weather conditions.

Post Completion

1. **As-Built Records:**
Construction projects including underground utility or irrigation lines should call for preparation of As-Built drawings at the construction site on a daily basis or as the work is being installed. The inspector or landscape architect should rigidly enforce compliance with this requirement to assure adequate recording of work as it is being installed. After completion and acceptance of the installation the As-Built information should be put on construction drawing originals and recorded as As-Built documents. The contract should not be accepted until any required As-Built records have been received from the contractor, usually delivered to the landscape architect on or before the date of final inspection.

2. **Catalogs, Manuals and Operating Instruments:**
Some construction projects will include manufactured parts and equipment where it is desirable for the owner and the owner's maintenance staff to have accurate records of the equipment installed including operating instructions. The contract documents should require one or more copies of all pertinent catalogs, spare parts lists, operating manuals, or instructions and guarantees to be delivered prior to final acceptance of the contract.

These should be delivered to the landscape architect for later delivery to the owner, or direct delivery to the owner with the contractor getting receipt for delivery to the landscape architect to assure compliance with the contract provisions.

3. **Spare Parts and Tools:**
For certain types of construction projects, including equipment requiring special tools, such as irrigation systems and maintenance equipment, some owners desire the contractor to supply these parts and tools as a part of the construction contract. The spare parts and tools should be delivered to the owner or to the landscape architect prior to final acceptance and payment for the total contract. If the contractor delivers them directly to the owner a receipt should be obtained and delivered to the landscape architect to assure contract complaince.

4. **Guarantees:**
A variety of guarantee types may be required by the landscape architect or the owner. These should be clearly specified in the construction documents and may be of two types—one, conditions of the guarantee specified in the contract documents, with the consigning of the contract being agreement to guarantee that portion of the work or materials; or, two, contractor delivery of a manufacturer's standard guarantee form to the owner, including a supplemental umbrella guarantee by the contractor for the same guarantee provisions. All guarantees should be delivered to the landscape architect prior to final acceptance for delivery to the owner. It is usually advisable for the landscape architect to retain a copy of all such guarantees in the project files.

5. **Replacements:**
Equipment failures are not unusual on any construction project. Guarantees include a one-time replacement of faulty equipment and parts. Any such replacements should be made with the same or equivalent acceptable product and installed in compliance with the original contract requirements. Reinstalled equipment or parts should bear the same guarantee life as the original part if reasonable and feasible. This must be evaluated carefully, however. If the original contract required, for instance, a one-year guarantee on a particular piece of equipment, and the original equipment installed and a replacement lasts one year, together they have satisfied the contract requirement and guarantee provisions. If the landscape architect and owner require full guarantee terms for original equipment and any replacement equipment it should be stated clearly in the construction documents, as it may influence the price of the contract.

6. Mechanics Lien Releases:

Before final payment to the contractor of amounts due to complete the contract and before notifying the bonding company, (if a bonded project) that the project is complete and acceptable, all mechanics liens should be cleared and releases obtained for all material, labor, suppliers, subcontractors and others that may have a financial interest in the contract. The contract documents may stipulate that all mechanic's lien releases are to be delivered to the landscape architect or to the owner. One or the other should carefully review all potential claimants to be sure that all possible releases have been obtained. Additionally, a general lien release should be obtained from the general contractor stating that all outstanding debts directly related to the contract have been cleared. In addition, the contract documents should stipulate that the owner would be held harmless in the event of any claims filed or law suits resulting from claimants after expiration of the lien period.

7. Follow Up:

The considerate and wise design professional will continue to provide a follow-up service well after the project is completed and the guarantee period over. This follow-up may be an annual or semi-annual visit to the project site followed by a written memorandum to the owner, outlining the observations recorded. The observations might deal with maintenance failures, changed uses affecting the original design, the availability of more modern and efficient equipment or fixtures, and so on.

It is usually difficult to charge for these follow-up services, but they can be highly rewarding in other ways. Satisfied clients are often repeat clients and they are a professional service enterprises best public relations and new client promotional source. Consistent follow-up practices show a special interest the client's need, and provide a meaningful on-going relationship with the client. Clients appreicate this, and are more likely to remain advocates for their consultants.

Of equal importance, follow-up activities can help insure that the original design intent is maintained and that the project continues to reflect the quality of the professional service enterprise's skills and capabilities. Poorly maintained projects as well as those which are arbitrarily changed without design help can be very poor public relations symbols which can become haunting evidence of poor follow-up procedures.

Completing the Project

Many design professionals find this final step to be the most difficult of all. Projects often tend to drag on and on. The last 10% of the effort seems to be the hardest to complete. More often than not, these problems arise from the lack of a clear understanding of what really constitutes a project's completion.

The preceeding section of this chapter dealt specifically with the subject of running the construction project and included information on "closing out the project". At this point it is appropriate, however, to state the importance of a clear and concise statement about what constitutes project completion, and how this will be determined and by whom. In the case of a construction project this is normally spelled out in the contract documents giving all parties a precise statement of completion requirements.

In non-construction activities, however, the method of articulating completion criteria is less clear. When the service activity involves a contract between a consultant and a client, the contract becomes the most appropriate instrument for defining completion criteria. Regrettably, very few consulting agreements recognize this most important concept. In the case of public agency or an academic program activity the completion criteria must be carefully defined in a project statement or program. In all forms of service activity completion criteria must be spelled out, and should not be changed without the expressed consent of all parties to the effort.

Chapter Fourteen Notes:

1. Faulkner, *Project Management with CPM*, R.S. Means Co., Inc., Duxbury, Mass., 1973
2. Samuel Bridges, These sections are reproduced in their entirety from the *Landscape Architects Handbook of Professional Practice* which is now out of print and has been replaced by this publication. In reuse, the Bridges material contains only minor changes and its use has been granted by the American Society of Landscape Architects.

Chapter Fifteen
Legal Concerns and Professional Liability

No design professional is immune to civil litigation resulting from claims of negligence.

Introduction

There was a time, not too long ago, when landscape architects could practice their profession without great concern for legal constraints or professional liability. Many landscape architects can still recall a time when practice, like life, was fairly simple and easily managed. A time when liability law suits were rare and when regulation of professional and project activity was mostly nonexistent. If such a time every really existed, it is today little more than a nostalgic memory.

Today, landscape architecture, like all professional endeavors, is practiced within a "maze-like" framework of Federal, State, and local laws, codes, regulations, ordinances, statutes, and bureaucratic pro-

cedures which are staggering in their complexity. Furthermore, the professions have been beset by a heightened public scrutiny which questions the reliability and benefit of nearly every professional act. The general principle laws governing contractural and civil responsibility are being applied with ever increasing frequency to professional activity. "We are witnessing what some authorities term a litigation explosion. The practice of a design profession seems particularly vulnerable."[1]

The increasing complexity and amount of regulatory law; the growing frequency of litigation against design professionals, and the generally minimal understanding most design professionals have of the

law and legal matters provides justifiable cause for concern. Together, these concerns threaten the very existence of the design professions.

The increased complexity and amount of regulatory law is an issue which must, for the most part, be addressed on a highly individualized basis. Practice impacts from this area of concern will vary greatly and will change according to practice form, location, size of organization, marketing approach, project types, and other variables. For these reasons a discussion of regulatory law goes well beyond the scope of this book. It is appropriate to mention, however, that this issue must be addressed by every prac-

tice firm and agency. Understanding the laws which govern practice is as important as having the other practice skills.

The issue of professional responsibility under contractual and civil law, however, applies without variation to all practice forms, regardless of size, location or activity. Contractural and civil law responsibilities cut through corporate or agency shields and directly affect each individual landscape architect on a personal as well as a professional basis.

Law and ethics demand that the (landscape) architect use reasonable care, be moderate in his (her) demands, and scrupulous in all professional relationships. Even this may not assure the (landscape) architect of freedom from litigation because he (she) may be sued as a result of an accident for which he (she) was not responsible.[2]

No design professional is immune from civil litigation. From the retired landscape architect providing gratuitous services, the teacher or government practitioner designing patios in their spare time, to the principals and employees of large multidisciplinary firms, all landscape architects face the possibility of litigation stemming from claims of negligence.

For a design professional to be charged with professional negligence is a serious matter. Even if the action proves unsuccessful or without merit and he (she) is vindicated, the damage to his (her) reputation lingers insidiously.[3]

Those who have suffered the emotional and physical strain of litigation will also report that win, lose or draw the financial costs are staggering. Even the financial protection offered by liability insurance fails to offset the full financial implications of litigation.

In this age of increasing legal complexity and the expanding doctrine of fault, it is not difficult to understand the rising number of litigation decisions against the design professionals. The reasons for concern over the perils of litigation are many and most compelling.

Cause for concern, however, should not become cause for panic. Studies have revealed, for instance, that most litigation can be traced to human rather than technical errors. Lack of interpersonal relationship skills, poor communication, and faulty problem solving and administrative decision making leads to more negligence suits than any other factor.[4] This book, throughout its course, has suggested that technical and theoretical competence was not sufficient to assure successful practice. There can be no more dramatic illustration of this point than the constantly increasing number of negligence suits which stem from human skill failings.

In spite of their obvious importance this chapter will not reiterate what has already been said in Part Three of this book about the human skills and their application to the practice of landscape architecture. This chapter will, however, provide an overview of the common legal issues involved in litigation which affect the design professions. This overview will place the utilization of human skills in perspective and provide the reader with a basic understanding of how they can be used to avoid financially and emotionally debilitating litigation.

The Law and Landscape Architecture

Almost every major construction project undertaken in the (years ahead) is likely to generate a lawsuit. In that lawsuit, it is almost certain that one of the accusations made by the complaining party will be that the party sued was somehow negligent and caused harm.[5]

Negligence is the primary culprit in litigation proceedings against design professionals. While everyone believes they understand the meaning of the term 'negligence', it has a special legal meaning and must be understood from that point of view. There are literally dozens of legal concepts which are encompassed by the term negligence. Too many, in fact, to discuss in this book. It is possible, however, to identify the most frequently encountered of these concepts as they relate to landscape architectural practice in all of its forms.

The Law of Tort:

The legal doctrine of fault or breach of duty forms the foundation for the law of tort. In lay terms, a tort is often defined as a civil wrong for which a legal court will grant a remedy.[6] In law this suggests that if someone has suffered damage; financial, property or bodily loss or injury, then someone else must be at fault. While the relationship between cause and effect is the issue of a tort case, both judges and juries, under encouragement of a proliferating number of high damage claims, are showing a marked propensity to shift the burden of proof from the accuser to the accused.

Tort Law is divided into two categories: unintentional and intentional. Intentional torts would include actions such as misrepresentation, deceit, and defamation of character. These practices are, gratefully, rare in the design professions, and cause little worry for the scrupulous practitioner. Unintentional torts, on the other hand, are of very real concern for they deal directly with the question of negligence.

Webster's New Collegiate Dictionary No. 8 defines negligence as the "...failure to exercise the care that a prudent person usually exercises". The courts and lawyers, however, apply a much more precise meaning than carelessness. In legal terms negligence usually involves four concepts:[7]
1. A duty of care,
2. A breach of the duty or standard of care,
3. Some causal connection between the breach of duty and,
4. Damages.

Each of these concepts requires some greater discussion:

1. Duty of Care: In every state the legal concept embodied in the duty of care doctrine follows a similar rationale. "All persons owe a duty to others to conduct themselves with a reasonable care in a way that an average, responsible and prudent person would in the same or similar circumstances."[8] The test of the duty of care is not what a specific person would do, but rather what an average reasonable person would do. The amount of care considered reasonable, however, increases as responsibility and skills required to perform a task increase. This is the duty or standard of care principle.

The design professional is an expert and as a result has an increased standard of care beyond that of the average person. The test of duty of care in the case of a design professional would be what a reasonable person with similar skills and specialized knowledge would do in similar circumstances. This suggests that in every profession there is a norm or level of skill and specialized knowledge to which all reasonable practitioners must adhere. For most landscape architects this presents little problem. For those professionals who wish to explore new areas or new technology, this concept of professional standard presents a real threat. Even simple deviations from the norm can present real problems. Varying the standard riser-tread relationship in the design of steps or stairways to create a special effect, for instance, might not be considered reasonable under the duty of care test.

2. Breach of Duty: A breach of duty or the standard of reasonable care occurs in two ways; an affirmative act or the failure to act (errors and ommissions), An affirmative act would include incorrect advice, drawings, details and/or specifications which resulted in some form of damage. Failing to provide necessary advice, or omission of a detail or specification which resulted in some form of damage, would be a failure to act type breach of duty.

3. Causal Connection: A connection between a breach of duty and damage must be shown to prove professional negligence. While it is often difficult to prove a connection between cause and effect, it is even more difficult to disprove a proported connection. With the burden of proof continually shifting to the accused this has become a serious problem.

Where the burden of proof rests with the accuser, the courts will normally apply one of two rules to determine the cause for damage in negligence cases:[8]

a. **The But-For Rule:** This rule is usually applied when a single act may have been the cause for damage and is used as follows: "If the complaining party would not have been damaged *but-for* the defendant's act or ommision, such act or ommision was then the cause of the damage."[8]

b. **The Main Factor Rule:** This rule is usually applied when two or more acts or ommissions may have been disproportionate causes for damage, or where one act or ommission alone would be insufficient to cause damage. Simply stated this rule says that the act which was the main or material factor should be the cause for damage. Frequently the term "proximate" cause is used to describe a main factor rule.

In many negligence cases every professional and contractor involved is named a defendent.

Courts and juries are affixing with increasing regularity, however, secondary and tertiary causes for damages. In most construction-oriented negligence suits all professionals associated, even remotely, with the project are named as defendants. In many cases judgements of causal connection are attributed to several and/or all of the parties named in the suit. In a single suit a judgement may be made against the prime consultant for overall responsibility, a sub-contract consultant for interim responsibility, and an individual professional for the causal act.

4. Damages: The complainant in a negligence suit must prove that damages or losses to person or property actually occurred. Since the basic purpose of damages in unintentional negligence cases is compensatory rather than punitive, the establishment of actual rather than perceived damage is necessary. This does not preclude, however, the assessment of damages for pain and suffering—assessments of often staggering proportions.

In any event, the complaining party must prove actual harm or loss, and cannot use the courts as a means of unjust enrichment, as shown by the following example:

A landscape architect designed a municipal swimming pool with a surrounding skid-free surface deck area. After construction bidding and the award of contract, but prior to commencing construction, a State Statute was discovered which required a 20% increase in the amount of deck area specified. The landscape architect redesigned the deck and modified the drawings and the contractor built the deck to its new dimensions. The contractor submitted an extras charge for the additional deck. The extra was approved and paid by the municipality. At the completion of the project, however, the municipality brought suit against the landscape architect to recover the extra costs. The suit claimed that the landscape architect committed an ommission error of negligence in the original design.

In this case, however, there was no actual damage. The municipality was, in fact, bound by the State Statute requiring the amount of deck actually built. The extra costs was appropriate to the amount of extra work. While the landscape architect's ommission act caused a "surprise" extra to the contract price, no real damage was caused. To make the landscape architect pay the difference between bid price and final cost would unjustly enrich the municipality.

In this example, the landscape architect's real error was human rather than technical. While it can be argued that the landscape architect should have more carefully researched regulations governing the design, any reasonable professional might have missed the statute which caused the extra. The real problem in this example was poor communication. The municipality approved and paid for the extra not really knowing why they were doing so. The landscape architect failed to clearly and fully explain the facts and to insist that all officials within the municipality's hierarchy agreed to the extra prior to its payment. In this case approval by the municipality's project director proved to be insufficient. The court ruled in favor of the landscape architect, but in fact the landscape architect suffered dramatic losses. To begin with, the liability insurance coverage did not include the first $5,000.00 of legal fees. More importantly, the trial was very time consuming and emotionally debilitating. The lost time represented thousands of dollars in lost fee production on other projects. The landscape architect also lost that particular municipality as a potential client for a good many years.

Special Duty Rules for Design Professionals:

Local legislation and jurisdictional precedent have imposed two specialized duties of care which impact most design professionals. The "expert" nature of the design professions makes them especially susceptible to the following two doctrines of law:

1. Doctrine of Respondeat Superior: This doctrine holds that employers are liable for the acts of their employees while performing within the scope of their employment duties. Even decisions and acts made without specific authorization would fall under this doctrine. This doctrine can even be applied when employees provide services outside of their normal employment duties, when such activity carries the implied endorsement of the employer. This is the major reason why most employers strictly prohibit "moon lighting" or outside the office consulting by their employees.

The doctrine of *Respondeat Superior* says that not only are individuals responsible for their actions, but also their superiors.

"Moonlighting" is frowned upon by most professional service enterprises and for good reason.

2. Doctrine of Gratuitous Service: This doctrine, sometimes referred to as the "good samaritan" doctrine, holds that volunteered and free services carry the same duty of care as do those services which have been solicited and for which a fee has been paid. This seems reasonable enough, but when one considers the nature and frequency of gratuitous service, the potential for liability disaster becomes evident. Consider the following example:

A landscape architect employed by a large consulting firm was called at work by a close friend. The friend was considering the purchase of a piece of property and called to seek zoning advice. The friend wished to know if the property could be developed in a certain way under its current zoning classification. Instead of suggesting that the friend come by the office to discuss the matter with the firm's zoning expert, the landscape architect decided to offer some gratuitous council. After a quick scan of the County Zoning Ordinance, the landscape architect reported that the desired use was allowed under the property's current zoning.

On the gratuitous advice received, the friend purchased the property only to find out later that the property was located in a special zoning district which overrode the County's zoning ordinance. Under the special district the property's development potential was severely limited. The friend had purchased nearly useless land.

In this example the landscape architect failed to exercise a reasonable standard of care. The advice was offered casually and without the normal expertise and concern shown by the consulting firm. Both the landscape architect and the employer would be liable for damages.

The Gratuitous Service Doctrine also has special applicability to those professional degree programs whose students provide gratuitous service to communities, neighborhood associations, park boards and so on. When Department or Program sponsorship is expressed or implied, as is normally the case with course work for credit, student efforts carry the same responsibility for reasonable care which is standard for the profession as a whole. This places the responsibility for student work squarely on the shoulders of the faculty under the *Respondeat Superior* Doctrine and no relief from liability is granted merely because the service was offered gratuitously.

Contract Pitfalls:

The subject of contracts was covered in some detail in Chapter Twelve. That discussion dealt with how to prepare a good contract. It did not deal with how to recognize and avoid a poor contract. Landscape architects are frequently required to sign contracts prepared by their clients or other parties. In most cases such contracts are perfectly legitimate documents and will recognize the two way nature of a contractural agreement. In some cases, however, clients may attempt to place greater than normal liability responsibility on the shoulders of the design professional. This is done in a number of ways but the most common are contract provisions which have one of the following headings:

Hold Harmless and Indemnity Clause
Warranty and Guarantee Clause
Defense and Indemnity Clause

The heading descriptions may vary, but in every case the purpose is to shift liability away from the client and to the design professional. Every design professional should be willing to assume fair and equitable responsibility to act in a reasonable way and to exercise the proper duty of care. To expect more is unreasonable and to sign a service agreement which codifies such an expectation could lead to professional disaster.

Business Records:

This section on the Law and Landscape Architecture concludes with a examination of the need to maintain proper business records. This subject was discussed in great detail in Chapter Twelve, but its significance to the issues discussed in this chapter makes it worthy of some reiteration.

A landscape architect does not need to be wrong to be sued. Innocent design professionals are sued frequently and they are required to offer as rigorous a defense as are those sued for legitimate reasons. The essential ingredient in a successful lawsuit defense is the accurate recreation of actual events. The claimant says one thing, the defendant says another. Who is right?'Deciding this question is the principal function of the Courts. Without admissible and reliable evidence it becomes difficult, indeed, to refute the claimant's position. If the actual facts cannot be documented, it may be difficult to prove innocence.

Written business records are usually considered a most reliable form of evidence, provided they are recognizably authentic and clearly a part of routine business procedures. The latter is perceived as a fundamental test of the authenticity of business records. If field inspection logs, for example, are not normally kept for projects under construction, the sudden appearance of a field inspection log as evidence will be highly suspect and may even be ruled inadmissible.

Maintaining clear and concise business records for every project must be standard operating procedure for every professional service firm. Moreover, these procedures must be designed to build chronological historical records of a service undertaking from its inception to its conclusion. The records must be detailed and clearly identify all decisions, instructions, changes, progress check points, inspection results, and other activities impacting the outcome of the work effort. In a court of law, unwritten evidence may be considered hearsay and is always considered less reliable than written records.

The American Institute of Architects recommends that the following written records be maintained for all projects:[9]

- Memoranda of all conferences
- Names and addresses of all parties concerned with the project
- A list of all data furnished by the client
- Copies of all communication to and from the client, to include memoranda of all telephone communication
- Memoranda listing all work product submitted to the client with date of submittal and date of acceptance and/or approval by the client
- Proposed and actual completion dates for each service activity or phase of service production
- Consultant's production budget and detailed costs for each phase of service
- Date of submission and approval of drawings and other required data by governmental review and regulatory agencies
- Final construction estimate
- Amounts of all bids and sub-bids

- Date of issuance and return of all documents by contractors and sub-contractors as well as agents of the client
- Date of approval or acceptance along with copies of surety bonds, certificates of insurance, progress schedules, tests, and schedules of values
- Dates and results of shop drawing and sample review
- Copies of certificates for payment and change orders
- Reports from project inspectors and field representatives
- Dates of approval or rejection of work or materials
- Copies of substantial completion, semi-final and final inspections, and certificate of completion
- Final construction costs
- Summary of all project service expenses
- Photographs taken before, during and after construction

Most of the data included in this record keeping list can be maintained on standard forms or check sheets. The actual appearance of these forms will vary from one service organization to the next and may also vary from one project type to another. The standardization approach not only simplifies the record keeping process, it adds to the routine nature of the process. Not only are these records important to effective project and business management, as Chapter Twelve pointed out, they could well mean the difference between winning and losing an unjustified lawsuit.

Professional Liability Protection

General:

To fully understand the precautions and tools available to protect against liability claims it is necessary to look at the fundamental cause for such claims.

> Litigation of any type is nurtured by controversy; and controversy results from a breakdown in understanding between the parties involved. Correspondingly, study reveals that a large number of lawsuits brought against design professionals are caused, not by technical errors or incompetence, but by deterioration in relations between the design professional and the claimant. Minor disputes are cumulative. They build up to the final breakdown. When it comes, it is too late for negotiation. A lawsuit is the result.[10]

Chapter Fifteen has already make it clear that communications breakdown, poor interpersonal relations, and inefficient business procedures can be viewed as a primary cause of liability claims. It may be said, therefore, that the best protection against liability claim is not formal insurance, but rather effective communications, good interpersonal relationship skills, and the employment of proper business procedures on a routine basis.

Even the most effectively and creatively run professional service enterprise, however, faces the potential of liability claims. With this concern in mind, this chapter concludes with a look at formal arbitration of potential claim situations, a method of limiting liability and finally at liability insurance.

Formal arbitration of contract disputes can provide a viable alternative to costly law suits, but the process has pitfalls which must be carefully understood.

Arbitration:

"Arbitration is a formal procedure for the resolution of disputes arising from the discharge of contract obligations."[11] The arbitration concept is based on the premise that settlement of potential claim disputes by an impartial panel of knowledgeable experts is far superior to resolution by the courts or lay juries. The premise also suggests that the arbitration process is both faster and less expensive than formal litigation. There is a considerable amount of contrary opinion concerning the later premises, but before considering that opinion, a look at the arbitration process itself should come first.

The arbitration process in most instances is used only when the parties have stipulated to it in their service agreement or contract. Such stipulations bind the parties to the arbitration process as a means of settling contractual disputes. The specific wording of such contract stipulations have been devised by the American Arbitration Association which has also established the Construction Industry Arbitration Rules normally followed in such proceedings.[12]

Arbitration procedures come into effect only when informal negotiations to settle a dispute have broken down. By contractural agreement both parties are bound to abide by the resolution of their dispute by an arbitration panel, usually appointed by the American Arbitration Association.

An arbitration panel is composed of three knowledgable representatives from the construction industry. They are selected in a number of different ways, with the actual procedure identified in the arbitration stipulation of the contract. One popular technique involves the appointment of one panel member by each of the two contracting parties. The third panel member is selected by the two original appointees.

In another popular procedure, the American Arbitration Association submits a list of qualified potential panelists to both parties. Each party may delete from the list those people who are not acceptable and then rank order the remainder from most acceptable downward. They must leave at least three names on the list. Both lists are returned to the American Arbitration Association which makes the final panel selection attempting to appoint the fairest possible group.

The arbitration panel will conduct a hearing allowing both parties to present their position in regard to the dispute in question. The panel will then, on the basis of the evidence presented, determine a final resolution of the dispute. As noted earlier, both parties have agree to abide by this decision.

On the surface, arbitration appears to be an ideal alternative to civil action in resolving disputes. In many situations it is exactly that. There are, however, many aspects of arbitration which can create problems for a design professional.

First of all, an arbitration agreement is a two party agreement. Arbitration decisions have no binding affect on third parties, who may in fact have a considerable stake in the decision. The design professional's liability insurance underwriter, for instance, may not feel obligated to abide by an arbitration decision in which they had no participating role. Of even greater concern, the two party arbitration concept precludes the direct involvement of a manufacturer or materials supplier whose product rather than professional error, may be at fault.

Secondly, the arbitration process does not allow discovery proceedings. In civil law a defendant has the right to examine a claimant's files and determine the exact extent of the evidence in support of the claim. This lack of discovery process in arbitration can create great difficulties in developing a rational and effective defense.

Finally, the arbitration process allows the introduction of any form of evidence no matter how irrelevant or non-authentic it may be. Irrelevant information can cause great confusion and non-authentic information can be severely damaging. The civil courts follow very carefully defined rules of evidence which, while strict, protect all parties involved.

For these reasons, arbitration must be viewed as a sometimes useful alternative to civil action, not a panacea for the courtroom. Professionals should check with their liability insurance underwriters and their attorneys before agreeing to an arbitration clause in a service agreement.

Limitation of Liability:

The search for a rational approach to professional liability protection inevitably leads to the Limitation of Liability concept. The Limitation of Liability concept is just what it says. Limits can and should be set on the amount of liability a design professional should assume. The concept recognizes that design professionals, like all humans, are not perfect, nor does the law expect them to be. The historical truth of the matter, however, points in a different direction. Design professionals are being sued for damages with increasing regularity, and the judgements become more excessive each day.

Not only have lawyers adopted the strategy of suing anyone connected with the project in hopes that someone will be made to pay, the courts and lay juries have shown an inclination to award judgements based more on sympathy for the injured party than on the often bewildering technical facts. Together these facts of American life prompt more and larger suits to be filed. The design professions have joined the medical profession on the civil action "chopping block".

While our legal system is flexible, it is unlikely that even the combined strength of all the design professions could effect a significant change in the current state of affairs. The legal profession's jealous defense of the right to redress and the prevailing sympathetic attitude of lay juries for consumer rights could take decades to modify. In the meantime, the design professions are in desperate need of reasonable protection from unjustified and extravagant liability claims.

The Limitation of Liability concept can provide exactly the kind of protection needed.

The concept implies a belief that a person acting in good faith on behalf of another will be responsible in a reasonable measure to that second person, but should not be jeopardized by enormous penalities when unexpected contingencies occur. Limitation of liability, as espoused by design professionals, would establish a reasonable assumption of liability on their part in proportion to their fee. It would have the effect of bringing some types of claims for damages back into a reasonable perspective so that the issues involved could be faced on a more realistic and less expensive basis, and still be equitable to all parties concerned.[13]

This concept is not new and is utilized by many other gorups and organizations, including the maritime shipping industry, Security and Exchange Commission lawyers, financial analysts, interstate truckers, railroads, hotels and others. The concept finds its origins with Phoenician ship captains before the birth of Christ. Faced with enormous penalties when their ships were sunk or lost, they solved the problem by contracting for a limitation on their cargo liability not to exceed the value of the ship's hull. This tradition has lasted for more than three thousand years and is now a doctrine of International Maritime Law.[14]

The Limitation of Liability concept can only be initiated through the service contract between the design professional and the client. A limitation of liability clause in the contract is not dissimilar to the one used by the Phoenician ship captains. It binds the client to a liability ceiling, usually equal to the total expected fees for the project. The same clause will obligate the client to include a similar proviso in all construction contracts binding the contractor and sub-contractors in the same way.

The Limitation of Liability concept is a fair and appropriate method of dealing with the increasing number and escalating costs of liability claims. These costs must eventually be returned to the consumer and any reduction in them will benefit all. It must be pointed out, however, that the limitation of liability approach does not bind anyone other than the signers to the service and construction agreements. Liability would not be limited in the event of a suit filed by anyone else.

Most professional liability suits, however, are brought by parties involved in the contract for services or construction. For this reason, the Limitation of Liability concept makes great sense. It is available now to all professionals. Its implementation requires only inclusion of appropriate provisions in professional service contracts and the ability to convince clients that such a concept is fair to all. This last concern might frighten some design professionals. Why would a client want to sign such an agreement? Wouldn't public clients be especially difficult to convince? These are reasonable questions. The historic record, however, clearly shows that both public and private clients can be convinced that the approach is fair and valid.

The overriding fact is that limitation of liability provisions are beneficial to all contracting parties. Liability costs must be passed along to the client in the long run and are frequently built into service fees. The limitation of liability provision often allows for a lower fee for services. Moreover, the limitation of liability provision puts everyone on notice that the project is to be run in the most businesslike fashion, and that casual interpretation of the plans and specifications will not be tolerated. This provides insurance against careless bidding and the subsequent rash of change orders and requests for extra construction costs. It is just good sensible business and every-

one benefits. *Untangling the Web of Professional Liability* (see note 1) offers excellent advice on selling the limitation of liability concept to both public and private clients.

Liability Insurance:

The ultimate protection against liability claims is insurance. In the insurance business, the term is "loss prevention", and there are several insurance underwriters who specialize in errors, ommissions, and breach of duty insurance for design professionals.

To understand how loss prevention insurance works it is necessary to understand the three categories of liability claims. First, are those involving only bodily injury or death. The second are those involving only property damage (remedial costs) or economic loss. The third category includes those which involve a combination of bodily injury and property damage or economic loss.[15]

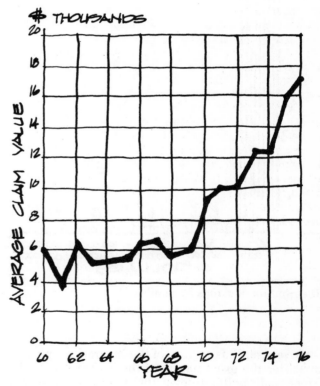

Severity of claims.
First $250,000.00 layer of insurance[15]

Most claims against design professionals fall within the second category. It is also interesting to note that the vast majority of all liability claims against design professionals are for $25,000.00 or less.[16]

Liability insurance underwriters, like all insurance

carriers, maintain detailed actuarial records, and predicate their insurance offerings and premium rates on these constantly changing data. The same data is helpful to the design professional in selecting the offering most appropriate to their specific practice form and the subsequent level of liability exposure. As a result, policies may be widely varied and it is difficult to describe a standard insurance coverage package. There are, however, certain elements of every policy that require careful attention and which can be used to tailor the final coverage to suit specific needs.

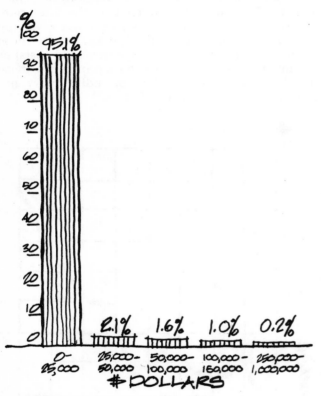

Distribution of claims by number.[15]

Coverage: This section of the insurance agreement specifies the exact nature of the coverage provided. Most basic policies cover the insured's liability for errors, ommissions or negligent acts arising from the performance of professional service activities. Coverage should also extend to all partners, directors, stockholders and employees while acting on behalf of the insured. The coverage can also be made retroactive to cover past activities, or extend to provide continued protection after retirement. The coverage options are many and must carefully reflect the specific needs of the insured. The exact amount of dollar protection is also determined in this section. Many policies are written with a deductible provision which eliminates coverage from zero up to a specified starting point. The higher the deductible amount, the lower the premium cost.

Exclusions: All liability policies contain coverage exclusions or specific liabilities against which the insurance will not protect. The number of exclusions can be reduced by increasing the premium costs. It is imperative that the exclusion section of the insurance policy be carefully examined. It is quite possible that a frequent activity of the insured may be excluded from coverage under the policy.

Territory: Liability insurance policies are normally written for specific time frames and for specific geographical areas. This is a reasonable provision and relates directly to premium costs. A firm or individual whose practice activity is confined to a single state need not pay for coverage in all fifty states. If a firm or individual suddenly expanded practice activity into several states, however, a single state policy would need to be modified.

Settlement: This policy section defines the conditions under which a claim may or will be settled out-of-court. These conditions will vary greatly from one policy to the next and it is important that the insured know exactly what they are. Some policies may prohibit out-of-court settlement, while others may set upper or lower limits to settlement. The design professional may have little choice in the matter unless this aspect is determined in the policy agreement.

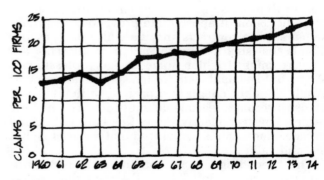

Frequency of claims[15]

The compelx and peculiar nature of the liability issue, as well as, the complicated nature of insurance terminology blend to make the question of liability insurance difficult for many design professionals whose decision to seek its protection is blocked by confusion and procrastination. The need for reliable protection, however, is very real. No practitioner is immune and even a small liability claim can be devastating without some form of protection. Not only does liability insurance protect against financial ruin in a very real sense, it provides an important measure of mental comfort to the insured.

Insurance underwriters in the liability field have proved to be important allies to the design professions. They provide valuable advice on business practices designed to eliminate liability causing procedures and the development of sound practices. In the event of a claim they are of immense value. Their counsel and advice can help make an otherwise debilitating claim at least go smoothly and with some sense of perspective. Liability insurance underwriters provide an important service to the design professions and they deserve great credit for their efforts.

Conclusion

The material covered in this chapter is complex, especially to those who have neither a legal nor insurance underwriters background. To further confound the situation, the scope of this book does not allow an indepth study of the subject matter. The chapter provides only an overview and an introduction to the primary areas of concern.

Four important references were used in the preparation of this chapter. Three of these were prepared by the principal insurance underwriters in the professional liability area. These references are noteworthy and important publications and should be in every landscape architect's library. The specific publications are given in the footnotes to this chapter. Those published by the Design Professionals Insurance Company of San Francisco, California, and by the Victor O. Schinnerer and Company, Inc. of Washington, D.C. are of special merit.

Chapter Fifteen Notes:

1. Howell & Howell, *Untangling the Webb of Professional Liability*, Risk Analysis & Research Corporation Publication, 2nd Edition, 1976, Design Professional Insurance Co., San Francisco, Cal.
2. American Institute of Architects, "Legal Concerns", Chapter 19, *Architect's Handbook of Professional Practice*, AIA, Washington, D.C., 1969.
3. Ibid 1
4. Ibid 1
5. Design Professionals Insurance Company, *A Collection of Information That Will be Valuable to Design Professionals in Private Practice Who Are Interested in Reducing Their Professional Liability Exposure*, DPIC San Francisco, Cal., 1974
6. Ibid 5
7. Ibid 5
8. Ibid 5
9. Ibid 2
10. Ibid 1
11. Ibid 2
12. Ibid 2
13. Ibid 2
14. Ibid 5
15. Victor O. Schinnerer & Company, Inc., "Types of Professional Liability Claims", *Guidelines For Improving Practice*, Vol, ix, No. 3, Washington, D.C., 1979
16. Ibid 15
17. Ibid 2

PART FIVE
CONCLUSION

Chapter Sixteen
Advocacy, Politics and a
Professional Association

Courtesy of the Student Chapter of The American Society of Landscape Architects at the University of Kentucky.

Introduction

So, you want to be a Landscape Architect? Surely it is safe to assume that most who read this book aspire to be, or are already, landscape architects. Some, in both categories, share a deep commitment to the profession and know exactly where they are going and why. Others may have small doubts and nagging fears about their skills or their ability to use their skills effectively. Still others may even wonder if they have chosen the right profession.

All of these feelings have been, historically, voiced by students and young professionals across the country, and always will be. These feelings, in their own way, are healthy. They represent the beginning of the maturation process, the soul searching which preceeds the highly refined commitment to landscape architecture so common among its practitioners.

While certainly some students and young professionals "drop out", the great diversity of the profession provides opportunity doorways for nearly every graduate. This unique practice diversity demands many different kinds of skills, and can accommodate professionals with varied personalities, outlooks, and interests. In these terms, very few landscape architects are alike. Some have beards while others are clean shaven. Some are skilled designers while others are public administrators. Some specialize in large scale land use computer modeling while others design roof-top gardens.

There is no landscape architect "mold"; no standard module or neat description which must be matched, in order to succeed in the profession. There is, of course, a common body of knowledge shared by those who practice the profession, but beyond that core of information and skill lies a world of application potential so vast it often staggers the imagination.

The profession, because of its great diversity, even has difficulty reaching a concensus definition of itself. As Chapter One of this book pointed out, the definition of the profession is constantly changing. It is a dynamic definition not a static one. Yet, throughout all of its many changes, the profession's ethic of land and people has always survived.

So you want to be a Landscape Architect? Bravo! The profession needs you and welcomes you. With this hearty welcome, however, the profession charges you with a special responsibility. You are charged with the special task of devoting every skill and energy you have to moving the profession forward. The profession has reached its maturity but has much growing yet to do. Your growth as a professional will correspond directly to the growth of the profession itself. What you give to the profession and what you get back as a practitioner will be directly linked.

Chapter Sixteen is devoted to explaining this special responsibility. The task is both an individual and a collective effort. Performing the task can be exciting and rewarding, but is occasionally filled with disappointment and what appears to be thankless labor. Those who have accepted the charge before you have found the rewards to far outweigh the disappointments. The task, nonetheless, must be undertaken and the charges are clear.

Firstly, you are charged with the task of becoming an advocate; a strong and powerful spokesperson for the profession. Secondly, you are asked to develop and utilize "clout" effectively and wisely for yourself, your organization, and your profession. Finally, you are asked to learn, understand and utilize the system of political power and governmental decision making within which the profession must function. You must become politically astute.

All of this suggests that if the profession is to grow and move forward, it must rely not only on the quality of its executed works, but also upon the advocacy, clout and political skills of its practitioners. If the profession is to assume any real leadership role and impact the decision making process which is the real force of change on the landscape, then the profession must place special demands on its practitioners to better understand the system, to speak out clearly and powerfully, and to act individually and collectively on behalf of the land and its people.

Much has been said in this book about human skills; what they are and why they are important to professional success. This chapter reiterates the special importance of human skills, for it is largely through them that effective advocacy, clout and access to the power systems is achieved.

Advocacy

There can be no question that the profession requires more and better skilled advocates. Advocacy, to be effective, requires highly developed communication skills, a highly refined dedication to and understanding of the profession, unquestionable professional competence, and a special aura of credibility.

Not all landscape architects will acquire this combination of talents, but all should aspire to achieve them. Many do possess them, however, and most could easily develop them with encouragement and practice. Moreover, every landscape architect will, at one time or another, be called upon to explain or support the profession, and some advocacy skill development is important to every practitioner.

Webster's New Collegiate Dictionary No. 8 offers the following definition:

ad.vo.cate, n. 1. one that pleads the cause of another. 2. one that defends or maintains a cause or proposal.

Lawyers are perhaps the best known and most highly skilled advocates. Functioning under Webster's first definition, lawyers plead the cause of their clients in the court room, in the preparation of contracts, in nearly every action they perform. They are skilled listeners and skilled communicators, able to speak in simple and passionate terms or in complex legal language. If their communication skills are not oral they use the written word. They must have at least one of the two skills in order to survive. And of course, they must possess a thorough understanding of a highly complex and technical body of knowledge.

Lawyers are also process oriented. They prepare their cases and legal positions in much the same way landscape architects apply process to design and problem solving. In many ways, the two professions are very much alike. Lawyers, however, know from the very first day in law school that advocacy is critical to their profession, and they work hard to develop the appropriate skills.

Upon serious consideration, shouldn't landscape architecture be just as advocacy oriented as the law profession? Are not landscape architects also called upon to advocate a client's cause or to support a larger cause like the fragility of the landscape? Whether a client's cause is an appropriate siting for a new home or a land use plan for thousands of acres, the landscape architect is responsible for advocating the work or service product. The answer to the questions posed is most definitely, yes.

In their professional responsibility, landscape architects can not afford to be any less effective as advocates than the most skillful lawyer. A client's problem, creatively solved but poorly advocated, runs the risk of remaining a problem with no solution at all.

In addition to the responsibility to advocate effectively for a client's cause, lies the special task of advocating the profession's cause. More closely aligned to Webster's second definition, this advocacy task becomes the responsibility of all landscape architects. Landscape architecture is the cause, and while some non-landscape architects may herald its virtues, its practitioners must become its principal advocates.

The cause may be championed in many ways, and certainly includes finely executed works and satisfied clients. The advocacy role cannot be left, however, to this approach alone. The advocacy process must begin in the city halls and county court houses and go beyond them to the state houses and the nation's capital as well. The process includes public speaking, volunteerism, community involvement, and a willingness to give of one's self.

Those who actively undertake the profession's advocacy role will find some very interesting spin-off benefits. In performance of the advocacy process, professionals can concurrently build personal clout and develop the skills and contacts necessary to access and influence the political power structure.

Being an advocate for the profession and developing clout are simultaneous functions. Together they open doors which might otherwise remain closed. Frequently, these are doors of access to the decision making process which guides and directs the look of the landscape in much more powerful ways than the individual landscape architect can.

Clout

Webster's New Collegiate Dictionary No. 8 offers eight vastly different definitions for the term clout. These range from a "blow with the hand" to "hitting a ball a long distance". The definition of interest here, however, is stated quite simply: "pull, influence, (informally); political power"

Of these rather straightforward terms the ones most appropriate to this discussion are influence and political power. The latter term, however, is not intended to conjure a "Boss Tweed" image, but rather to suggest the development of power sufficient to influence the political decision making process in ways sensitive to the land and its people.

Taken together, clout building and advocacy are really selling procedures. The process includes selling one's self, one's work organization, and one's profession. They are usually accomplished in that order. Each part of the process is, however, mutually supportive and for most seasoned practitioners they merge into a single function.

Selling Yourself: Developing clout begins with selling one's self. This strongly suggests that before someone can begin to sell a product, a skill, or a profession, they must be accepted as a living, feeling, human being. Every successful salesperson understands this simple fact of life. There must be a rapport established between seller and buyer before a transaction of any significance can be consumated.

Lee Davis of the Goodkin Executives consulting firm in Westlake Village, California suggests that goal-orientation is the most important starting point in effective personal selling.[1] Davis suggests that goal-oriented people have consciously made, and usually reduced to writing, four basic decisions:

1. They have established professional, civic, and personal goals for specified time periods.
2. They have honestly and carefully identified their strengths and weaknesses.
3. They have quantified and set out their most significant accomplishments and noted their most saleable features.
4. They have developed a set of immediate objectives, any one of which will put them on the road to achieving their goals.

Those people who are goal-oriented and who have reduced this orientation to writing are well on their way to developing real clout for themselves. They know what tools they have to work with and how they can be most effectively used. They are ready to begin the personal selling process.

At this point, the most important element in selling one's self becomes involvement. for the young practitioner this must be implemented on several fronts. Involvement in the affairs of one's neighborhood, community, employment organization, and professional organization should be undertaken simultaneously.

Selling one's self means involvement.

Initially, this multi-faceted involvement will be very demanding and the inclination to remain comfortably behind one's drafting table will be strong. Involvement means giving, not taking. It means listening, learning and participating. Involvement means work. There is, however, no substitute for involvement in the clout building process.

Throughout the clout building process it is the human you, not necessarily the professional you, which provides the foundation for real clout. It will be your organizational and leadership skills that will be put to work. When the community learns that you are good at organizing a fund raising drive or a special event, they will inferentially assume that you are equally good in your professional endeavors. Effective involvement, that which is freely given and competently done, soon manifests into leadership roles. People and groups will begin to seek you out for increasingly more important tasks. Your network of contacts will expand. Your ability to move freely about the community and within the profession will

be greatly enhanced. Your role within your organization will also expand as your community and professional involvement increases. You are building clout. People seek your help and advice and you are being listened to. As long as you have the ability to deliver what you promise, your clout will increase in direct proportion to your involvement efforts.

The process continues throughout your professional career. While it begins modestly, its potential to grow is unfettered. Soon, you may be asked to serve on a very important special committee of the Mayor's. Next you may well be asked to chair an equally important task force. As a result you will have gained access to one of the community's most important people and those who serve with you are among the most influential people in the community. Your volunteer involvement can also lead to other important and clout filled community positions. You may be asked to serve on the Planning Commission or to be a director of the Historic Commission. There is no mystery to this clout building process. The part is clearly marked and the rewards can be spectacular.

As your network of contacts expands, your ability to access the community system and leadership is greatly enhanced.

The rewards for community involvement come in dozens of packages. There is the emotional satisfaction which comes from helping people and supporting worthwhile causes. There is the intellectual high which accompanies the hundreds of encounters with people of diverse and stimulating interests. There is the psychological satisfaction derived from dozens of lasting and very special friendships which go hand in glove with meaningful involvement in community and professional affairs.

From a pragmatic point of view there are also direct financial rewards. Job advancement results as involvement contacts become clients or provide access to potential projects. As your firm or agency grows, so do you, and your clout has a direct bearing on the growth of your organization. Your clout becomes your organization's clout and your organization's prestige will grow in proportion to its total clout and, so too, will the organization's ability to reward those who serve it best.

At some point along the clout building path, the opportunity to become an effective advocate for the profession will present itself on an ever increasing basis. You may, for example, be asked to speak to the Kiwanis Club or the League of Women Voters about landscape architecture or some aspect of it which interests you most. A case in point is a Cleveland, Ohio landscape architect, who in 1978 was asked to speak about landscape architecture to the Downtown Rotary Club. The landscape architect did so and also showed the film "Legacy for Living". At the conclusion of the presentation 600 Rotarians presented the profession and its advocate with a standing ovation.

"Legacy For Living" gets a standing ovation from the Cleveland Rotary Club.

Selling Your Organization: Building clout for and selling your organization is markedly similar to selling one's self. Goal-oriented organizations who are prepared to involve themselves in their community and their profession will have little difficulty in building clout.

The process begins when each member of the organization is encouraged to sell themselves and build personal clout. To a very large extent, an organization's clout is a measure of the collective clout of its employees. Beyond this encouragement of individual clout building, the organization's principal officers must devote a considerable portion of their time and effort to the clout building process. While an organization may survive with employees who have not developed clout, it cannot survive the absence of clout in its' principal officers. Unlike the major product and service organizations who build substantial clout through media promotion and financial assets, most landscape architectural service enterprises must rely, almost exclusively, on people power.

Within the profession there is a collective role in the clout building process. Both self-selling and organizational-selling can be dramatically assisted by the collective efforts of the entire profession. The film "Legacy for Living" which brought 600 Rotarians to their feet, was a collective professional effort under the sponsorship of the American Society of Landscape Architects. The role of a professional society as a collective tool will be discussed at the conclusion of this chapter. It is important to recognize at this juncture, however, the value of collective effort to the clout building process.

Clout building has another important goal. It provides access to the political and community power structure and the accompanying ability to influence those decisions which so dramatically impact the world in which we live. Landscape architects possess very special skills and insights which, when put to effective use, can aid in very positive ways the future of the natural and man-made environment. The really important decisions about these matters, however, are not being made on the drawing boards, but in very different, and to many landscape architects, very alien places.

Politics

Landscape architecture has been called, by some of its practitioners, the most politically naive profession in the United States. While the fairness of this statement may be questioned, there can be no doubt about the profession's comparative lack of political awareness. Among the design professions, landscape architecture has a most meager track record on political astuteness. The civil engineers are aware, from their earliest college training, that their work effort is constantly monitored by and filtered through the political and bureaucratic machinery.

Too few landscape architects really understand the political and decision making systems of their communities.

The civil engineer quickly becomes efficient at understanding, accessing, and functioning within the political system. They are politically astute. The other engineering professions, the planning profession, the environmental professions, and most others who represent or serve the design professions have developed equally keen political acumen. Only architects and landscape architects seem to stand alone in their special world, exhibiting a kind of political aloofness which has greatly minimized their ability to impact the real decision making process in this country.

Certainly there are notable exceptions to this situation. Most highly successful landscape architectural practitioners have trained themselves to be politically effective. They have learned the political system and how to work within it. These skills are utilized on an almost daily basis. Their success as practitioners, in fact, can usually be directly attributed to their political skills.

The preponderance of landscape architects, however, exhibit a strong reluctance for political involvement. They hold rather deep seated reservations about mixing political activism with the creative function. They feel that compromise, a mainstay of the political process, will impair their creativity and cause design solutions of an unacceptable nature. Moreover, there is a kind of unspoken belief that politics is undignified, even "dirty", and that association with the process will degrade both their personal and professional lives. This latter feeling has been further reinforced by the popular wave of mistrust and disrespect for politicians which swept the nation following the Viet Nam War and Watergate.

Psychological profiling also points out the common link between creativity and introverted personality traits. Highly creative people are inclined to be less outgoing and much more reserved in the nature of their personal contacts. Since most political figures are extroverts and exhibit very different personality traits, many creative landscape architects will feel uncomfortable in their presence.

Obviously, not every landscape architect is an introvert. Neither are all introverts incapable of developing political acumen. What does seem apparent, however, is a kind of anti-political mind set which permeates the profession and fosters an attitude of political inaction. To help offset this problem, the landscape architectural professional degree programs need to take a page from the civil engineering curriculums. Political understanding must be viewed as a critical part of the landscape architect's package of skills.

The aspiring landscape architect must realize that the political system can be understood, can be accessed and can be influenced. Citizen participation in the political process became a by-word during the early 1970s and has grown more popular with each passing year. Landscape architects need to become citizen and professional participants in the process if they are to exert any real influence over the future of the natural and man-made environment.

The other design professions have learned this simple lesson well and they continue to develop and sharpen their political skills. If landscape architects fail to follow suit, the profession may never have the opportunity to nurture its ethic and play the important role its skills so well suit it for. Assumption of a participatory role in the political decision making process is relatively simple. It requires only a strong desire to assume an important role and the development of well understood and easily learned skills. Little more can be said about stimulating the desire, but a discussion of the skill development process would be most appropriate.

Understanding the System: Developing the skills necessary to influence the political decision making process begins with understanding or knowledge. Knowledge is power, and developing this power requires the accumulation and synthesization of data and information about how the system works.

It is incredible to find landscape architects practicing in communities and regions about which they know little or nothing politically. It is equally incredible to learn that many of these same professionals don't even know much about the power structure of their own employment organization. This venture into the incredible is further intensified by the relatively simple effort needed to find the information and understand its meaning. This is a homework procedure.

Understanding the political system begins with a homework process.

The home work process begins the moment a landscape architect enters employment. It begins, like the design process, with the collecting of data. Typically this data could include.

- Annual Reports issued by all government agencies: state, regional, and local.
- State Fact Book: Most states produce an annual Fact Book which provides a wealth of information about the state and its political institutions.
- *The Governmental Guide:* This document is published privately and includes important data about the political structures of cities and counties in every state.[2]
- Local Chamber of Commerce Reports
- Policy statements and reports issued by local

political action groups such as the Tax Payers Association and the League of Women Voters. In some areas the League of Women Voters produce and distribute a primer on local politics.

- Special policy reports issued by Planning Departments, Park Boards, and Transportation Authorities. and so on.
- *The Municipal Year Book,* published annually by the International City Management Association.[3]

This basic information source list will frequently stimulate interest in collecting data of a more specific nature and may lead the homework search to sources such as: Minutes of governmental meetings, news clipping services, local libraries, and state, regional and local periodicals and special interest publications.

The personal interview with elected and appointed officials will provide much useful information and add to your network of contacts.

The second step of the homework process involves a more personalized method of data collection, and provides an important framework for synthesizing the data collected. This step involves interviews with key elected and appointed officials and attendance at governmental meetings. Most local officials are delighted to spend some time with their constituents. When asked, they are more than willing to discuss their jobs and their role in the overall decision making process. A tremendous amount of insight can be gained through interviews with city and county managers, elected representatives, planning directors, city and county attorneys, and other members of the political hierarchy. This part of the process, in addition to yielding very useful information, is the first step in building a network of contacts and developing clout for you and your organization.

Attending public meetings as an observer will also yield valuable information and aid the synthesizing process. While public meetings frequently represent only the tip of the political decision making process, they are an important part of the system. Public meetings can often be long and dull. They can also be very exciting. Both types, however, when viewed over the course of time, provide unique insight to the political process.

The time necessary to learn and understand the political system and its process will vary greatly and will depend to a large extent on community size and organizational complexity. In smaller political jurisdictions the learning and understanding process will be very easily accomplished. In the more complex systems the process may take months of effort. In these overwhelming situations it is best to start with the smallest political units first. Determine the overall framework of the system then develop a refined understanding from the bottom up.

Keep in mind that the political system is community wide and involves more than the elected and appointed officials. The system involves business leaders, social and cultural leaders, a host of special interest groups, and a voting constituency that can come alive almost instantly. When the workings and the nuances of the system are understood, accessing the system takes only the simpliest of skills.

Accessing the System: Accessing and utilizing the political system to the advantage of our professional and personal lives follows swiftly on the heels of understanding the system. The knowledge accumulated during the homework process will have a direct and immediate benefit. Knowing the system assures you of access to information. You will have learned, for instance, that the Tax Assessor's office has aerial photographs which have ownership information for every parcel of land in the county. You will have learned that the planning department maintains a cumulative file on all properties considered for rezoning. This is information that could prove invaluable when suggesting zoning changes to a client.

Your knowledge of the political system will serve you in a pragmatic sense as well, providing continuing access to information and people within the system. Your understanding of the system, and its often cumbersome procedures, will enable you to provide greater service to your clients and their projects. The scope of your services can be greatly expanded and your ability to get the job done greatly enhanced.

Your knowledge of the system will provide opportunity for direct involvement in the process itself. Understanding the system means that you will be able to communicate with the system in its own language. In doing so, your chances of being understood and listened to are greatly improved.

If you are a public practitioner and work as a member of the system, your complete understanding of the system can lead to greater responsibility and increased access to the system's power base. The more you know about the structure you work within, the easier it is to function within it. To the public practitioner, the power structure may rest outside the political system itself. The political activist may be vastly more important to the public practitioner than those people within the system.

If you are a private or academic practitioner your knowledge and enhanced communication abilities will also lead to broader involvement opportunities on planning commissions, park boards, special advisory committees and so on. Accessing the political system and the building of clout are linked functions, and they grow together. As your knowledge of the system increases, so also will your clout, and vice-versa.

Influencing the System: In addition to the professional advantages which insure to those who access and utilize the political system, an ultimate reward is the ability to influence the system's decision making function. It is at this level where the profession of landscape architecture can make the most important and beneficial contributions to the future of both the natural and man-made environment.

The ability to influence the political decision making process in positive ways does not come easy. It can take years of effort and credential building. Generally, however, there are four overriding criteria. The first is unquestionable professional competence. As a landscape architect, your ultimate ability to influence the political decision making process will rest on your credibility as a professional.

Second, your perspective and understanding of the world around you must go beyond parochial interests. While it is important to be committed to local interest, you must be able to maintain a broader view to include regional, state, national and even global concerns.

Third, you must have highly developed human skills. Those skills discussed in Part Two of this book are critical to your influencing abilities.

Fourth, you must become involved. Involvement provides credibility through proven accomplishments rather than rhetoric. Involvement also provides access to other influential members of the community and allows for coalition building and the development of often needed support for a cause. Serving on advisory boards and task forces, actively working for political candidates, assisting neighborhood associations, helping appropriate special interest groups, and even being a candidate for office (especially if you should win) will all add greatly to your influence potential. There is no substitute for this final criterion. In fact, without involvement the other criteria become meaningless in the clout building process.

Understanding and accessing the political system is a highly individualized activity. Only bits and pieces of the process can be done for you. You must accomplish most of the process yourself. Influencing the political decision making process, on the other hand, is both an individual and a collective effort. The dramatic and continuing power of special interest groups provides a good example of collective influence. Such groups exist for nearly every cause imaginable. They can appear almost overnight and disappear just as quickly. Understanding and working with appropriate special interest groups can often provide an important influence base.

The effectiveness of collective power applies to the profession of landscape architecture as well. The profession's collective base is the American Society of Landscape Architects. Without this organization the profession is nearly powerless. With its help and continuing effort the profession has a strong and effective voice in the political decision making process.

A Professional Association

The establishment of a professional association, as Caplow pointed out in Chapter Six of this book, is the initial step in the evolution of a trade or craft to a profession.[4] Landscape architecture took this step in 1899 with the founding of the American Society of Landscape Architects (ASLA). From its inception, ASLA has been a guiding force in the profession's growth. There is no way to measure where the profession might be today without the efforts of literally thousands of landscape architects who have worked collectively through ASLA since its founding. It is safe to say, however, that the profession would be little more than a scattering of individual practitioners whose impact would be minimal.

The constitution of ASLA states the Society's purpose as follows:

... The advancement of education and skill in the art of landscape architecture as an instrument of service in the public welfare.

To insure accomplishment of its purpose, ASLA has adopted seven specific goals, each with a corresponding set of objectives. The objectives are modified and are added to as they are accomplished or as conditions change. The goals, however, remain the same and are outlined here:

1. **Membership Opportunity:** To provide membership opportunity in the American Society of Landscape Architects for all qualified individuals to strengthen the landscape architectural profession.

2. **Chapter Development:** To provide direct assistance and guidance in chapter operations and development, recognizing that chapters are the basic operational unit of the society.

3. **Educational Advancement:** To provide for the advancement of landscape architectural education in order to identify and educate the best qualified individuals to enter the field.

4. **Professional Development:** To broaden the scope of landscape architecture and assist landscape architects to fully develop their capabilities.

5. **Public Service:** To insure that the landscape architecture perspective shall be brought to bear continually and effectively on appropriate issues of concern in the public domain—internationally, nationally, and locally.

6. **Public Relations:** To develop optimum exposure and visibility for the landscape architecture profession at the national and local levels.

7. **Administrative Standards:** To provide for development and maintenance of the professional society to the highest possible standards of efficiency and effective service for the members and the public in order that the goals of ASLA may be achieved.

To accomplish these goals ASLA undertakes a wide variety of programs and service activities designed to meet both short and long range needs. The services and activities are designed to serve each goal area and its objectives. In the broadest sense, however, the entire effort of ASLA is two fold: Direct service to its members, and continuing advancement of the profession as a whole.

Direct membership services include but are not limited to the following:

• **LAND** (*Landscape Architectural News Digest*): LAND is a monthly newsletter containing important and timely information about the activities of the Society and its members and also includes highlights of legislative activities and other events which have an influence on landscape architectural practice.

• **LAM** (*Landscape Architecture Magazine*): LAM is a quality bi-monthly magazine which features the executed works of the profession in all its diverse forms. While owned and published by the Publication Board of ASLA, the magazine has a readership which goes well beyond the Society's own membership. In this regard LAM provides both a direct member service, as well as, advancing the profession.

- **LATIS** (*Landscape Architectural Technical Information Series*): LATIS is published periodically and is designed to bring state-of-the-art information on the profession to the Society's members.
- **Members Handbook:** The ASLA Members Handbook is published annually and includes membership listings, a yearly calendar of events, and a wealth of information about the Society and its activities.
- **Educational Seminars:** Traveling educational seminars are developed and presented throughout the year by ASLA. Subjects of a timely and critical nature are presented along with traditional concerns for ongoing skill maintenance. The seminars provide a valuable continuing education service.
- **Practice Specific Services:** To insure a continuing flow of information and service activities to the private, public, academic, and boundary expanding practice forms, ASLA established the Professional Practice Institute in 1978. The Institute is responsible for producing and disseminating direct services to each practice specific area. An example of the Institutes activities is the annual publication of the *Directory of Landscape Architectural Firms*.
- **Annual Meeting and Educational Exhibit:** The Society's annual meeting provides unique and exciting educational programs and an industry wide trade exhibit. The Society's annual meeting provides its members with the opportunity to upgrade their skills and to view hundreds of new products, services and systems of special interest to professional practice.
- **Administrative Services:** ASLA's paid professional staff deals with hundreds of individual member problems and concerns each month. By phone and mail the staff provides information and counsel on issues ranging from membership qualification to political activism.

ASLA services directed toward the overall growth of the profession include but are not limited to the following:

- **Professional Awards Program:** Each year ASLA identifies and formally recognizes the most outstanding works of landscape architectural design, planning, analysis, and research accomplished by its members. While considered a direct benefit to those who receive awards, the program is specifically designed to promote the activities of the whole profession. The annual award ceremonies are held in Washington, D.C. and are attended by a wide variety of specially invited nationally prominent people.
- **Government Agency Liaison:** ASLA's professional staff monitors the federal legislative process on a continuing basis and takes appropriate action in support of or in opposition to legislation of interest to the profession. The Society's staff will call upon the most appropriate and knowledgable of its members to prepare and present position papers and testimony as needed to support the profession's best interest.
- **Professional Liaison:** ASLA maintains close and effective liaison with the other design profession socieities and represents the landscape architectural profession on national commissions, councils, federations and other collaborative groups and organizations.
- **Visibility:** ASLA promotes the highest possible visibility for the profession through the production of films, public service announcements, news releases, promotional brochures and other methods.
- **Education:** In keeping with the educational emphasis in its constitutional purpose, ASLA devotes considerable effort to the promotion of the highest possible standards in landscape architectural education. Through the Council on Education and the Landscape Architectural Accreditation Board, ASLA advises and evaluates professional degree programs, sets accreditation standards, and offers a wide variety of special assistance to the educational process.
- **Public Information Services:** ASLA prepares and distributes, on a continuing basis, information about the profession and its mission to the general public, aspiring landscape architects, organizations, and special interest groups.

In addition to these ongoing membership and profession advancement activities, ASLA provides a variety of specialized services and programs through the activities of its committees and task forces. These services and programs usually involve efforts dealing with very immediate concerns and they are often most valuable.

ASLA is a national organization with more than 40 local chapters around the country. All members belong to one of the local chapters, and it is important to note that most of the service activities just described are also conducted by each of the local chapters. The services provided by the local chapters deal with parochial interests and they are fully coordinated with the counterpart service at the national level.

ASLA is landscape architecture's collective voice. It is the profession's most powerful advocate and maintains a level of clout no individual alone could achieve. It has access to the power structure and has learned to utilize that access effectively. It has become an influential force and it will continue to serve the profession well.

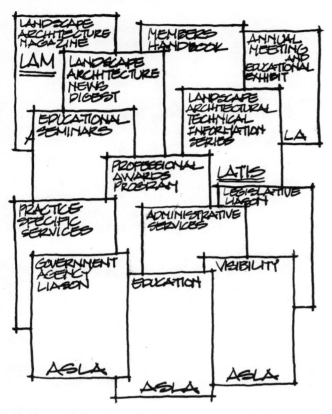

ASLA serves the individual practitioner and the profession in many ways.

Every man owes a part of his time and money to the business or industry in which he is engaged. No man has a moral right to withhold his support from an organization that is striving to improve conditions within his sphere.

It must be understood, however, that ASLA is a collective body of volunteers. The Society's strength and vigor is a direct reflection of its membership; their numbers and their energies. ASLA has approximately doubled its membership in each decade of the twentieth century. Should this growth continue, ASLA will be 10,000 strong by 1990 and 20,000 strong by the turn of the century. Historically, however, the membership of ASLA in any given year has been less than a quarter of the total number of practicing landscape architects in this country. While that regretable ratio seems to be improving it is interesting to speculate how much further ahead the profession might be today if all landscape architects had pooled their collective energies and resources over the same period.

While participation by all landscape architects in a collective effort on behalf of the profession seems most unlikely, the profession deserves and requires a maximum collective effort. Teddy Roosevelt put it this way:

As ASLA's membership, energies, and financial resources grow, so too will the profession. The growth of the profession and the corresponding rewards to its practitioners is directly and inexorably linked to ASLA's collective effort. It has always been so, and will always remain so.

To the profession of landscape architecture, advocacy politics and the professional society are linked concepts. They include individual and collective concerns, efforts and skills. They move forward simultaneously and in lockstep toward common goals. Every landscape architect must play a role in moving the profession forward and giving it a strength which belies its relative numbers. The profession has something to give and something to say. Whether its gift will be accepted and its voice heard may well depend on how effective it can be as advocate and political activist. The individual and collective effort must be skillfully and wisely handled, and the task will be mighty. The results, however, can be well worth the effort.

Chapter Sixteen Notes:

1. Lee Davis, "Goal-oriented Profit Centers: Requisite for Survival", A Goodkin Executives Report, Westlake Village, Cal., 1972
2. Editors, *The Governmental Guide* Governmental Guides, Inc. Madison, Tenn. published annually.
3. International City Management Association, *The Municipal Yearbook*, Printed annually, 1140 Connecticut Ave., Washington, D.C.
4. Theodore Caplow, *Harvard Educational Review*, Winter 1955, Cambridge, Mass.

Chapter Seventeen
A Profession for Tomorrow

LANDSCAPE ARCHITECTURE IN THE 21st CENTURY

Frederick Law Olmsted, through his executed works, writings, and special energies, founded a profession of truly unique proportions. He was a visionary, and while his example remains today for all to emulate, it is doubtful that even he could have predicted his profession's dramatic growth, its diversity, or the prestige it enjoys today.

From Olmsted's legacy, landscape architecture has grown and matured into a highly visible and a highly regarded profession. A special devotion to the land and to people has become a touchstone for all forms of landscape architectural practice, however diverse. This ethic has served the profession well and will carry it forward for generations yet to come.

A mere handful of landscape architects crossed the threshold of the twentieth century. When the twenty-first century dawns, the number of practitioners could exceed 30,000, and more than 100 years of professional accomplishment will be impressive indeed.

Landscape architecture has grown, matured, and prospered during the twentieth century, and stands today facing the twenty-first century with expectation for continued prosperity and a commitment for continued maturation. An exciting future lies ahead for the profession, but to see it clearly demands a brief look toward the past.

Landscape architecture enjoys its current status, for the most part, because of its wise and prompt reaction to the changing world around us. Albert Fein noted the special reactive nature of the profession in his *Study of the Profession of Landscape Architecture:*

In short, the profession has been compelled, almost periodically, owing to external forces, to alter its focus. World War I, the 1920s, the Depression, World War II, post war expansion in housing, education and highways, and now a new ecological awareness have compelled such changes.

The profession's reaction to these compelling forces of change have been highly successful, but there can be no denying the largely reactive posture of the profession since its founding. Why should this historical reactive nature of the profession be of any concern? Will not the profession continue to grow and mature by reacting wisely to future change in the same way it has in the past? The answer may well be no.

Two reasons stand out clearly. First, the profession has reached a state of maturity that demands a greater leadership role for it in the future if it is to continue to grow. This will be expected of the profession in the same way it is expected of any young person who reaches maturity. Secondly, and of equal importance, the very nature of change in the years ahead may preclude the same level of successful reaction the profession has used in the past.

Peter F. Drucker, in his recent book, *Managing in Turbulent Times*, suggests that the years ahead will be irregular, non-linear, and erratic. The future, Drucker advises, will be governed by the "unique event" which cannot be planned for, but which can be forseen. Drucker suggests that those who are willing to slough off the past and look thoughtfully ahead will be the ones most likely to survive in such turbulent times.

The profession of landscape architecture must follow Drucker's advice. The profession can no longer afford to be merely reactive to change. It must learn to predict and direct change. It must be a forward looking profession with leadership ambitions and the skills to match them. The profession's tomorrow can be bright indeed, but it will depend on the development of predictive and leadership skills as finely tuned as the traditional design and technical skills so common to the profession.

In large measure, this book has been dedicated to the belief that landscape architecture is a profession for tomorrow. The book has attempted to look at landscape architectural practice not only in a traditional sense, but also through a lens toward the future. The book suggests that successful practice is today, and will continue to be, predicated on a great deal more than the traditional skills. It urges the utilization of the broadest possible spectrum of skills across an ever expanding practice base.

By its very nature and diversity, landscape architecture enjoys a dynamic rather than a static posture. It has changed and modified its definition of itself over the years and will continue to do so, allowing it the flexibility and the reach to grasp the future. The profession's diversity will continue to expand and its practitioners will serve an ever broadening base. With this will come greater exposure and increased potential for meaningful leadership across a full range of future-oriented issues, from energy to aging population concerns.

Formal education and the educational continuum must also be untethered by traditional limitations. The professional degree programs can have the flexibility to meet the needs of an ever-expanding profession. Already, there is a diversity in the educational programs that matches the diversity of the profession. Furthermore, the increasing number of women, older adults, and career change students in the professional degree programs reflects accurately societal trends and gives the profession a truly modern mantle.

The influx of older and career change students also brings a stepped up maturation process and will allow the profession to more closely stay in step with an aging society. The body of knowledge which supports the profession has also neared the critical mass needed to insure the scholarly framework necessary for meaningful discovery and the corresponding leadership potential.

The profession's potential to access the future is excellent. The book suggests, however, that some sharpening of existing skills and the acquisition of some new skills is in order. Assessing the future may well depend on greater emphasis being placed on human skill development. The advocacy and political skills the profession so desperately needs are directly linked to these human skills. Interpersonal relationship skills, effective communication skills, and sound decision making skills are all essential ingredients for the profession's future growth.

The book also emphasizes that landscape architecture is a business, but a service-oriented, not a product-oriented business. Consequently, the book looks at the business of landscape architecture from a new point of view. No longer can landscape architecture be seen as a profession dominated by the private practice office. While such offices may well remain the backbone of the profession they will not dominate the future as they have the past. There are, however, business threads common to the practice of landscape architecture in all its many forms, and the book looks at ways to strengthen these in the future. When concepts like marketing management are viewed as essential aspects of all practice forms and applied within the framework of the professional service enterprise as distinct from the product-oriented enterprise, the profession takes on greatly enlarged growth potential.

While the book breaks from traditional views of professional practice, it continues to recognize that executed works of landscape architecture will continue to plow new ground for the profession, and those activities associated with the built project are discussed in some detail. Emphasis is placed on management as a critical aspect of future practice. Management skills cross-cut professional practice and as projects and collaborative project teams become more complex these skills become increasingly important. Much of the more tedious work of the future will be handled by the computer. Moreover, the computer has the capacity to assist with many of the highly creative tasks of the future. The profession must, if it is to survive, become computer literate.

Landscape architecture is a profession for the future. Its practitioners possess the expertise and the sensitivity to move through the future with continued success. The combination of foresight, and human and political skills with those traditional skills of the profession will allow landscape architecture to grow, mature and prosper. The future, of course, rests, as it always does, with today's students. Many of today's practitioners will have the opportunity to continue to practice in quite traditional ways. Today's students, however, will find tomorrow's practice placing altogether different skill demands on them without a lessening of demand for the traditional skills.

This book is dedicated to today's student and the future leaders of the profession. They are a bright, dedicated, and energetic group and the future of the profession is in excellent hands.

Appendix

Appendix A
Bibliography

Chapter One: The Profession Defined

Fein, Albert, *A Study of the Profession of Landscape Architecture,* Washington, D.C. ASLA, 1972

Fein, Albert, *Frederick Law Olmsted, 1822-1903* N. Y, N.Y., G. Braziller, 1972

Jellicoe, G. A., *The Landscape of Man, Shaping the Environment, From Prehistoric to the Present Day,* N. Y., N. Y., Viking Press, 1975

Newton, Norman T., *Design of the Land: The Development of Landscape Architecture,* Cambridge, Mass: Belknap Press, 1971

Sutton, S. B., Ed., *Civilizing American Cities,* Cambridge, Mass. The MIT Press 1979

Tobey, G. B., *A History of Landscape Architecture: The Relationship of People to Environment,* N. Y., N. Y., Elsevier, 1973

Chapter Two: Practice Diversity

American Society of Landscape Architects, *Landscape Architects in Government Practice; A Special Profile Survey,* Washington, D.C., ASLA 1977

Fein, Albert, *A Study of the Profession of Landscape Architecture,* Washington, D.C. Landscape Architecture Foundation, 1972

Griswold, Ralph E., *Opportunities in Landscape Architecture,* N. Y., N. Y., Vocational Guidance Manuals, 1970

Laurie, Michael, *An Introduction to Landscape Architecture,* N. Y., N. Y., American Elsevier Publishing Co., Inc. 1975

McHarg, Ian, *Design With Nature,* Garden City, N. Y., Doubleday & Co., 1971

Preiser, Wolfgang, F. E., ed., *Environmental Design Perspectives: Viewpoints on the Profession, Education and Research,* Christainburg, VA, Virginia Polytechnic Institute, College of Architecture, 1972

Shillaber, Caroline, *Landscape Architecture/Environmental Planning: A Classified Bibliography,* Monticello, Illinois, Council of Planning Librarians, 1975

Simonds, John, *Landscape Architecture; The Shaping of Man's Natural Environment,* N. Y., N. Y., McGraw-Hill Book Co., Inc. 1961

Chapter Three: The Industry; A Service Base

American Society of Landscape Architects, *Landscape Architects in Government Practice, A Special Profile Survey,* Washington, D.C., ASLA 1977

American Society of Landscape Architects, *Marketing Landscape Architectural Services to the Federal Government,* Washington, D.C., ASLA 1974

Fein, Albert, *A Study of the Profession of Landscape Architecture,* Washington, D.C. Landscape Architecture Foundation, 1972

Robinette, Gary, ed., *Award Winning Landscape Architecture,* Washington, D.C., Landscape Architecture Foundation, 1974

Chapter Four: Formal Education

American Society of Landscape Architecture, *List of Accredited Programs in Landscape Architecture,* Washington, D.C., ASLA, published annually

Fishman, Lois R., *Profiles of the Design Professions,* Background Paper prepared for Architecture, Planning and Design Program, National Endowment for the Arts, 1978

Lohman, Karl B., *Fundamentals of Landscape Architecture,* Ed. 4, Scranton, PA: International Correspondence School, 1974

Robinette, Gary, *Landscape Architectural Education,* Dubuque, Iowa, Kendall/Hunt, 1973, 2 vols.

Chapter Five: The Educational Continuum

Marshall, Lane L., "An Exciting Future for Landscape Architecture", *Landscape Architecture Magazine,* Nov. 1978

Wolfe, J. K., "Keeping Up to Date in Career Training in the USA", *Electronics and Power,* August 1965

Chapter Six: Professionalism

American Society of Landscape Architects, *Members Handbook,* Washington, D.C., ASLA, published annually

Carr-Sanders, A. M., "The Professions", *Untangling the Web of Professional Liability,* The Design Professionals Insurance Co., San Francisco, CA, 1976

Caplow, Theodore, *Harvard Educational Review,* Winter 1955

Miller, Sam, *Professional Licensure of Landscape Architects: An Assessment of Public Needs and Private Responsibilities,* ASLA, Washington, D.C., 1978

Reimann-Buechner-Crandell Partnership, *Candidate Review Manual Uniform National Examination in Landscape Architecture,* Reston, VA., Environmental Design Press, 1978

Wagner, H. A., "Principles of Professional Conduct in Engineering", *The Annals of the American Academy of Political and Social Sciences,* 197, January 1955

Chapter Seven: Interpersonal Relations

Bennis & Schein, eds., *Leadership and Motivation,* Essays of Douglas McGregor, Cambridge, Mass. MIT Press 1966

Cooper, Gary L., ed., *Behavioral Problems in Organizations,* Newark, N.J. Prentice Hall, Inc., 1979

Covert, Colin, "Things Your Alma Mater Never Told You", *TWA Ambassador,* May 1980

Doran, Bernadette, "Does Your Job Have Personality?" *TWA Ambassador,* May 1980

Rosenberg, Morris, "Occupations and Values" Research Paper, Cornell University, 1975

Sommers, Robert, *Personal Space,* Englewood Cliffs, N. J., Prentice-Hall, Inc., 1969

Editors, *A Collection of Information that will be valuable to Design Profesionals who are interested in reducing their Professional Liability Exposures,* San Francisco, CA, The Design Professionals Insurance Co., 1974

Chapter Eight: Making Decisions

Churchman, C. A., *Design of an Inquiring System,* Basic Books

Fuller, Buckminster, *Intuition,* Doubleday Book Co.

Koberg & Bagnall, *The Universal Traveler; A Soft-Systems Guide to: creativity, problem-solving, and the process of reaching goals.* Los Altos, CA, William Kaufmann, Inc., 1974

LaBrecque, Mort, "On Making Sounder Judgments", *Psychology Today,* June 1980

Nesbitt & Ross, *Human Inference: Strategies and Shortcomings of Social Judgment,* N. Y., N. Y., Prentice-Hall 1980

Slovic, Flieschoff & Lichenstein, "Risky Assumptions", *Psychology Today,* June 1980

Chapter Nine: Effective Communications

Bloom, Benjamin, ed., *Taxonomy of Educational Objectives,* N. Y., N. Y., Longman Co., 1954

Gibb, Jack, "Defensive Communication", *Journal of Communications*, Vol. XI, No. 3 Sept. 1961

Jones, Gerre L., *How to Market Professional Design Services*, N. Y., N. Y., McGraw-Hill Book Company, 1973

Nichols & Stevens, *Are You Listening?* N. Y., N. Y., McGraw-Hill Book Company, 1957

Weiss, Allen, *Write What You Mean*, N. Y., N. Y., Amacom, 1977

Howell & Howell, *Untangling the Web of Professional Liability*, San Francisco, CA, The Design Professionals Insurance Co., 1976

Chapter Ten: Basic Business Principles

American Institute of Architects, 'The Architects Office", Chp. 6 *Architect's Handbook of Professional Practice*, Washington, D.C., AIA, 1971

American Institute of Architects, *Small Office Practice Handbook*, Washington, D.C. AIA, 1972

Burstiner, Irving, *The Small Business Handbook*, Englewood Cliffs, N. J., Prentice-Hall, Inc., 1979

Coxe, Weld, *Managing Architectural & Engineering Practice*, N. Y., N. Y., John Wiley & Sons, 1980

Day, William H., *Maximizing Small Business Profits*, Englewood Cliffs, N. J., Prentice-Hall, Inc. 1978

Foote, Rosslyn, *Running an Office for Fun and Profit*, N. Y., N. Y., McGraw-Hill, 1978

Sibson, Robert E., *Managing Professional Service Enterprises*, N. Y., N. Y., Pitman Publishing Corporation 1971

————, "Hiring Criteria", Journal No. 9, March 1966, Palo Alto, CA, Stanford Research Institute

Chapter Eleven: Marketing Management

Coxe, Weld, *Marketing Architectural and Engineering Services*, N. Y., N. Y., Van Nostrand Reinhold Co., 1971

Drucher, Peter F., *Managing in Turbulent Times*, N. Y., N. Y., Harper & Row, 1980

Enis, Ben M., *Marketing Principles: The Management Process*, Pacific Palesades, CA Goodyear Publishing Co., Inc., 1974

Jones, Gerre L., *How to Market Professional Design Services*, N. Y., N. Y., McGraw-Hill, Inc. 1973

Kotler, Philip, *Marketing Management: Analysis, Planning and Control*, 2nd ed., Englewood Cliffs, N. J., Prentice-Hall, Inc., 1972

Rewoldt, Scott, Warslaw, *Introduction to Marketing Management*, Richard D. Irwin, Inc., N. Y., N. Y., 1977

Stanton, William J., *Fundamentals of Marketing*, N. Y., N. Y., McGraw-Hill, 1975

Editors, *The Encyclopedia of Marketing of Professional Services*, Washington, D. C., PDR Publications, 1980

Chapter Twelve: Business Administration and Office Procedures

Abbett, Robert W., *Engineering Contracts and Specifications*, 2nd Ed., N. Y., N. Y., John Wiley and Sons, 1948

American Institute of Architects, "The Architect's Office", Chapter 6, *Architect's Handbook of Professional Practice*, Washington, D. C., AIA, 1971

American Institute of Architects, "Owner-Architect Agreements", Chapter 9 *Architects Handbook of Professional Practice*, Washington, D. C., AIA, 1970

American Society of Landscape Architects, *Guidelines for Personnel Management*, Washington, D. C., ASLA 1977

Burstiner, Irving, *The Small Business Handbook*, Englewood Cliffs, N. J., Prentice-Hall, Inc., 1979

Coxe, Weld, *Managing Architectural and Engineering Practice*, N. Y., N. Y., John Wiley and Sons, Inc., 1980

Paterson, John, *Architecture and the Microprocessor*, Somerset, N. J., John Wiley and Sons, Inc., 1980

Chapter Thirteen: Construction Documents

Abbett, Robert W., *Engineering Contracts and Specifications*, N. Y., N. Y., John Wiley & Sons, Inc., 1967

American Institute of Architects, "Construction Documents—Specifications," Chapter 14, *Architects Handbook of Professional Practice*, Washington, D. C., AIA 1972

Arnell, Alvin, *Standard Graphic Symbols*, N. Y., N. Y., McGraw Hill, 1963

Buss, Truman C., *Simplified Architectural Drawing*, Chicago, Illinois, American Technical Society, 1947

Meier, Hans W., *Construction Specifications Handbook*, Englewood Cliffs, N. J., Prentice-Hall Inc., 1978

Polon, David D., ed., *Dictionary of Architectural Abbreviations*, N. Y., N. Y., Odyssey Press, 1965

Editors, *Bidding Procedures and Contract Awards*, The American Institute of Architects and The Associated General Contractors of American, AIA, Washington, D.C., 1969

Chapter Fourteen: Project Management

Clough and Sears, *Construction Project Management*, 2nd Ed., Somerset N. J., John Wiley & Sons, Inc. 1979

Clyde, James E., *Construction Inspection: A Field Guide to Practice*, Somerset, N. J., John Wiley & Sons, Inc., 1979

Faulkner, W., *Project Management with CPM*, Duxbury, Mass., R. S. Means Co., Inc. 1973

Halpin and Woodhead, *Construction Management*, Somerset, N. J., John Wiley & Sons, Inc., 1980

Chapter Fifteen: Legal Concerns and Professional Liability

American Institute of Architects, "Legal Concerns", Chapter 19, *Architect's Handbook of Professional Practice*, Washington, D.C., AIA 1969

Dib, Albert, *Forms and Agreements for Architects, and Contractors*, Vol 1 & 2, N. Y., N. Y., Clark Broadman Co., Ltd 1977

Howell & Howell, *Untangling the Webb of Professional Liability*, Risk Analysis & Research Corporation Publication, 2nd Edition, 1976, Design Professional Insurance Co., San Francisco, Calif.

Design Professionals Insurance Company, *A Collection of Information That Will be Valuable to Design Professionals in Private Practice Who Are Interested In Reducing Their Professional Liability Exposure*, DPIC San Francisco, Calif., 1974

Victor O. Schinnerer & Company, Inc., "Types of Professional Liability Claims," *Guidelines for Improving Practice*, Vol. ix, No. 3, Washington D.C., 1979.

Chapter Sixteen: Advocacy, Politics and a Professional Association

Caplow, Theodore, *Harvard Educational Review*, Winter 1955, Cambridge, Mass.

Davis, Lee, "Goal-Oriented Profit Centers: Requisite for Survival," A Goodkin Executives Report, Westlake Village, Cal., 1972.

International City Management Association, *The Municipal Yearbook*, Printed annually, 1140 Connecticut Ave. N.W., Washington D.C.

Editors, *The Government Guides*, Governmental Guides, Inc., Madison, Tenn. published annually.

Appendix B
Index

Appendix C
Curriculum Content

The following matrix is reprinted from the *ASLA Bulletin*, May, 1974. It was prepared by Professor David Young, FASLA.

The matrix catagories fall into four broad components titled *Substance* (core knowledge), *Design* (creative process), *Communications* (expression of ideas), and *Implication* (application of a design to the land). Since this matrix was developed, there have been many changes in the substantive content of Landscape Architecture programs throughout the country. This matrix does not represent those most recent developments.

LANDSCAPE ARCHITECTURAL CURRICULUM
CONTENT AND DEPTH CHART

MINIMUM REQUIRED DEPTH IN TOPIC

CURRICULUM CONTENT BY CATEGORY (Physical Skills & Basic Knowledge)	ABILITY LEVEL				ATTITUDE LEVEL				REMARKS
	AWARE (Associate/Recall)	COMPREHEND (Restate/Explain)	APPLY (Principles/Techniques)	CREATE (Synthesize/Evaluate)	INTEREST (A desire to know overview)	INVOLVEMENT (A desire to know in detail)	APPRECIATION (A desire to fully understand)	EVOLVEMENT (A desire to advance knowledge)	
SUBSTANCE (core knowledge)									
PHYSICAL SCIENCES									
Resources									
Natural — Characteristics & Limitations									
climate									
macro									
factors									
patterns									
regions									
micro									
factors									
orientation									
earth									
geology									
origin of materials									
material properties									
distribution patterns									
form/process relationships									
soils									
origin of materials									
distribution patterns									
engineering properties									
agricultural properties									
water									
hydrologic cycle									
storage & diversion									
quality control									
life									
animal									
basic requirements									
behavioral patterns									
plant									
anatomy and physiology									
species identification									
trees									
shrubs									
groundcovers & vines									

LANDSCAPE ARCHITECTURAL CURRICULUM
CONTENT AND DEPTH CHART (continued)

MINIMUM REQUIRED DEPTH IN TOPIC

CURRICULUM CONTENT BY CATEGORY (Physical Skills & Basic Knowledge)	ABILITY LEVEL				ATTITUDE LEVEL				REMARKS
	AWARE (Associate/Recall)	COMPREHEND (Restate/Explain)	APPLY (Principles/Techniques)	CREATE (Synthesize/Evaluate)	INTEREST (A desire to know overview)	INVOLVEMENT (A desire to know in detail)	APPRECIATION (A desire to fully understand)	EVOLVEMENT (A desire to advance knowledge)	
SUBSTANCE (core knowledge) — continued									
annuals & perennials									
turfs									
cultural requirements									
ecological associations									
installation & maintenance									
inter-relationships									
closed system									
food chains									
natural balance									
regional character									
Cultural — Requirements & Standards									
building									
housing									
shopping									
industrial									
recreational									
institutional									
warehousing									
parking									
circulation									
inter-site									
air									
rail									
boat									
bus									
car									
intra-site									
transit									
cycle									
walking									
service									
off-site sewer systems									
public water supply									
power distribution									
refuse collection									

LANDSCAPE ARCHITECTURAL CURRICULUM
CONTENT AND DEPTH CHART (continued)

MINIMUM REQUIRED DEPTH IN TOPIC

CURRICULUM CONTENT BY CATEGORY (Physical Skills & Basic Knowledge)	ABILITY LEVEL				ATTITUDE LEVEL				REMARKS
	AWARE (Associate/Recall)	COMPREHEND (Restate/Explain)	APPLY (Principles/Techniques)	CREATE (Synthesize/Evaluate)	INTEREST (A desire to know overview)	INVOLVEMENT (A desire to know in detail)	APPRECIATION (A desire to fully understand)	EVOLVEMENT (A desire to advance knowledge)	
SUBSTANCE (core knowledge) — continued									
fire, police, delivery									
recreational									
wilderness									
parks									
playfields									
playgrounds									
totlots									
specialized									
agricultural									
pasture									
tilled land									
orchard									
timber									
mining									
surface									
subterrainian									
Technology									
Structural design									
light framing									
post and beam									
reinforced concrete									
Utilities									
storm water									
run-off estimation									
surface drainage									
subsurface drainage									
hydraulic principles									
waste water									
on-site disposal									
off-site disposal									
water supply systems									
well pump									
municipal									
irrigation									
fuel supply									
steam distribution									

LANDSCAPE ARCHITECTURAL CURRICULUM
CONTENT AND DEPTH CHART (continued)

| | MINIMUM REQUIRED DEPTH IN TOPIC | | | | | | | | |
| | ABILITY LEVEL | | | | ATTITUDE LEVEL | | | | |
CURRICULUM CONTENT BY CATEGORY (Physical Skills & Basic Knowledge)	AWARE (Associate/Recall)	COMPREHEND (Restate/Explain)	APPLY (Principles/Techniques)	CREATE (Synthesize/Evaluate)	INTEREST (A desire to know overview)	INVOLVEMENT (A desire to know in detail)	APPRECIATION (A desire to fully understand)	EVOLVEMENT (A desire to advance knowledge)	REMARKS
SUBSTANCE (core knowledge) — continued									
power distribution									
circuit design									
standard lighting									
low voltage lighting									
Land description									
scaling									
planimetering									
taping									
leveling									
traversing									
interpolation									
sections									
grading									
earthwork									
road alignment									
traverse calculations									
Remote sensing									
photography									
black & white									
color									
infra red									
thermal imagry									
radar imagry									
Computers									
principles of operations									
desk top model									
terminal model									
graphic display unit									
Construction materials									
soils									
asphalt									
concrete									
masonry									
wood									
metals									
synthetics									

LANDSCAPE ARCHITECTURAL CURRICULUM
CONTENT AND DEPTH CHART (continued)

MINIMUM REQUIRED DEPTH IN TOPIC

CURRICULUM CONTENT BY CATEGORY (Physical Skills & Basic Knowledge)	AWARE (Associate/Recall)	COMPREHEND (Restate/Explain)	APPLY (Principles/Techniques)	CREATE (Synthesize/Evaluate)	INTEREST (A desire to know overview)	INVOLVEMENT (A desire to know in detail)	APPRECIATION (A desire to fully understand)	EVOLVEMENT (A desire to advance knowledge)	REMARKS
SUBSTANCE (core knowledge) — continued									
coatings									
Construction methods									
standard details									
equipment									
field practices									
maintenance									
SOCIAL SCIENCES									
Physiology									
Dimensions									
Proportions									
Movements									
Psychology									
Instincts									
Emotions									
Time									
Behavioral norms									
Learning process									
Sociology									
Cultural geography									
Proxemics									
Economics									
Market analysis									
Construction financing									
Government assistance									
History									
European									
Oriental									
Western world									
pre WW II									
post WW II									
current trends									
cultural context									
Planning									
State of the art									
Land use policies									

LANDSCAPE ARCHITECTURAL CURRICULUM
CONTENT AND DEPTH CHART (continued)

	MINIMUM REQUIRED DEPTH IN TOPIC								
	ABILITY LEVEL				ATTITUDE LEVEL				
CURRICULUM CONTENT BY CATEGORY (Physical Skills & Basic Knowledge)	AWARE (Associate/Recall)	COMPREHEND (Restate/Explain)	APPLY (Principles/Techniques)	CREATE (Synthesize/Evaluate)	INTEREST (A desire to know overview)	INVOLVEMENT (A desire to know in detail)	APPRECIATION (A desire to fully understand)	EVOLVEMENT (A desire to advance knowledge)	REMARKS
SUBSTANCE (core knowledge) — continued									
Land use controls									
Construction controls									
Health controls									
HUMANITIES									
Art									
Architecture									
Art/Architectural History									
DESIGN (creativity)									
THEORY									
Perception									
Art elements									
Design principles									
Lighting effects									
Material relationships									
Scale relationships									
Spatial relationships									
PROGRAM									
Resources									
Natural									
Cultural									
Requirements									
Needs									
Relationships									
Controls									
Guides									
Standards									
Laws									
Costs									
Design									
Implementation									
Maintenance									
PROCESSES									
Scientific method									
Problem solving									

LANDSCAPE ARCHITECTURAL CURRICULUM
CONTENT AND DEPTH CHART (continued)

CURRICULUM CONTENT BY CATEGORY (Physical Skills & Basic Knowledge)	AWARE (Associate/Recall)	COMPREHEND (Restate/Explain)	APPLY (Principles/Techniques)	CREATE (Synthesize/Evaluate)	INTEREST (A desire to know overview)	INVOLVEMENT (A desire to know in detail)	APPRECIATION (A desire to fully understand)	EVOLVEMENT (A desire to advance knowledge)	REMARKS
MINIMUM REQUIRED DEPTH IN TOPIC	ABILITY LEVEL				ATTITUDE LEVEL				
DESIGN (creativity) — continued									
Design process									
Intuition									
Simulation									
Computer packages									
comparative analysis									
process scheduling									
Variations & combinations									
ATTITUDE									
Comprehensive consideration									
Rational approach									
Aesthetic attention									
Social accommodation									
Pragmatic solution									
COMMUNICATION (expression)									
VISUAL									
Drawing									
drafting & lettering									
basic equipment									
techniques & media									
hardware aids									
software aids									
working drawings									
orthographic									
isometric									
perspective									
computer aided									
symbolic mapping									
flatbed plotter									
drum plotter									
sketching									
media properties									
composition									
shades & shadows									
reflections & entourage									
techniques									

LANDSCAPE ARCHITECTURAL CURRICULUM
CONTENT AND DEPTH CHART (continued)

CURRICULUM CONTENT BY CATEGORY (Physical Skills & Basic Knowledge)	AWARE (Associate/Recall)	COMPREHEND (Restate/Explain)	APPLY (Principles/Techniques)	CREATE (Synthesize/Evaluate)	INTEREST (A desire to know overview)	INVOLVEMENT (A desire to know in detail)	APPRECIATION (A desire to fully understand)	EVOLVEMENT (A desire to advance knowledge)	REMARKS
COMMUNICATION (expression) — continued									
rendering									
media properties									
techniques									
Models									
assembled									
sculptured									
Reproductions									
photographic									
offset									
diazo									
Layout Composition									
VERBAL									
Voice									
Gesture									
WRITTEN									
Grammar									
Style									
correspondence									
technical									
expository									
MULTIA-MEDIA									
Visual-verbal									
Visual-written									
IMPLEMENTATION (application)									
BUSINESS MANAGEMENT									
Personnel Administration									
Work Scheduling									
Cost Accounting									
Taxes & Contributions									
Forms of Practice									
Scope of Practice									
Service Contracts									

MINIMUM REQUIRED DEPTH IN TOPIC

ABILITY LEVEL — ATTITUDE LEVEL

LANDSCAPE ARCHITECTURAL CURRICULUM
CONTENT AND DEPTH CHART (continued)

MINIMUM REQUIRED DEPTH IN TOPIC

CURRICULUM CONTENT BY CATEGORY (Physical Skills & Basic Knowledge)	ABILITY LEVEL				ATTITUDE LEVEL					REMARKS
	AWARE (Associate/Recall)	COMPREHEND (Restate/Explain)	APPLY (Principles/Techniques)	CREATE (Synthesize/Evaluate)	INTEREST (A desire to know overview)	INVOLVEMENT (A desire to know in detail)	APPRECIATION (A desire to fully understand)	EVOLVEMENT (A desire to advance knowledge)		
IMPLEMENTATION (application) — continued										
Promotion & Fees										
Files & Reference Systems										
Professional Standards										
PROJECT MANAGEMENT										
Site Development										
job programming										
cost estimating										
contract documents										
bid & contract forms										
general conditions										
technical specifications										
job sequence										
procedures										
inspections										
modifications										
acceptance										
Planning Program										
project programming										
capital budgeting										
report preparation										
report publication										
public presentation										
project acceptance										

Biographical Data

The Author: Lane L. Marshall

Lane received his Bachelor of Landscape Architecture degree from the University of Florida in 1960. In 1961 he founded his own landscape architectural firm in Sarasota, Florida. During the 1960's Lane was an active member of the Florida Chapter of the American Society of Landscape Architects, serving as chairman of the gulf coast section, secretary-treasurer of the chapter, and founder and first chairman of the chapter's annual environmental design conference.

In 1972 Lane was elected by the Florida Chapter of ASLA to serve as their national trustee, a position he held for nearly five years. In 1976 Lane was elected national secretary-treasurer of ASLA. Throughout this period Lane's professional practice firm grew and matured, with projects ranging from the Bahamas to Canada. In 1977 Lane was selected to membership in the American Society of Golf Course Architects and was honored as the first receipient of the University of Florida's Department of Landscape Architecture Distinguished Alumnus Award.

The membership of ASLA elected Lane their national president in 1977. During his term as president he spearheaded ASLA's dramatic change to self manangement and traveled more than 250,000 miles visiting landscape architectural education programs and ASLA chapters throughout the country.

Following his term as ASLA president, Lane decided to return to college. Serving as both visiting instructor and graduate student Lane received his Master of Landscape Architecture from the University of Illinois in August of 1980. During the fall of 1980 and spring of 1981 Lane served as adjunct associate professor in the Department of Landscape Architecture at the Ohio State University while continuing to manage his Florida based practice.

In July of 1981 Lane was selected to serve as head of the Department of Landscape Architecture at Texas A & M University and in September of that year he merged his firm with William A. Behnke Associates Inc. of Cleveland, Ohio. While still maintaining a consulting role in the combined firms, Lane's committment now rests in furthering the profession through academic pursuits.

The Illustrator: James E. Hiss

Jim is a native of Sandusky, Ohio. He received a Bachelor of Science in Architecture in 1972 and a Master's of Architecture in 1975 from Ohio State University. While working on his master's degree Jim was a teaching assistant in the Department of Landscape Architecture and in 1976 he was hired as a full time faculty member. Like most trained architects who chose to pursue a landscape architectural career, Jim has the special ability to bridge the two professions and brings a unique sensitivity to his teaching and his private practice activities.

Jim's teaching specializations tend toward residential and small scale site design, wood construction techniques and the full range of graphics and presentation media skills. Jim is an affiliate member of the American Society of Landscape Architects.